On the Track of a Prehistoric Economy

To my son
Morten
for his keen
and humorous
spirit

H.P. Blankholm

ON THE TRACK OF A PREHISTORIC ECONOMY

Maglemosian Subsistence in Early Postglacial South Scandinavia

AARHUS UNIVERSITY PRESS

Printed by Cambridge University Press, England
Cover design: Inga Friis
ISBN 87 7288 439 8

AARHUS UNIVERSITY PRESS
University of Aarhus
DK-8000 Århus C
Fax (+ 45) 8619 8433

73 Lime Walk
Headington, Oxford OX3 7AD
Fax (+ 44) 865 750 079

Box 511
Oakville, Conn. 06779
Fax (+ 1) 203 945 9468

ANSI/NISO
Z39.48-1992

Preface

This book presents a study of the Maglemosian economy in South Scandinavia. It is based on selected faunal assemblages and follows a novel theoretical and methodological approach.

Previous treatments of the economy generally have not gone beyond descriptions of the animal species present, an estimate of their relative numbers or importance, and a general appreciation of their utility as sources of food, hides, and raw material for tools. In general, no attempt has fully been made to integrate the zoological material and its bearing on the economy from a larger number of sites into the cultural-historical treatment and interpretation of the Mesolithic.

During more than a decade of commitment to the study of spatial analysis and behavioural interpretation of the Early Postglacial Maglemose Culture in South Scandinavia (ca. 7500-6000 BC) (e.g. Blankholm 1984, 1987a, 1990, 1991), it became clear that the study of the Maglemosian economy needs a change in its direction of research and a renewal of its procedures. The present investigation was largely carried out and written up in 1991-92.

I am greatly indebted to a number of people and institutions, all of whom, in one way or another, contributed to the project.

First of all, I wish to thank the curator Knud Rosenlund for guiding me through the archives and faunal collections of the University Museum of Zoology, Copenhagen, for many fruitful discussions, and for his great help in making a new bone count of the faunal assemblage from Lundby II.

I also greatly acknowledge the fine work of my old friend and colleague, Dr. Peter Rowley-Conwy, of the Department of Archaeology, University of Durham, England. Besides giving me access to his unpublished faunal data from Sværdborg I, 1917-18, Sværdborg I, 1923, Lundby I & II, and Holmegård I, he contributed with many helpful discussions and suggestions, and also carried out the linguistic revision of the manuscript. Peter and I have had (and still have) long and fruitful discussions on various aspects of paleoeconomic and multicausal approaches. We may not always agree, but I hope our discussions will continue for our mutual benefit.

Thanks are also due to Dr. Kim Aaris-Sørensen, University Museum of Zoology, Copenhagen, and to Dr. Jane Richter, School of Conservation, Royal Academy of Arts, Copenhagen, for giving me access to their private files on Sværdborg I, 1943-44 and Ulkestrup I & II, respectively.

Likewise, I wish to thank mag.art. Gitte Jensen for permission to use her unpublished files on Sværdborg I, 1923, professor Lars Larsson, of the Department of Archaeology, University of Lund, Sweden, for providing original distribution plans of faunal remains from Ageröd I:B and I:D, and lecturer Erik Brinch Petersen, of the Department of Archaeology, University of Copenhagen, for briefing me on his excavations at Mullerup Syd.

Thanks are also due to lecturer Bjarne Grønnow, Department of Archaeology, University of Copenhagen, who critically read the manuscript in detail and offered many helpful suggestions; to Dr. H. Thrane, Fyns Oldtid, likewise for many helpful editorial suggestions; to Dr. Helle Juel Jensen, of the Department of Prehistoric Archaeology, Aarhus University, for many discussions on use-wear analysis; and to Dr. Bodil Bratlund, Schleswig, Germany, for interesting discussions of Late Paleolithic and Ertebølle faunal assemblages.

Moreover, thanks go to draftsperson Inga Friis at Aarhus University Press for her ever ready assistance and excellent cooperation in the production of the book.

However, all shortcomings or errors remain my own.

Financial support was generously provided by Carlsbergfondet (The Carlsberg Foundation), who also financed the actual production. Statens Humanistiske Forskningsråd (The Danish Research Council for the Humanities) financed the linguistic revision.

Forlaget Sesam and Politikens Forlag are acknowledged for permission to reproduce Figures 1 and 2, and 3 respectively.

For all this I am very grateful.

Thanks are also due to my fellow musicians of Tumbleweed Blues Band, with whom once a week I share the fun and relaxation of getting away from work and cranking out tunes on old 100W Marshall amps.

Finally, my sincere thanks go to my wife Karen Marie and sons Anders and Morten without whose support, patience and goodwill this work would never have materialized. Many of the hours and days devoted to this book really should have been spent with them.

Beder, December 1993
H.P. Blankholm

Contents

List of tables

List of figures

1 Introduction

1.1 Theory

From the outset I wish to make explicit the theoretical approach adopted in this study.

The number of current approaches to interpreting the past is large, shows considerable variation, and is becoming ever more difficult to grasp, classify and discuss.

Recently Hodder (1988) discussed archaeological theory in terms of the systems approach (liberally interchanged with processual and 'New Archaeology'), structuralist archaeology, Marxist archaeology, contextual archaeology, and post-processual archaeology, which in turn were characterized as either materialist or idealist. In this scheme economic and ecological archaeology is dealt with only in passing and is generally subsumed under the systems approach. On the other hand, middle-range theory and ethno-archaeology receives much attention; the former being rejected and the latter's potential being narrowed considerably.

In a contemporary view, Schiffer (1988) takes another stand and discusses theory (middle-range theory in particular) and methodology in terms of social theory, reconstruction theory (comprising Correlates, C-Transforms and N-Transforms; see also Schiffer 1976), and methodological theory (including recovery, analysis and inference).

Following Kuhn (1964) it may be argued that it is not possible to compare such different frameworks and approaches. There may be some truth to this. In fact, some years ago Rowley-Conwy, Zvelebil and the present author argued:

In our view, each approach must be judged on the capacity of its associated methods for answering the questions and achieving the goals the approach sets itself. (Rowley-Conwy et al. 1987b)

This, however, is not to say that all approaches are equally valid or that any are flawless.

Although the various frameworks may be explicit and competitive among themselves, there is nevertheless a considerable degree of overlap and inter-dependence. This is seen not least in attempts to reconcile, in the broadest sense, the ecological and social approaches (Sheridan & Bailey 1983), but also is emphasized by Hodder (1988, 127):

The two types of meaning (the functional, systemic and the ideational content) are necessarily interdependent — it is not possible to talk of one without at least assuming the other.

In extension, and assuming a multivariate nature of past archaeological data and societies, I will propose a broad framed multicausal approach, which initially permits all imaginable agents or aspects (natural or human) to play a role and thus for any time and place allows the most important variables and parameters to be elucidated and explained. In essence, this is a holistic and heuristic approach allowing, for example, ecology, economy, formal structure, meaning, content and historical circumstances to play their roles (from nil to complete domination) in any time, place or societal context. From a still larger perspective it permits the building of a prehistory of mankind, showing both local and regional details and the most conspicuous mega-trends, be they cross-cultural, basically human, or whatever.

The notion of multicausality is far from new. Excellent work has, for example, been done by McGovern (1980, 1985a & b) on the issue of Norse extinction in Greenland, and a more modest contribution is my own on the transition to farming in South Scandinavia (Blankholm 1987b).

This is the general framework adopted in this volume. In the following two sections we will look at the Mesolithic as a concept (Section 1.2), and at various particular approaches used for the study of the Early Postglacial economy in South Scandinavia (Section 1.3).

1.2 The Mesolithic

The Mesolithic was the last major prehistoric era on the stage of European archaeology. The history has been excellently told elsewhere (Clark 1978, Zvelebil 1986, Rowley-Conwy 1986). In the following I will concentrate on points of relevance for the present study.

A product of the three-age stadial archaeology, the Mesolithic was originally introduced in the 1870s (Zvelebil 1986, 5) and was gradually accepted during the beginning of the 20th century. Initially it functioned to plug the gap between Late Glacial hunters and Neolithic farmers, after the hiatus theory that Europe was not occupied during this intervening period was proven false (Clark 1978, 1980, Zvelebil 1986, Rowley-Conwy 1986).

Until the middle of the 20th century, however, the Mesolithic was regarded as an embarrassing step-child in much archaeological thought and practice. In the first place, the apparent cultural impoverishment never fitted with the uniliniar models of the social evolution of mankind prevailing well into the first half of the century. Even the onset of historical and anthropological perspectives in the 1920s and 1930s did not do much to change the general view of the Mesolithic. Although the new perspectives did away with the notion of absolute stages in the development of mankind, the view of the Mesolithic as a low status chronological stop-gap and a period of basically little cultural or evolutionary interest was retained. In essence, it was the pariah of Stone Age research — an insignificant period of degeneration and decline.

It took the excavation of a large number of South Scandinavian, German and English sites with richly varied content, including organic remains, plus the pioneering work of Grahame Clark and many of his South Scandinavian and German colleagues to show the multivaried nature of the period and to give real impetus to Mesolithic research (Sarauw 1903, Friis-Johansen 1919, Broholm 1924, Mathiassen 1937, 1943, Mathiassen *et al.* 1942, Brøndsted 1938, 1957, Becker 1945, 1951, 1953, Troels-Smith 1953, Schwabedissen 1944, Althin 1954, Clark 1936, 1952, 1954).

Slowly but surely the Mesolithic gained importance and recognition as a period worth studying in its own right. Further momentum was gained with the theoretical developments of the 1960s and 1970s coupled with the recognition of the large range and variability of recent hunter-gatherer economy and sociology, and with, as Zvelebil (1986, 6) puts it:

...the replacement of the notion of cultural progress — an heir to the unilinear evolutionary views — by a more flexible concept of adaptation as a measure of cultural competence. Thus even technologically and socially simple cultures could now be perceived as 'successful' and effective within their niche.

Today it is widely recognized among hunter-gatherer archaeologists that Mesolithic cultures may be both affluent and complex (Rowley-Conwy 1986, Price & Brown 1985). Yet along with increasing research and appreciation of the wide range of cultural constructs and phenomena has come a bewildering array of definitions and terminology (see Rowley-Conwy 1986, Figures 1 & 2), which continues to cause much confusion. Indeed, much time and energy has been, and still is, spent on finding an appropriate definition and standard terminology or nomenclature for the Mesolithic. Some prefer strict definitions for the Mesolithic, while others, including myself, feel content merely to see it as a broad and convenient frame of reference. Perhaps it is about time to abandon the old worn-out 3-age system? From a scientific point of view both the classic Stone-Bronze-Iron Age and the Paleo-Meso-Neolithic systems seem very much obsolete, although they may continue to be useful for basic antiquarian work in museums for registration, for cultural heritage administration, and so on.

Certainly, with the realization that stone age societies may be as complex as any late Iron Age manifestation (some of their materials may differ, but their economic and social organisation and behaviour may not) there is no

urgent need to keep the old nomenclature. In fact, the sooner we get accus-
tomed to thinking that the entire variability of economic and social behaviour
and cultural phenomena probably was potentially achievable from the emergence of *Homo sapiens* the better (see also Gamble 1986). *Then* we can begin to
investigate what, where, when, how and why things really happened.

1.3 Maglemosian subsistence in history

The study of Maglemosian subsistence has followed a variety of research
traditions and approaches. This is not the place for a review or discussion of
hunter-gatherer theory *per se* (the reader is referred to Sheridan & Bailey 1981,
Binford 1968, 1973, 1978a & b, 1979, 1980, 1981, 1983, Hodder 1982a & b,
Jochim 1976, 1981, Winterhalder & Smith 1981, Wiessner 1983, 1984, Sackett
1982, Price & Brown 1985, Bettinger 1991, and Gamble & Boismier 1991, to
mention but a few). Rather, this section serves as a brief overview of factually
used approaches within the study area.

Nearly all studies from the turn of the century until about 1970 followed
the traditional approach or broad stadial views prevalent at the time (Rowley-
Conwy *et al.* 1987). No general survey was made until the late 1930s (e.g.
Clark 1936, Brøndsted 1938). Instead, subsistence was dealt with in a series of
Maglemosian site publications (e.g. Sarauw 1903, Friis-Johansen 1919, Broholm
1924, K. Andersen 1960) in which detailed, but rarely complete, lists of the
faunal material were compiled by zoologists (e.g. Winge 1903, 1919, Møhl
1960).

However, the primary investigator's treatment of the economy rarely went
beyond mere descriptions of species present, an estimate of their relative
numbers or importance, and a general appreciation of their utility for food,
hides, and raw material for tools. Typically, no attempt was fully made to
integrate the zoological material's economic impact into the cultural-historical
treatment and interpretation of the Mesolithic.

On the other hand, investigators in the early part of the century did not
possess the theoretical and methodological concepts and approaches of the
present day. It would, perhaps, be fair to say that had it not been for the
foresight of the earlier generations and the early development of high
excavation standards, there would probably not have been much left today for
analytical treatment using new lines of research.

There were exceptions to the general treatment of zoological materials,
however. As to the Late Paleolithic, the treatment by Rust, Krause and Kollau
of the zoological evidence and economic interpretation of the Hamburgian site
of Meiendorf and the Ahrensburgian site of Stellmoor (Rust 1937, 1943, Krause
1937, Kollau 1943) was exemplary for its time, and Grahame Clark's first
synthesis of the Mesolithic settlement of Northern Europe (Clark 1936), his

book *Prehistoric Europe: The Economic Basis* (Clark 1952), and his treatment of Star Carr (Clark 1954, 1972), signalling the onset of the economic approach, certainly broke new ground and heralded a new era.

Yet it took a while before this approach made any real impact on Scandinavian research. Studies may loosely be divided into three groups, comprising (a) site-specific investigations, (b) general Mesolithic subsistence studies, and (c) general surveys or textbooks on the Scandinavian Stone Age.

Among the site-specific studies, a deeper concern with the use of zoological evidence for paleoecological and paleoeconomic reconstruction — notably within the realms of the carrying capacity and optimal foraging models — is evident. Site catchment analysis (Vita Finzi & Higgs 1970, Jarman 1972, Blankholm 1976) in various forms is central for the estimation of biomass and population on sites and for modelling settlement patterns. Good examples are Larsson's detailed analysis of the Late Maglemosian sites Ageröd I:B and I:D (Larsson 1978) and the Early Atlantic site Segebro (Larsson 1982); another example is Skaarup's investigation of the Early Maglemosian site Flaadet (Skaarup 1979). If there is a weakness to the economic reconstructions, it is the rather mechanical and static use of classical site-catchment analysis. Other site-specific studies include an interesting study by Møhl (1980) of the elk skeletons from Skottemarke and Favrbo, Aaris-Sørensen's (1984) and P.V. Petersen & E.B. Petersen's (1984) study of the Prejlerup aurochs, and a number of important contributions by quaternary zoologists in more recent site publications, for example, Rosenlund on Sværdborg II and Lundby II (Rosenlund 1972, 1979), Aaris-Sørensen on Sværdborg I, 1943-44 (Aaris-Sørensen 1976), and Richter on Ulkestrup I and II (Richter 1982).

Among the more generally oriented works, we find Hatting's (1969) study of beaver teeth as tools, Noe-Nygaard's (1974, 1988) investigations of hunting technique, marrow processing and taphonomy; and my own studies of various other aspects of the Maglemosian (Blankholm 1984, 1987a, 1990). Other studies include Bay-Petersen's (1978) investigation of animal exploitation in Mesolithic Denmark, and Mithen's (1987) study of prehistoric red deer hunting strategies. If there are weaknesses to the two latter contributions, one certainly is their lack of source assessment. For example, of the 19 sites used by Bay-Petersen (1978, Table 1), 10 were generally considered unsuitable to represent Mesolithic subsistence activities as early as the time of her investigation. Much the same pertains to Mithen's study, which in turn drew its Danish data from Bay-Petersen as a secondary source. Among the Boreal or Maglemosian sites they employ, in fact only Sværdborg I, 1917-18 (they completely omitted Sværdborg I, 1923 and I, 1943-44), would pass a first screening (see Section 4). I do not claim that their results necessarily are wrong, but their arguments certainly lack the substance and corroborative power of a well assessed database.

Finally, Maglemosian exploitation has been dealt with in general, but often brief, terms in a number of surveys and textbooks on the Scandinavian or Danish Stone Age or wildlife. In brief we may mention Brøndsted's (1937, 1957) now classic trilogy *Danmarks Oldtid I-III*, Brinch Petersens (1973) much quoted *A Survey of the Late Palaeolithic and Mesolithic of Denmark*, Grahame Clark's (1975) *The Earlier Stone Age Settlement of Scandinavia*, S.H. Andersen's (1981) popularily oriented *Stenalderen I*, and Aaris-Sørensen's (1988) *Danmarks Forhistoriske Dyreverden*. Other contributions to the discussion of general developments are found in Fischer (1978), Price (1985), and Blankholm (1987b).

For two reasons, I have so far refrained from detailed discussion of results. The first is redundancy caused by the fact that the basic material — the database — to a very large extent remains the same; the second is that although we cannot claim full concensus, there are trends in the more recent literature towards general agreement on the developments that occurred particularly concerning economy and settlement patterns:

1. The Maglemosians were full hunter-gatherers of mammals, fish, birds and plant foods.
2. The hunting of mammals was chiefly directed towards dispersed, non-migratory species living in small groups.
3. The 'big game' were aurochs, elk, red deer, roe deer, and pig. These animals were 'ambulatory stores of necessities' (Brinch Petersen 1973) providing food, hides, and raw material for tools. Smaller mammals such as beaver, marten, wolf, fox, brown hare, red squirrel, badger, otter and wild cat were primarily hunted for their fur, except for beaver, which was possibly also hunted for its meat. Fishing was directed towards non-migratory species, particularly pike, but the exploitation of anadromous fish is also very probable. Birds were probably hunted both for food and for feathers. Egg collecting has not been documented. The gathering of plant foods is documented by hazelnuts and water lily seeds.
4. During the warmer part of the year the Maglemosians lived in small social/economic units along river and lake margins in the interior, while winter camps, perhaps in the form of larger aggregation camps, were probably on the now largely submerged coastline.

However, most ideas on the subject have been based on generalized extractions of original site reports or on secondary or tertiary sources. It also is evident that most models are static in character, that there has been too much reliance on the band level of social structure and ecologically determined group size, and the narrow scope provided by only considering a fraction of the variability found among extant and recent hunter-gatherers (see also Newell 1984).

A thorough and more detailed assessment of the archaeo-fauna is needed in order to reach more firm conclusions about the economy and its role in Maglemosian times and its relationship with other aspects of the society in time and space.

2 Environment

This chapter describes the topography, raw material availability, conditions of preservation, and the main environmental trends of the study area from ca. 7500 BC to ca. 6000 BC.

2.1 Topography, raw materials and conditions of preservation

2.1.1 Topography

The relief and outline of South Scandinavia is largely the result of the last glacial (Weichselian) processes and their Holocene isostatic and eustatic aftermath.

Modern Denmark and Schleswig-Holstein (northern Germany) is a low relief region with the highest point (Ejer Bavnehøj) reaching 173 m above sea level. To the east of the main still-stand line (also the present main watershed) of the last glaciation (Fig. 1a), the landscape generally is gently undulating moraine with fertile soils, intersected by narrow fjords and river valleys. Jutland west of the still-stand line, however, mostly consists of flat, sandy and podzolized outwash plains interspersed with higher, more diverse moraine dating from the Saalian glaciation (A.V. Nielsen 1967, Figs. 290, 291). Scania in Sweden in many respects is similar to eastern Denmark, but, like the Baltic island of Bornholm, is notable for its conspicuous rock outcrops and spits (e.g. Kullen).

2.1.2 Raw materials

Flint is the basic geological raw material for tool production within the area. Flint nodules may be found in morainic country and in river beds all over the study area. Freshly outwashed flint may be of as good a quality as embedded chalk-flint, but nodules generally are smaller in size. The chalk-flint is associated with the lime deposits and cliffs notably in the Limfjord area, the Gjerrild Klint area of northeastern Djursland (both in Jutland), Stevns Klint on Zealand, and the Malmö region in Scania. This is good quality flint, suitable for mining and extraction for the fabrication of larger implements like picks, axes, sickles, and daggers. Mining and surface extraction is evident from the early Neolithic (Becker 1951, 1958, 1981), but exploitation and collection may have taken place earlier. Another source, in areas lacking naturally embedded or larger nodules of flint, is pebble-flint, particularly characteristic for the

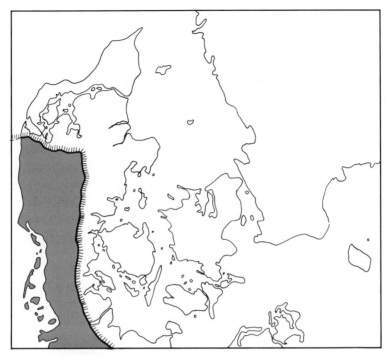

Fig. 1a. Topography.

Mesolithic of the Baltic island of Bornholm (Becker 1951) and in some parts of western Jutland. It is not currently possible to trace flint to particular sources by quantitative or physical methods, and qualitative estimates by experienced observers may not be reliable.

2.1.3 Conditions of preservation

There are marked differences across the study area. Flint, of course, is preserved everywhere, but calcification and decalcification may be more or less pronounced depending on the local geochemical setting. Good preservation conditions for bone and antler, however, are only found in waterlogged deposits with high alkaline content or in anaerobic marine deposits. This essentially means Scania and the eastern Danish islands, and to a much lesser extent certain parts of the Jutland peninsula. Shell middens may by their very content of shells preserve organic materials, which otherwise would not survive in the local soil.

Conditions of preservation are rapidly deteriorating, however. Particularly since the latter part of the 19th century drainage has lowered the water table in most lake basins and bogs, resulting in devastating dry-outs of potentially rich archaeological sites. Deep ploughing is another constant threat to sites, as peat cutting was formerly, particularly during the extensive workings of the two World Wars. Although one could argue that peat-cutting helped to locate a great number of sites, many of which were later surveyed or partially excavated, there is no doubt that it has also forever destroyed most possibilities for research-oriented excavation projects of well-preserved and potentially rich and informative sites.

2.2 Vegetation, climate, temperature and fauna

Because of a long tradition of pollen analytical research (Jessen 1935a and b, Iversen 1960, 1967, Jørgensen 1954, 1963, Nilsson 1935, 1967, Berglund 1966), the general vegetational history of South Scandinavia is well known (see also Clark 1975).

The problem remains, however, that partially incompatible zonation systems (e.g. Jessen 1935b, Jørgensen 1954, Nilsson 1935) render comparisons both between regions and site datings difficult (see also Larsson 1978). Specific pollen samples also are difficult to compare, because relatively few pollen grains were counted from each sample in earlier work.

2.2.1 Zone IV. The Preboreal. The oldest postglacial period, ca. 8300-7000 BC

Following the open Late Glacial (Younger Dryas, Zone III), the landscape changed to light, open forest conditions first characterized by birch (*Betula pubescens, Betula verrucosa*), European aspen (*Populus tremula*), willow (*Salix* sp.) and rowan (*Sorbus*). This was later followed by pine (*Pinus sylvestris*) spreading from the southeast and gradually replacing the birch; hence the name birch-pine period.

The onset of the postglacial is marked by a rapid and steep rise in temperature (Fig. 1b). While the summer temperature (mean July) is estimated at ca. 10°C for the Younger Dryas (zone III), hops (*Humulus lupulus*) and cladium (*Cladium mariscus*) suggest a corresponding figure for the Preboreal of 15°C, i.e. slightly below the present 16°C. The 'Friesland phase' in the beginning of the period suggests a short climatic recession, marked by a short decrease of birch and a temporary rise of grasses and sedges (Iversen 1967).

This open pioneer forest biotope was rich, supporting a wide range of wildlife species. The big game of the Late Glacial — reindeer (*Rangifer tarandus*), bison (*Bison bonasus*) and horse (*Equus ferus*) — seem to disappear at, or shortly after, the transition to the Preboreal and is initially replaced by elk (*Alces alces*) and aurochs (*Bos primigenius*) (Iversen 1967, Aaris-Sørensen 1988). The poor preservation conditions on most Maglemosian sites in South Scandinavia from this period preclude detailed assessments of the relative importance or exploitation patterns of the species. However, Star Carr throws

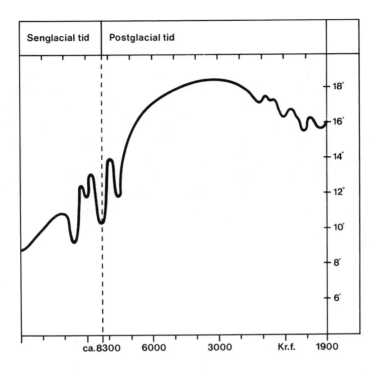

Fig. 1b. Temperature (reproduced from S.H. Andersen 1981 with permission of the publisher).

light on such aspects (Clark 1954, 1972, Legge & Rowley-Conwy 1988) and shows intensive use of red deer (*Cervus elaphus*), roe deer (*Capreolus capreolus*), and to some extent pig (*Sus scrofa*) from very early on. Other animals present are bear (*Ursus arctos*), beaver (*Castor fiber*), badger (*Meles meles*), wolf (*Canis lupus*), fox (*Canis vulpes*), pine marten (*Martes martes*), hare (*Lepus europaeus*) and hedgehog (*Erinaceus europaeus*). Bird species include crane (*Grus grus*), black stork (*Ciconia nigra*), black-throated diver (*Gavia arctica*) and goosander (*Mergus merganser*) (E.B. Petersen 1973). The only fish and plant foods documented are pike (*Esox lucius*) and hazelnuts (*Corylus avellana*).

2.2.2 Zone V. The Boreal, ca. 7000 – 6200 BC

Generally, the Boreal is characterized by hazel (*Corylus avellana*) and pine in its early stage, and later by the immigration of nearly all the broadleaved trees, e.g. oak (*Quercus robur, Querqus petraea*), ash (*Fraxinus excelsior*), alder (*Alnus glutinosa*), lime (*Tilia cordata*) and elm (*Ulmus* spp.). The spread of hazel was primarily at the expense of birch. The reason was probably entirely ecological, but it has also been argued that its occurrence in southeastern

Denmark about a thousand years earlier than in the western part of the country could be attributed to man (Iversen 1967). While this remains an open question, there is, on the other hand, no evidence whatsoever of more sophisticated manipulation, such as fire-ecology, as often claimed for the British Mesolithic (e.g. Smith 1970, Mellars 1975, Simmons 1975, see also Edwards 1990), and even these cases seem doubtful. The delayed spread of hazel across the region is, however, a warning to avoid terms like Preboreal or Boreal Maglemosian! It also indicates that vegetational cover and arboreal species composition was far from homogeneous across South Scandinavia.

As from the zone Va/Vb transition, i.e. the hazel maximum, the big shade-giving and warmth-demanding broadleaved trees replaced the hazel and pine forest in suitable places. The oak and elm arrived first, followed by lime and alder; the latter was a strong competitor to hazel on wet soils (Iversen 1967).

The amelioration of the climate continued (Fig. 1b). European pond tortoise (*Emys orbicularis*), ivy (*Hedera helix*) and mistletoe (*Viscum album*) suggest a mean summer temperature of 18-20°C towards the end of the period, and a winter temperature (mean January) of between -1 and -1.5°C (Iversen 1960, 1967, Troels-Smith 1960). The climate was warm and dry, and because of the land bridges with England and South Sweden continental in character.

The light, open pine and hazel biotope was even richer than the Preboreal in species composition. Again the 'big game' were aurochs, elk, red deer, roe deer and pig, the two latter documented for the first time in South Scandinavia proper (Iversen 1967, Brøndsted 1957). Aside from the other species mentioned for the Preboreal, otter (*Lutra lutra*), wild cat (*Felix sylvestris*) and lynx (*Lynx lynx*) were hunted. Bird species were abundant, e.g. woodpecker (*Picus viridis*), white-tailed eagle (*Haliaeetus albicilla*), kite (*Milvus milvus*), and a wide range of waterfowl (Brinch Petersen 1973). Documented fish include pike, wels (*Siluris glanis*), and perch (*Perca fluviatilis*), and vegetational food comprised hazelnuts and yellow waterlily seeds (*Nuphar luteum*). Among the reptiles European Tortoise is common.

2.2.3 Zone VI

Jessen (1935b) defined the beginning of this period as the rational limit for alder (*Alnus glutinosa*). Generally this occurs later than the rational limit for the so-called mixed oak forest, but may also coincide with this limit, or may even occur before it. To get rid of the confusion, Jørgensen (1954) redefined the period as the rational limit for mixed oak forest *and* the first occurence of ivy (*Hedera helix*) and mistletoe (*Viscum album*). Jessen (1935b) placed the zone VI/VII limit at the intersection of the rising mixed oak forest curve and that of the declining pine curve. Jørgensen (1954), however, argued that this limit would always be a point on a continuum and thus redefined the limit to the end of the rise of the mixed oak forest curve. In essence, Jørgensen's zone VI generally covers parts of both zone V and VI in Jessen's system.

When Jessen's system was current, zone VI was most often considered either as an integrated part of the Boreal, or as a short, but unlabelled, phase of the transition to the ensuing Atlantic period. Following the above redefinitions by Jørgensen it comprises a part of the Atlantic (often the whole of Jessen's zone VIIa). The correct term probably should be Early Atlantic. However, regarding both vegetation and climate it is a transitional phase, and for this reason I have retained the term: Zone VI (*ex.* Jørgensen).

All this clearly reiterates the warning against the use of terms like Boreal or Atlantic Maglemosian culture. This simply causes too much confusion!

In essence, Zone VI marks the end of the transition from light open pioneer to mature climax forest. Right from the onset all the essential climax trees are present and the ensuing time is one of competition. Lime and elm dominate the rich soils, oak holds its ground on the more meagre soils, while alder is characteristic of swamps and lake and river margins.

At the Boreal/Atlantic transition the climate changes from dry to humid. The continuous rise of the production of pollen from ivy and mistletoe suggests a further rise in temperature to 18-21°C (Iversen 1967, Troels-Smith 1960), which is the postglacial (or present interglacial) maximum (Fig. 1b). Increasing humidity and temperature — coastal climate — is seen as a result of the continuous rise in global sea level, which caused the North Sea, Kattegat Sea and Baltic Sea to inundate the surrounding lowlands until the study area approximated its present geographical shape (Iversen 1967, see also Fig. 1c).

Variability of wildlife was essentially the same as for the former period. Some have claimed that the general biomass declined considerably during this time because of the expansion of the climax forest with almost no undergrowth (e.g. Iversen 1967, Troels-Smith 1960). However, the continuous human settlement along lakes and rivers through the period does not corroborate such arguments. At least the lake and river margin ecotonal zones must have supported a wide spectrum of resources. It has also been claimed that aurochs, elk and bear disappeared from the Danish islands during the Atlantic period due to a combination of the vegetational changes, absence of immigration of fresh stock from the Continent due to isolation, and over-exploitation of breeding populations (Degerbøl 1964, Møhl 1979, Aaris-Sørensen 1980, 1988). Following a re-assessment of the evidence, however, this argument has recently been severely contested (Newell 1990).

Towards the end of the period, during the Late Kongemose Culture, the first documented coastal sites appear with intensive exploitation of marine resources.

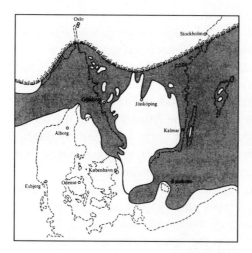

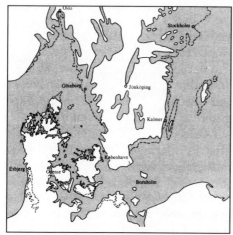

Fig. 1c. Land-Sea relationship at approximately 8000, 6500 and 4500 BC (reproduced from J. Iversen 1967).

2.3 Isostatics and eustatics

Most postglacial change in land-sea relationships is the aftermath of de-glaciation and has recently received some attention (e.g. Mörner 1969, K.S. Petersen 1985).

The iso/eustatic relationships are very complex globally, regionally and locally. In the following the North Sea and the Baltic Sea will be dealt with separately. Figure 1c shows land-sea relationships at approximately 8000, 6500 and 4500 years BC.

The North Sea

From about 13,000 BC down to c. 6000 BC the coastline encroached from a line running approximately from the middle of the Skagerak over to Flamborough Head in England, back to a line lying not far northwest of the present coast.

The English Channel was finally inundated around 6500 BC (Jacoby 1973). Solid documentation of human occupation of this vast, former lowland is provided by numerous finds of trawled and beached Maglemosian bone tools, most dated to the Preboreal or Boreal (Clark 1975, Louwe-Kooijmans 1971). A great number of bone tools, mostly barbed bone points, have also been excavated from reclaimed land in Holland (Verhart 1988, 1990).

The Baltic Sea
The Baltic seems more complex. After the Baltic Ice-lake was breached at Billingen ca. 8300 BC, the lake gradually changed to the Baltic Ice-sea. Because of the ongoing deglaciation salinity remained low. About 7000 BC the continuing isostatic uplift of North Scandinavia cut the connection to the Skagerak and Kattegat seas, whereafter the Ancylus Lake (after the common freshwater snail *Ancylus fluviatilis*) was formed. At the beginning the lake's outlet was still over the threshhold in Götland, Sweden (via the so-called Svea Elv), but the continuing isostatic uplift rapidly raised this area, so that later the outlet ran south of South Sweden and the eastern Danish islands and up through the present Great Belt (the Dana Elv).

However, the ongoing eustatic rise in sea level gradually forced the sea to penetrate the Belts and change the salinity of the Ancylus Lake, first to brackish waters, later to the more saline Litorina Sea. This, in essence, was the result of the first Atlantic transgression.

3 Subsistence equipment

Theoretically, Maglemosian subsistence equipment may be classified into four groups (Table 1 & 2):

1. Equipment used directly or primarily for hunting, fishing or gathering.
2. Equipment used for the processing or consumption of food, whether in domestic or hunting contexts.
3. Equipment used for the manufacture of tools for groups 1 and 2 above.
4. Equipment used for non-subsistence related activities, e.g. hide preparation.

With only a few direct or indirect pieces of functional evidence within each of the four classes, however, most functions of the wide range of Maglemosian equipment must still be assumed rather than demonstrated. It should also be emphasized that a number of formal tool types could easily have been used purposively or expediently throughout the functional areas suggested above.

3.1 Equipment used directly or primarily for hunting, fishing or gathering.

Arrows/projectile components

Within the Maglemosian proper the use of the flint-tipped arrow (Mathiassen 1948, Nos. 75-89, 210-15, E.B. Petersen 1966, Nos. 39-41, 44-45, 48-51, 53) is only demonstrated with absolute certainty in one single case: the aurochs bull from Vig (Hartz & Winge 1906, Noe-Nygaard 1974) in which two ribs contained embedded arrow-tips (Type A). One lesion was healed, whereas the other was unhealed showing that the bull escaped its pursuers at least once.

However, embedded flint-tipped arrows are plentiful from other Mesolithic and Late Paleolithic contexts. In the Hamburgian and Ahrensburgian, respectively, 4 and 27 specimens are now known from Stellmoor Site A in northern Germany (Bratlund 1991). At Schwenningen am Nechar a Tardenoisian point was found embedded in an aurochs bone (Ströbel 1959). The wild boar from Aldersro (Noe-Nygaard 1974) showed a healed lesion containing flint; highly suggestive of a flint-tipped arrow. The pollen date is Jessen's zone V, but its affinity with the Maglemosian is not clear. From the eponymous Kongemose site (S. Jørgensen 1956) an oblique transverse arrowhead was found embedded in an unhealed lesion in a red deer male humerus (Noe-Nygaard 1974), and another oblique transverse arrowhead was found in an unidentified piece of

Table 1. Maglemosian subsistence equipment

Group 1
Arrows
Projectile components
Bows
Unret. blades
Backed blades
Flint picks
Slotted daggers
Slotted spears
Antler picks
Bone picks
Barbed bone points
Plain bone points
Fish hooks
Harpoons

Group 2
Unret. blades
Backed blades
Notched/denticulated items
Slotted daggers
Tusk knives
Daggers
'Skinning' knives
Borers

Group 3
Cores
Hammer stones
Flint flakers
Unret. blades
Backed blades
Scrapers
Trunc. blades
Burins
Notched/denticulated items
Axes/adzes of flint, green-
  stone, bone or antler
Awls

Group 4
Flint axes/adzes
Unret. blades
Backed blades
Scrapers
Burins
Borers

Table 2. 'Big Game', elements and tools

	Aurochs	Elk	Red deer	Roe Deer	Pig
Antler		Axes Adzes Picks Chisels Percussion/pressure sticks	Axes Adzes Socketed axes/adzes Picks Chisels Barbed points Percussion/pressure sticks Handles Shafts	Fish hooks	
Tooth	Pendants	Pendants	Pendants		Pendants Tusk-knives Chisels
Rib	Barbed points		Barbed points Fish hooks		
Scapula	Wedges				
Humerus	Axes				
Radius	Axes	Knives		Bodkins	Picks
Ulna	Picks Axes	Daggers	Daggers Picks		Daggers Picks
Metacarpus	Mace-heads Faceted scrapers	Points Bodkins Slotted points	Points Bodkins Barbed points Slotted points Knives Faceted scrapers	Slotted points	Handles Faceted scrapers
Tibia			Knives	Awls Faceted scrapers	Faceted scrapers
Fibula					Awls
Metatarsus	Axes Picks Mace-heads	Axes Adzes Chisels Points Bodkins Barbed points Slotted points Knives	Points Bodkins Barbed points Slotted points/daggers Knives Awls Fish hooks	Points Bodkins Barbed points Slotted points	Handles

bone at Klampenborg (Westerby 1927). Typologically, both points may be associated with the Vedbæk phase of the Late Kongemose Culture or the Norslund/Bloksbjerg phase of the Early (aceramic) Ertebølle Culture. From the end of the sequence (probably early Neolithic), two ribs with healed lesions containing a transverse arrowpoint and small pieces of flint came the Maglelyng Complex in Åmosen, Zealand (Noe-Nygaard 1974).

Indirect evidence is more plentiful. A comparison of cross-sections or approximate measurements of tips and lesions has led to a multitude of shot holes being recorded (i.e. Noe-Nygaard 1973, 1974), particularly in shoulder blades of various animals. Healed lesions (Noe-Nygård 1974, 1975, Legge & Rowley-Conwy 1988, Rowley-Conwy n.d.) are, of course, suggestive of hunting, but otherwise this methodology has been recently, and in my view correctly, contested by Bratlund (1991, 194), who states that:

...it cannot be ruled out, that scapulae from Stone Age contexts were damaged in connection with activities other than hunting.

From a comparison with other cultural contexts she concludes that the alleged hunting lesions could equally well have been caused by the hanging of meat for smoking (Bratlund 1991, 193). Consequently these alleged hunting lesions will not be further discussed.

Other indirect evidence exists, however. At Prejlerup the nearly complete skeleton of an aurochs bull was associated with a number of Maglemosian type microliths; highly suggestive evidence of hunting by bow and arrow (Aaris-Sørensen 1988, P.V. Petersen & E.B. Petersen 1984).

From a number of sites microwear analysis has proven a case for microliths as projectile points for hunting (e.g. Star Carr and Mount Sandel (Dumont 1987)). In an excellent review of the state of the art of microwear analysis Dumont states:

...no single tool type can be confidently correlated to either a single manner of use or worked material on a scale greater than that of the individual site. (Dumont 1987, 88)

Apparently this still holds true (although see H.J. Jensen 1994 on blade sickles) so there is every reason to be cautious in making broad statements about the correlation of morphology and function.

Hafted flint-tipped arrows have been found in various Mesolithic contexts, e.g. the Maglemosian arrow from Lilla Loshult, Scania (Malmer 1969) and the Ertebølle transverse arrowhead from Ejsing, Jutland (Brøndsted 1957, Mathiassen 1948, No. 104).

In addition, unmistakable arrowshafts with grooves for flint insets, but without the armatures actually in place, have been found at, for example,

Fippenborg, Vinkelmose (S.H. Andersen 1979), Hohen Viecheln (Schuldt 1961), and in the Late Glacial Ahrensburgian context of Stellmoor (Rust 1943, Bratlund 1991).

The two latter categories of finds do not by themselves demonstrate hunting, but everything considered it seems fair to conclude that the bow and arrow was part of the hunting equipment.

Bows

Bows have been found in Maglemosian settlements, e.g. Holmegaard IV (Becker 1945, Mathiassen 1948, No. 209, Clark 1975). These are fully developed weapons; a testimony to a long tradition of craftmanship. They were made from split elm wood, were 160-180 cm long and had an estimated range of 150-200 m. These were fine and powerful weapons.

Unretouched blades

While formerly relegated to the debitage in the techno-hierarchy, recent microwear analyses have confirmed a broad range of long suspected or anticipated uses (Dumont 1987, 85). Again functions vary in time and between sites, and commonly only the more robust pieces were selected for use.

Generally the evidence suggests that these tools were used in a variety of contexts: hunting and manufacture, in both mobile and domestic contexts.

In a wider perspective it is also interesting that this simple tool — a companion in all subsistence related activities — is also the tool most often found as grave goods in the later Mesolithic, in contrast to decorated or personalized gear. This may suggest that status was played down in funeral rites and that ascribed status or power was not automatically reproduced or legitimized through ritual or ancestorship.

Backed blades (knives)

Quoting Dumont (1987, 86), the function of backed blades '...clearly varied through time and space.' The materials worked with backed blades include wood, antler, bone, meat or hide, and unidentified materials (Dumont 1987, 86, Keeley 1978, 82, Cahen et al. 1979, 665). Apparently, and not surprisingly, this was a versatile tool, and thus has tentatively been listed along with the hunting equipment.

Picks (Mathiassen 1948, Nos. 45-6)

Picks have not been found in contexts suggesting direct use for hunting or killing animals (again disregarding the 'hunting lesions' suggested by Noe-Nygaard). Also they do not seem to have been subjected to microwear analysis. Their inclusion with the hunting equipment is thus purely suggestive. They could easily have functioned in other areas as well.

Slotted daggers and spears (Mathiassen 1948, Nos. 178-82)
A substantial proportion of the slotted daggers and spears with flint insets (microblades) are stray finds. They are frequently heavily decorated, have often been extensively worn, and have sometimes been curated or repaired. All this indicates that they were heavy labour input, prestige/personal tools, and suggests a good deal of off site use — probably hunting.

Long antler picks (e.g. Mathiassen 1948, Nos. 137-40)
Long antler picks are as intriguing as they are uncommon. Their long twisted and often heavily decorated appearance suggests high labour investment and that they are personalized gear symbolizing status, rather than an efficient hunting tool.

Picks of aurochs, deer or pig metacarpus/tarsus, ulna or radius (e.g. Mathiassen 1948, Nos. 133-5)
These tools are often decorated, are only found in small numbers, but occur both on settlements and as stray finds. They indicate heavy labour input and suggest personalized prestige gear for both domestic and off site use, in the former case probably for butchering and the manufacture of bone implements, in the latter possibly for hunting or digging up edible matter.

Barbed bone points (e.g. Mathiassen 1948, Nos. 168-176)
Barbed bone points have been found in great quantities both on and off site and like microliths (*sensu stricto*) constitute a key artifact in Maglemosian typology. In the literature, barbed bone points have usually been associated with hunting and fishing, but direct evidence is rare.

As to fishing, barbed points have been found in association with pike skeletons at Kunda, Estonia (Indreko 1948, Clark 1975), but the evidence from at least one of these cases (Indreko 1948, Fig. 15) is, in my view, inconclusive. Aside from one hafted specimen, Ulkestrup I provided two additional points which were once probably parts of a composite leister and on which traces remained of rotting fish (K. Andersen *et al.* 1982). Corrosion from rotting fish was also reported from Mullerup Syd (Sarauw 1903, 258) and Sværdborg I, 1923 (Broholm 1924, 70). Other indirect evidence of fishing leisters is suggested by finds from, for example, Horne, Vendsyssel and Mullerup Nord, where 5 and 6 points, respectively were found in close association. More suggestive evidence comes from the so-called fishing sites in the Åmosen basin, Zealand, where several hundred bone points have been found with their tips still sticking into the lake bottom and often with broken bases, i.e. presumably lost during the act of spearing fish. Also at the fishing sites groups of from three to five bone points (of which one almost always is unbarbed) have been found in great numbers (K. Andersen *et al.* 1982).

Hunting of mammals with these implements is more dubious. The numerous hunting lesions reported by Noe-Nygaard (1974, Bratlund 1991) are basically inconclusive, and the find associations at sites like High Furlong, Lancashire England (Hallam *et al.* 1973), and Taaderup, Falster, Denmark (I. Sørensen 1980) seem unconvincing. That is, the association of the points with the actual hunting activities is not clear.

Most evidence then seems to point to a primary use for these artifacts as components of fishing gear.

Unbarbed bone points (e.g. Mathiassen 1948, Nos. 150-1)
Unbarbed bone points have not been documented in unambiguous hunting contexts in the Maglemosian. Finds of an unbarbed bone point in the vertebra of a roe deer from the Ertebølle site Trylleskoven (P.V. Petersen 1978), and another in a human skeleton at the Ertebølle cemetery at Bøgebakken (Albrethsen & E.B. Petersen 1976), may indicate that they also were used earlier on for hunting and aggression/defence against humans. Their frequent occurrence in association with groups of barbed points (leisters, see above), on the other hand, testifies to their use as fishing gear. They may also have been put to more peaceful uses, however (see below).

Fish hooks
Fish hooks are rare indeed. Although they never have been found embedded in fish, their use seems unambiguous.

Harpoons
True harpoons with line-holes or line-grips and detachable shafts are not known with certainty from Maglemosian contexts. There are a few specimens from older contexts, probably Ahrensburgian (e.g. Mathiassen 1948, Nos. 159-60), that suggest that the tool was known, used or stored on inland sites in the Late Glacial.

3.2 Equipment used for the processing or consumption of food, whether in domestic or hunting contexts.

Unretouched and backed blades
See section 3.1 above.

Notched and denticulated pieces

These were only recently officially recognized in South Scandinavian Stone Age typology (e.g. E.B. Petersen 1966, Nos. 28-30), and were thus not re-covered in a large number of pre-1960s excavations from which all debitage, except for 'elegant pieces', were discarded on site after counting. As to function, microwear analyses suggest a variety of primarily domestic uses (H.J. Jensen, personal comm.). H.J. Jensen, however, emphasizes that this goes for actually retouched notches and denticulates. The role of pieces with un-retouched notches and denticulates, many of which seem to be the accidental results of trampling, excavation, or post-excavational handling, is less certain.

Slotted daggers

See Section 3.1 above.

Knives of wild boar tusk (e.g. Mathiassen 1948, No. 187)

Their function(s) remains obscure; they may have served in all kinds of activities in a variety of economic and domestic areas.

Ulna daggers (e.g. Mathiassen 1948, No. 186)

These naturally sharp, pointed implements also await detailed functional analysis. Like tusk-knives they may have functioned in a variety of economic and domestic areas.

'Skinning knives' (e.g. Mathiassen 1948, Nos. 184-5)

These have been interpreted in various ways, but await detailed functional analysis. If used for skinning or butchering, they belong in the present Group 2, if used for hide preparation they belong to Group 4 (below).

3.3 Equipment used for the manufacture of tools for groups 1 and 2 above

Cores, hammer-stones, and pressure-flakers

Basic to the manufacture of most flint implements were, of course, cores from which blades and flakes were struck or pressed by means of hammer-stones and pressure-flakers. Cores are omnipresent on all excavated sites as are core rejuvenation flakes. They may be counted as basic domestic equipment, although they also may have served as mobile gear for *ad hoc* production of hunting or maintenance equipment.

Knives and unretouched blades

See section 3.1.

Flake and blade scrapers (including truncated blades)

This is probably the major tool category most heavily investigated by micro-wear analysts (e.g. Dumont 1987, Moss 1983, Keeley 1978, 1981, Plisson 1982, H.J. Jensen 1982a & b).

While only a few studies pertain directly to the Maglemosian or Early Mesolithic (e.g. Star Carr and Mount Sandel) the general wide variety of uses is clear. It seems fair to suggest, however, that they basically served in domestic or on-site activities such as the manufacture of tools for other economic activities (Group 1 and 2) and hide preparation (Group 4). For many years it has been customary to draw a simple analogy with recent and extant hunter-gatherers, and suggest that scrapers were used primarily by women. Appealing as such analogies may be for behavioural modelling, however, I believe that such sex-specific relationships should be demonstrated rather than assumed.

Burins

This tool class (e.g. E.B. Petersen 1966, Nos. 11-19) was not introduced into South Scandinavian archaeology until 1927 (Westerby 1927) and even thereafter up through the 1940s was often overlooked. In many instances these tools were thus discarded on site with the debitage after completion of the excavation.

Microwear research (e.g. Dumont 1987, Moss 1983, Keeley 1978) has thrown some light on their uses. Formerly they were frequently assumed to have been associated only with the working of bone and antler (Clark & Thompson 1953, Clark 1954).

The overall impression is one of primarily domestic manufacturing and curative activities, which also is supported by the common presence on settlements of burin spalls.

Borers (e.g. Mathiassen 1948, Nos. 38-41, 44, E.B. Petersen 1966, Nos. 8-9)

Microwear research (e.g. Dumont 1987, Moss 1983, Keeley 1978, 1981) indicates that their primary, but not exclusive, task was to bore holes in bone and antler. Their use for piercing hides sorts under Group 4 below.

Notched and denticulated pieces

See Section 3.1 and 3.2 above.

Axes and adzes of flint (e.g. Mathiassen 1948, Nos. 54-7)

Domestic use is manifest in re-sharpening flakes left at many sites. Core-axes were almost exclusively used on wood (both chopping and planing) at Star Carr and Mount Sandel, whereas the Mount Sandel flake axes were exclusively used for planing and adzing (Dumont 1987). Hideworking has been identified on resharpening flakes, but this does not necessarily imply this was part of the parent tool's function.

Although their role for hunting cannot be ruled out, the evidence so far suggests domestic manufacture of tools, curation, construction, and cutting of firewood.

Axes and adzes of greenstone (e.g. Mathiassen 1948, Nos. 109-10)
These are fairly uncommon on Maglemosian sites. No conclusive evidence of their use(s) exists. Probably they served in domestic manufacture and curation of equipment.

Axes and adzes of red deer and elk antler (e.g. Mathiassen 1948, Nos. 118-9, 121-2, 124, 126-8)
Maglemosian type antler axes are commonly found both on settlements and as stray finds. The red deer antler axes are frequently decorated. Some have been furnished with adze blades of flint. They are also often heavily worn and some show signs of repair and/or re-arrangement of the shafthole. This may indicate heavy labour input and suggests personalized prestige gear for both domestic and off site use. According to G. Jensen (1991) they were predominantly used on wood.

Awls
Awls of bone await functional analysis. Most (e.g. S.H. Andersen 1981) interpret them as hide working tools with a piercing function, but uses connected with binding and cordage cannot be excluded.

3.4 Equipment used for non-subsistence related activities

A great number of expected activities and tool functions clearly remain to be discovered and documented. Most construction work, i.e. for dwellings, racks, and means of transportation (except for paddles) remains unknown. It is tempting to think in terms of stone axes, and to some extent antler axes, for heavy duty work (Blankholm 1991, Grøn 1983, G. Jensen 1991), but many other implements may have been used.

Scrapers, knives, unretouched blades, borers, and burins have all been documented to have been used to various degrees for cutting, scraping or piercing hides. Hides may have been used for a wide range of necessities: clothing, containers, bags, covers, straps, etc., and awls, 'seam-smoothers' and sewing needles may also have served in their manufacture. However bark and plant fibre may also have been used for a wide range of necessities. How such materials were worked and by which tools largely awaits discovery (though see

H.J. Jensen 1983) unless, of course, the microwear category 'wood working' is equated with bark working.

Knives, borers and burins have also been used for decorative art on bone, antler and amber, and once again long decorated antler picks may have had symbolic or ritual rather than practical functions.

3.5 Hunting technique

Hunting technique is not to be confused with hunting strategy. In this context, technique relates solely to the way(s) prey was hunted, killed or caught. The evidence is clearly scanty, but some suggestions have recently been forwarded.

Mithen (1987, 1990; see also Woodman 1991 for a review) proposes selective stalking for the major five species (aurochs, elk, red deer, roe deer, and pig), but bases his research on only a very small and temporally biased sample of South Scandinavian Mesolithic sites, and on secondary or tertiary sources (see also Section 1.3). Moreover, he argues that a preponderance of certain ungulate species was one of the reasons for the development of new types of microliths, and that differentiation in microlithic form may have been a quick means of producing weapons, with each form intended to kill different species. These are unwarranted assumptions.

Firstly, the actual finds of skeletal elements with embedded points do not seem to corroborate his argument. Secondly, as to the South Scandinavian Mesolithic and in particular to the postulated change in ungulate population and composition on Zealand (i.e. elk and aurochs disappear at some point in time during the Atlantic; Aaris-Sørensen 1980) is highly questionable (Newell 1990). Thirdly, gross changes in preferred microlithic form may have other connotations (Blankholm 1980, 1990). Certainly, in this particular case these changes do not correlate with changes in animal species composition or preferences for prey.

In essence, Mithen's argument is in line with other notions about change in general hunting equipment from the Upper Paleolithic and into the Mesolithic (Gamble 1987). Probably more research is needed in this respect, but in both eras large and small hunting equipment was produced. Perhaps it is only in sheer numbers that gross categories such as microblades and microliths characterize the Early Mesolithic, but then again the numbers may not seem so large if the microliths are divided into preforms, serviceable, used and discarded and the numbers then compared with duration of occupation or frequency of re-use of the sites. As to the socio-stylistic meaning of microliths, see Blankholm (1990).

Opposed to Mithen's view is Grøn's (1983) notion that, for instance, the Prejlerup aurochs (Aaris-Sørensen & E.B. Petersen 1986, P.V. Petersen & E.B. Petersen 1984) was hunted by a cooperative band. This may have been the case, but also his argument lacks convincing evidence. Based on a wider analysis of Maglemosian microliths (Blankholm 1980, 1990) individual hunters cannot be identified and thus group composition cannot be estimated.

The excavators of the Prejlerup bull are more cautious. In his latest account, Aaris-Sørensen (1988) raises some interesting points on the hunt. Most of the microliths were found in association with the rear part of the animal and would not have inflicted fatal wounds. Aaris-Sørensen (1988, 172) asks: does this mean that blood loss and pain from wounds, and stress from the hunter and dogs not leaving it alone for a moment, were enough to do the job? Could hunting by a single marksman aided by dogs thus have been the common way to hunt aurochs? He tends to believe so himself (*ibid*). Today it is only possible to guess; any number of hunters, drivers or dogs may have participated. A twist to Aaris-Sørensen's story is that he also (1988, 172) raises the questions: did the bull really escape and later die unattended? Or was it driven into the lake without intent of retrieval, or did they try to retrieve the animal, but gave up? Or, was there some tabu against the retrieval of things from open water?

If the latter were the case it would link up well with the later and more widespread phenomena of lake/bog sacrifices, votive deposits, weapon offerings, etc. of the Neolithic, Bronze, and Iron Ages.

In the early 1970s, Noe-Nygaard (1974, 237f) reviewed Late Paleolithic and Mesolithic hunting techniques, particularly pertaining to wild boar. Ruling out sacrificial killings, she states:

It is difficult to tell what type of weapon Mesolithic man used in hunting the wild boar, but we have evidence for bow and arrow, probably spear, and an axe-like implement. The hunting methods employed were probably both long distance shooting with bow and arrow by groups, and single man participation for close-range hunting with short-range weapons. (Noe-Nygaard 1974, 239)

Although her understanding of shoulder blade lesions has recently been contested (Bratlund 1991), this essentially means communal hunting.

Comparing shoulder blade lesions from the Ahrensburgian site of Stellmoor with those from the mesolithic she further notes:

It would...be reasonable to conclude that the different distributional patterns should ...have resulted from the employment of different hunting methods for reindeer and Mesolithic game animals owing to dissimilarity in mode of life. (Noe-Nygaard 1974, 241)

This seems to be an overstatement. Firstly, the exact meaning of the alleged shoulder blade lesions is not clear (Bratlund 1991). Secondly, it may well be that the Ahrensburgians used fencing and drives to kill reindeer, but the hunting technique may have differed with season, age and sex of the animals (Binford 1978), not forgetting that even single hunters may be able to drive, trap and kill considerable numbers of reindeer all by him/herself. Furthermore, there is not necessarily any correlation between mode of life and hunting technique. It may well be that:

...Mesolithic hunters probably concentrated on the individual animal, finding, tracking, chasing and killing it. (Noe-Nygaard 1974, 242)

This apparently is also her view of how the Vig bull was hunted:

...arrows were probably used to exhaust the animal by loss of blood whereafter the spear was applied. (Noe-Nygaard 1974, 244)

Yet theoretically nothing would speak against communal hunting of smaller herds, or the use of drives by humans or dogs. Perhaps the most detailed assessment of prehistoric hunting technique is Bratlund's (1991, 199, 205-6) study of Stellmoor. Her conclusions seem ambiguous, however, in one place arguing for a communal drive hunt (*ibid* 199), while in another for ambushing the reindeer on dry land followed by shooting them while they escaped by swimming.

It often has been claimed that hunting of different species required different weapons (e.g. S.H. Andersen 1981, 97). At the level of large herbivores, carnivores, seals, fish or birds this may be true. Yet in theory nothing would speak against standardized hunting gear for, say, the terrestrial animals.

Animals like beaver, fox, wolf, lynx, bear, marten, otter and wild cat probably were hunted mostly for their fur. Conspicuous depressed fractures in the rear parts of several crania of these species suggest trapping, while the fact that almost complete articulated skeletons often are found in the settlement refuse (e.g. the wolf skeleton at Sværdborg I, 1943-44, Area B; Aaris-Sørensen 1976) suggests that the meat itself (save perhaps for beaver) was not always important.

Lake fishing using spears or leisters tipped with barbed bone points is indirectly documented by the several fishing sites where numerous complete or broken points have been found still oriented tip downwards in the old lake bed. Examples from Ulkestrup, Mullerup and Sværdborg I, 1923 clearly show marks made by rotting fish, and the Kunda-Lammasmägi example of a pike skeleton probably with an embedded bone point (the evidence is inconclusive) may also indicate fishing (see also Section 3.1). Fish traps are known from the Neolithic (e.g. Halskov, L. Pedersen 1992), and fishing nets have been found in Early Mesolithic settings from Finland (Clark 1975, 221f). Both of these passive, but efficient, devices may well have been employed by the Maglemosians too.

In conclusion, we have solid information on the weapons used in a small number of hunting and fishing incidents. However, the behaviourally and culturally more important questions of whether individual or communal hunting (or both) were employed, or whether stalking, ambushes or drives were used cannot be further discussed.

Too much speculation has probably been based on too rigid notions of ecology and animal behaviour, e.g. open tundra versus dense forest, migrating versus generally stationary species living in small herds. In particular, it seems as if the long-lived scenarios of forest succession provided by Jessen (1935b), Iversen (1967), and S. Jørgensen (1954) have hampered more nuanced views. Even taken at face value, the Preboreal/Boreal of the Maglemosian era showed considerable ecological and geographical variation through time, so even if one follows a strictly ecological paradigm, there should be plenty of room for more variability in both hunting technique and strategy than has been allowed for so far.

4 Selection of material and general source assessment

The main criterion by which sites were selected for inclusion in this study is systematic excavation with artifacts of stone, bone and antler recorded in square meters. Moreover, a minimum of 50 skeletal elements is required for a usable representation of at least one individual, regardless of species.

It is impossible to set the same lower limit for areal extent of excavations as previously used in investigations of hut floors (Blankholm 1981, 1984, 1987a). Yet in order to gain insights into behaviour around, for example, hearths, the areal extent of contiguous excavated squares should exceed 5 x 5 m.

The sites enumerated below satisfy the above criteria. However, they vary in quality. Some are homogeneous units, others are probably heterogeneous, while others again are stratified and documented to an extent that permits only general conclusions. Moreover, some sites can be split into smaller analytical units.

Local preservation conditions for bone and antler vary, but are in general good. Notably, certain of the least resistant bones from pig, for instance vertebra and sternum, are among those most frequently preserved. In fact, there is a notable degree of consistency in data representation between or among sites with differing preservation conditions. Activity by dogs is visible in many sites, but is negligible in analytical terms.

A perusal of South Scandinavian sites with special regard to zoological data shows the following. Figure 2 shows their geographical distribution.

Mullerup Syd

The site, of which 300 m^2 were systematically excavated in 1900, was published by the excavator in 1903 (Sarauw 1903).

Within a smaller area of the highest part of the site in Main Section I (Sarauw 1903, Figs. 2 & 3), a series of new, artificial sections (not displayed) shows two possible horizons separated by a layer with lower artifact frequencies. This may have been caused by the plotting of arbitrary, rather than naturally separated, excavation layers. This is often a problem when layers are not themselves horizontal (which they seldom are). Another probable explanation is recent disturbances (Sarauw 1903, 163), and possibly it could also indicate an actual sequence of occupation. A series of C-14 samples (K-1609-11, Tauber 1970) yields dates between 6710 and 6550 BC.

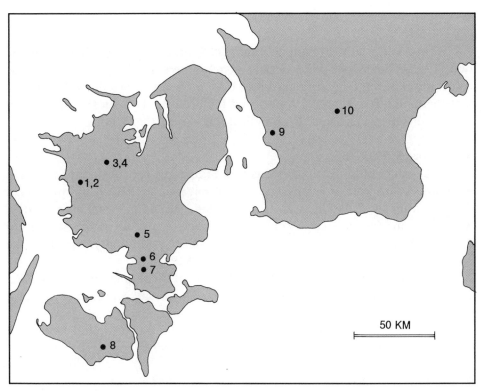

Fig. 2. Site distribution. 1) Mullerup Syd, 2) Mullerup Nord, 3) Ulkestrup I, 4) Ulkestrup II, 5) Holmegård I, IV & V, 6) Lundby I & II, 7) Sværdborg I & II, 8) Skottemarke, 9) Segebro, 10) Ageröd I:B, I:D & V.

The stratigraphy of the remainder of the site, however, shows the expected clines in frequency distributions and as a whole the material is homogeneous. Also refittings of bone fragments (Sarauw 1903) across the site indicate homogeneity. However, reuse over a shorter span of years cannot be excluded.

Ulkestrup I & II
Excavated by Knud Andersen in 1947-50. A preliminary report was published in 1951 (K. Andersen 1951) to be followed by a full publication three decades later (K. Andersen *et al.* 1982). 89 m² were excavated at Ulkestrup I and 92 m² at Ulkestrup II (the connecting trenches amount to 53 m²) (K. Andersen *et al.* 1982).

Ulkestrup I is a single, homogeneous unit, the dating of which (6190 BC (K-2174, K. Andersen *et al.* 1982)) is, however, questionable (Blankholm 1990). Ulkestrup II, however, represents at least two occupations (K. Andersen *et al.* 1982) for which reason conclusions about the latter must remain general. An average of three C-14 samples yields a date of 6130 BC (K-1507-9, K. Andersen *et al.* 1982).

In her zoological treatment, Richter (1982) did not distinguish between the two sites, i.e. the respective materials were lumped and dealt with *in toto*. The distribution of the faunal remains (see Figs. 5c & 6c), however, clearly shows that the material is spatially segregated between the two sites and that they can be considered as separate analytical units in further studies.

Sværdborg I, 1917-18

The areal extent of the various excavation campaigns at Sværdborg I is shown in Figure 7. This part of Sværdborg I was excavated in 1917-18 and published the year after by Friis-Johansen (1919). A total of 404 m² were excavated of which 314 m² forms a large coherent area and is the focus of the present analysis (Friis Johanssen 1919, 112 & Fig. 3). A preliminary report of the zoological material was provided by Winge (1919).

A compound plot of the spatial distribution of the faunal remains (see Fig. 8b), based on Winge's original accounts in the University Museum of Zoology, Copenhagen, indicate four possible units (see also Section 6). However, a division of the site into units does not allow for reliable quantitative treatment. Consequently this part of the site is treated as a whole.

Sværdborg I, 1923

Excavated and published by Broholm (1924) in a more summary fashion than Sværdborg I, 1917-18. A total of 267 m² was excavated (Broholm 1924, 92 & Fig. 37).

The zoological material was never published, but has recently been investigated by Gitte Jensen (report in the files of the University Museum of Zoology, Copenhagen) and by P. Rowley-Conwy (1993 and private files). Both have kindly given me access to their data. Plots of the spatial distribution of the faunal remains from this unstratified site allows for general assessments of human behaviour.

Sværdborg I, 1943-44

Excavated by C.J. Becker and published by B.B. Henriksen (1976). Altogether 642 m² were excavated: 288 m² in Area A, 124 m² in Area B and 230 m² in Area C. The zoological material was treated by Aaris-Sørensen (1976) as part of the same account. Plots based on Aaris-Sørensen's private files (kindly placed at my disposal) makes possible the division of this part of Sværdborg I into smaller analytical units, except for Area B (Figs.10c, 11c, 12c).

Sværdborg II

Excavated by C.J. Becker (60 m^2 excluding trial pits) in 1946 and published by E.B. Petersen in 1972. In the same account the zoological material was treated by K. Rosenlund. It is a small unit, chronologically and culturally homogeneous, albeit with a very limited amount of bone and antler.

Lundby I

Excavated by Th. Thomsen in 1929-31 and published by B.B. Henriksen (1979). A total of 276 m^2 were investigated: 1929: 39 m^2, 1930: 64 m^2, and 1931: 173 m^2. (B.B. Henriksen 1979, 16 & Fig. 5). Some of the zoological material from the 1929 campaign was identified by Degerbøl (1933), and tools and worked pieces were identified by Rosenlund (1979) for B.B. Henriksen's publication. Recently, the faunal remains were reidentified by Peter Rowley-Conwy (1993 and private files), who kindly placed his data at my disposal.

Unfortunately, the original level of documentation does not permit detailed analysis or assessments (see also B.B. Henriksen 1979, 15f). In fact, the chronological homogeneity of the site is dubious and conclusions about behaviour are thus restricted.

Lundby II

Excavated by C.J. Becker in 1945 (124 m^2) and published by B.B. Henriksen in 1979. The zoological material was identified by Rosenlund (1979) for the site publication. A supplementary check of aurochs, elk, red deer, roe deer and pig was made by Rosenlund for the present author in 1991.

There are two horizons, which can be separated only in some places because of the original level of documentation. This of course restricts more specific assessments.

Skottemarke

Excavated in 1902 by G.A. Rosenberg. The site is published in part by Sørensen (1980) and a very detailed treatment of the zoological material is provided by Møhl (1980). This site is unique as the zoological material consists almost entirely of the remains of six nearly complete elk skeletons.

Opinions are divided as to the character of the find, particularly on whether or not the elk skeletons are associated with the flint artifacts from the same site (Sørensen 1980). My own impression is that originally the two material components may very well have been associated. In any case, it is possible to regard the elk bones as the remains of a brief episode of human activity at or near the site, directly involving the animals.

Ageröd I:B
Excavated by Althin (1954) in 1946-49 and Larsson (1978) in 1971-73. The site is divisible into several analytical units (Larsson 1978). The three most reliable C-14 samples (LU-599, 698 and 873) give an average date of 6040 BC (Larsson 1978). Unfortunately, the zoological material is highly fragmented. It was identified by Lepiksaar (1978), but the MNIs (see below) are so small that the site can only serve as a general source of information.

Ageröd I:D
Excavated similarly to Ageröd I:B and C-14 dated by the probably most reliable sample to 5990 BC (LU-751, Larsson 1978). A small homogeneous unit, the zoological material identified by (Lepiksaar 1978) is unfortunately also so fragmented and has so small MNI totals that it is only possible to give a vague assessment of the economy.

Ageröd V
Excavated by Althin (1954) in 1947-48 and by Larsson (1983) in 1972 and 1977-80. A homogeneous unit from the younger part of the Kongemose Culture, but with rather fragmented zoological data identified by Lepiksaar (1983). This non-Maglemosian site is only included for comparative purposes.

Segebro
Excavated during several campaigns by Salomonsson (1964), Gerber in 1971 and Larsson (1982) in 1973 and 1976. Several occupations range in time from the Late Glacial through the Atlantic. Only the Atlantic Kongemose material (Lepiksaar 1982) is included in the present context for comparison.

Three other, non-Scandinavian, sites have been included for comparison: The Maglemosian site Star Carr in England (Clark 1954, 1972, Legge & Rowley-Conwy 1988), the Hamburgian site Meiendorf, and the Ahrensburgian site Stellmoor, both in northern Germany (Rust 1937, 1943, Krause 1937, Kollau 1943, Grønnow 1987, Bratlund 1991). These three sites have all recently been subjected to modern archaeo-zoological analysis and need no further presentation.

Unfortunately it is necessary to exclude Holmegård I, IV and V.

Holmegård I was generally excavated in 2.0-2.5 x 7-9 m strips over an area of 2044 m² (Broholm 1924, 7). At best only a very small portion of the zoological material can be referred to either half of any particular strip. Several occupations and analytical units are likely, although Rowley-Conwy's (1993) investigations of the faunal assemblage indicates a fairly homogeneous settlement, allowing for very generalized statements about certain economic aspects of the site.

Holmegård IV (Becker 1945) must also be excluded for reasons of incomplete documentation (Blankholm 1980).

Holmegård V is similar in this respect. A perusal of the original documentation by the present author (Blankholm 1980) showed up to six horizons (see also Troels-Smith, unpublished report in the files of the National Museum, Copenhagen), within which it is only possible to locate a minor part of the flint and bone material.

As to its often postulated status as a winter site (e.g. Becker 1953, E.B. Petersen 1973, Grøn 1987) this has proven premature. On the contrary, most indicators unequivocally point towards occupation within the summer half of the year (anonymous report in the Zoological Museum, Copenhagen; Rowley-Conwy 1993).

For more detailed assessments of the sites, see Chapter 6.

5 Analytical method

Basically the level of resolution of the investigation is contingent upon the detail and documentation of the zoological identification. This varies to some extent between sites such as, for example, Mullerup Syd and Sværdborg I, 1917-18 (Winge 1903, 1919), Sværdborg I, 1923 (Rowley-Conwy 1993), Sværdborg I, 1943-44 (Aaris-Sørensen 1976), Lundby I (Degerbøl 1933, Rowley-Conwy 1993), Sværdborg II and Lundby II (Rosenlund 1972, 1978), and Ulkestrup I and II (Richter 1982). This is hardly surprising. Just as lithic specialists may differ in their opinion of the typology of a site or on the meaning, or probable function, of implements, so archaeo-zoologists may vary in their opinion as to which species or skeletal element a certain bone or fragment belongs. The differences however seem mostly to result from the degree to which the individual archaeo-zoologists have wished to get involved with the difficult task of identifying small fragments. It is also interesting to note that in those present cases where more than one archaeo-zoologist has worked on one and same material (e.g. G. Jensen and P. Rowley-Conwy for Sværdborg I, 1923, and K. Rosenlund and P. Rowley-Conwy for Lundby II), the trends of the distributional profiles of skeletal element representation (representation graphs; see Section 5.4) remain almost identical.

On balance there is a basis for an investigation at the level of *identifiable elements*, which in any case also seems to be the most apropriate level (see below).

5.1 Fragments versus elements

As noted by Klein & Cruz-Uribe (1984), Grayson (1984), and Noe-Nygaard (1988) there may be several severe problems involved with analyses solely based on number of identified specimens (NISP) or fragments and their relative frequencies. Not least, the calculation and estimation of minimal number of individuals (MNI) and the relative importance of species may be heavily biased as a result of taphonomic loss, varying butchering and marrow fracturing processes, etc.

Basically the same pertains if only the relative number of elements is considered. As shown in Figure 3, there is indeed a significant correlation between the number of identifiable elements and the minimum number of individuals per species if the entire assemblage is considered. However, the number of identifiable elements cannot be used as a local estimator for the rank-

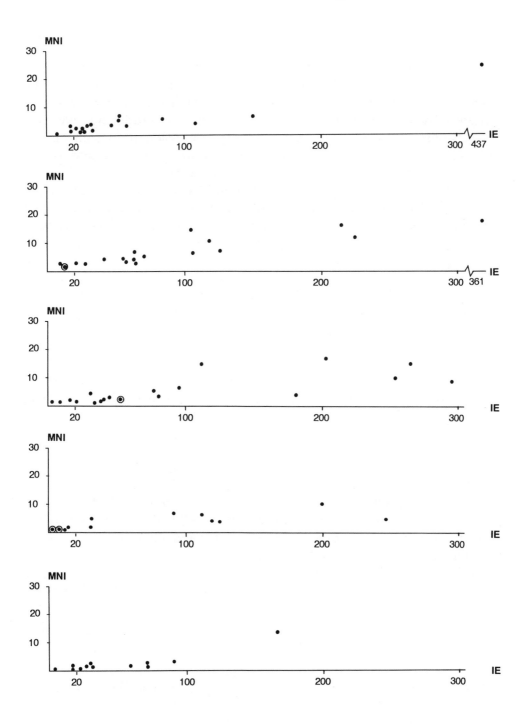

Fig. 3. The relationship between number of identifiable elements and MNI (excl. antlers and skulls): a) red deer, b) roe deer, c) pig, d) elk, e) aurochs.

order between species; out of 18 cases the rank-order is only unambiguously preserved in 3!

Analysis must thus be based on more detailed investigations of skeletal elements and derived indicators (such as MNI's, articulations, presence/ absence, etc.), while fragments *per se* may deliver supplementary information of various kinds, e.g. on degrees of fragmentation, marrow processing, and so on.

The list of elements is shown in Table 3. Aside from some minor differences the system and nomenclature follows that of Binford (1978), Grønnow (1987) and Legge & Rowley-Conwy (1988).

Partly because of preservation conditions, and partly because of the varying level of identification and documentation in the original files and records, a number of less significant elements have been omitted from analysis: caudal vertebrae, patellas, carpals, tarsals (except for astragalus (AST) and calcaneus (CAL)) and sesamoids. Moreover, it has been necessary to lump the cervical (3-7), thoracic and lumbar vertebrae into one group (VERT), and phalanges I-III into another (PHAL). On the other hand, it proved possible to treat ribs (R), sternums (ST) and ulna (UL) separately, although they occur less frequently.

In order to provide an adequate level of representation for the most important elements for further assessments, the minimum requirement is 50 identifiable elements per species per analytical unit or site. This number may seem low in some respects, but is acceptable, and most often the actual numbers greatly exceed this value (see Table 4).

5.2 Calculation of MNI (minimum number of individuals)

MNI is a key quantity in archaeo-zoology. Among the several methods of calculation, e.g. White 1952, Noe-Nygaard 1988, Chaplin 1971, Binford 1978 (see also discussions by Klein & Cruz-Uribe (1984) and Grayson (1984), Binford's has been singled out as the most realistic and attractive.

Binford's method is based on the principle that

...it is desirable to relate frequencies to the basic reference unit, the anatomy of a complete animal. (Binford 1978, 69),

thus,

...all MNIs will be calculated by dividing the observed bone count for a given identification unit by the number of bones in the anatomy of a complete animal for that unit. (Binford 1978, 70)

Table 3. Abbreviations for skeletal elements (partly after Binford 1978).

ANT(shed)	Shed antler
ANT(mass)	Massacreed antler
SK+Ant	Frontlet
SK(frag)	Cranial fragment
MAX	Maxilla
MAN	Mandible
AT	Atlas
AX	Axis
VERT	Vertebra, less cerv. 1 & 2. and caudals
SAC	Sacrum
PELV	Pelvis
RIB	Rib
ST	Sternum
SC	Scapula
PH	Prox. humerus
DH	Dist. humerus
PR	Prox. radius
DR	Dist. radius
PU	Prox. ulna
DU	Dist. ulna
PMC	Prox. metacarpal
DMC	Dist. metacarpal
PF	Prox. femur
DF	Dist. femur
PT	Prox. tibia
DT	Dist. tibia
FIB	Fibula
AST	Astragalus
CAL	Calcaneus
PMT	Prox. metatarsal
DMT	Dist. metatarsal
PHAL	Phalange

Table 4. MNI's per species per site.

Site	Red deer	Roe deer	Pig	Elk	Aurochs
Mullerup South	5.5	10.5	17.0	4.5	3.0
Mullerup North	1.0	1.0	1.0	5.0	2.5
Ulkestrup I	2.0	2.0	2.0	–	1.5
Ulkestrup II	4.5	3.0	1.0	1.0	2.0
Lundby I	2.0	5.0	6.5	2.0	2.0
Lundby II	3.5	4.5	9.0	4.0	3.5
Sværdborg 1917/18	6.0	6.5	14.5	7.0	4.0
Sværdborg 1923	6.5	16.0	14.5	6.5	2.0
Sværdborg I:A NE	1.5	4.0	2.0	1.0	–
Sværdborg I:A S	4.0	2.5	1.5	1.0	–
Sværdborg I:A Total	4.0	7.0	3.0	1.5	–
Sværdborg I:B	2.5	4.0	2.5	1.0	–
Sværdborg I:C NE	3.0	6.0	5.0	–	–
Sværdborg I:C SW	4.0	12.0	3.0	–	–
Sværdborg I:C SE	–	2.0	1.0	–	–
Sværdborg I:C Total	7.0	17.5	8.0	1.0	–
Sværdborg II	3.5	2.5	2.0	–	–
Skottemarke	–	–	–	5.0	–
Ageröd I:B	2.5	4.0	2.5	1.0	–
Ageröd I:D	1.5	1.0	1.0	–	–
Ageröd V	6.5	2.0	2.0	1.5	–
Segebro	20.0	18.0	14.5	3.0	–
Star Carr	25.0	14.0	4.0	10.5	14.0

	Reindeer
Meiendorf	71
Stellmoor A	247

This method ignores differences in side, age and sex, which however, may often

...distort the character of the assemblage and present a poor estimate of the number of animals actually killed. (Binford 1978, 71)

In other words, it is not so much the absolute number of animals that is important, but the way they were butchered and used.

Compared to that of Chaplin (1971), for instance, Binford's MNI is a conservative estimator, but the rank-order among species seems preserved.

MNIs per species per site are listed in Table 4. The minimum requirement for analytical treatment is MNI ≥ 4, which is just acceptable for the calculation of %MNI (see below).

5.3 Site-catchment analysis and estimation of meat weight

For the Late Glacial and Early Postglacial, site-catchment analysis (e.g. Vita Finzi & Higgs 1970, Jarman 1972, Blankholm 1976) can only include the most general aspects of the topography and vegetation (see also Chapter 2) and hence animal populations. In fact, site-catchment analysis cannot make a real contribution to the study and has thus been omitted.

The same pertains to estimates of available biomass for the various species. In general terms the calculation of biomass is based on a weak foundation (more often than not speculative comparisons and estimates are based on modern populations from environments not directly comparable with those in question). Moreover, estimates of potential biomass for a given area are dependent on the parameters of site-catchment analysis, which has been omitted in the first place.

In fact, the aim of the present study is to investigate the actual, rather than the theoretical, exploitation of the species (see also Rowley-Conwy 1993).

5.4 %MNI, utility indices and representation graphs

For comparative analyses, it is useful to standardize zoological data by means of %MNI (percent MNI).

This quantity is calculated for each species per site by dividing the MNI for each element by the highest MNI, and multiplying by 100 (Binford 1978). For the same reasons as given by Legge & Rowley-Conwy (1988) antlers and skulls are excluded from the calculations.

Utility indices such as MGUI (Modified General Utility Index) and IMGUI (Inverse Modified General Utility Index) (Binford 1978, 72f) have played an important role for the assessment of economic behaviour in prehistoric societies (e.g. Speth 1983, Grønnow 1987, Legge & Rowley-Conwy 1988). Criticism and refinements of the MGUI were offered by Metcalfe & Jones (1988), who developed the less complex FUI (Food Utility Index).

Such indices are problematic, however. Originally developed by Binford for reindeer and sheep, they were only based on investigations of one and two animals of these species respectively (Binford 1978, see also Speth 1983, Grønnow 1987, Legge & Rowley-Conwy 1988, Metcalfe & Jones 1988).

Moreover, it remains an open question whether or not utility index values may be reasonably transferred to other species in other biotopes (as done by for example Speth (1983) and Legge & Rowley-Conwy (1988)). Probably the best way to use Binford's indices archaeologically would be in situations where one is dealing only with reindeer (or sheep) in an arctic biotope as exemplified by Grønnow's (1987) investigation of the Hamburgian site Meiendorf and the Ahrensburgian site Stellmoor in northern Germany. This is far from a broadly mixed economy using several species in a boreal biotope, where the weighting of the utility of the various skeletal elements may have been different.

It also remains to incorporate into the weighting procedures a most important factor: the utility of the various skeletal elements for tool manufacture. Intuitively, only one of Binford's indices, the IMGUI, would give a weighting corresponding to what may be anticipated from the knowledge of the Maglemosian tool tradition. However, because of the above inherent problems this will be omitted.

The same pertains to representation graphs for %MNI (e.g. Binford 1978, Figs. 2.11 & 3.12; Legge & Rowley-Conwy 1988, Figs. 35-37). Generally %MNI graphs for a single animal across several sites, or for several species from a single site, are placed together in a single presentation. The problem is, however, that there is no standardized or rigorous technique available to compare the curves. Very much depends on a subjective estimate based on eyeballing — exactly as in the early days of spatial analysis (Blankholm 1991). Moreover, it is difficult systematically and consistently to compare graphs for a larger number of sites.

Instead, I have chosen a multivariate method, Correspondence Analysis (e.g. Bølviken *et al.* 1982, Blankholm 1991 with references), which allows the simultaneous evaluation of units and variables. This method is not to be confused with the clustering procedures used by Binford & Stone (1986). As an initial methodological step, Correspondence Analysis was successfully tested on 40 of Binford's Nunamiut sites (not shown), including 4 dispersed kill-butchering locations by season, 2 spring kill-butchering sites, 3 spring intercept hunting stands, 9 hunting stands, 1 early summer high mountain hunting camp, 1 mountain hunting camp, 5 August lower hunting camps, 2 late summer hunting camps, 6 fall hunting stands, 3 late fall hunting stands, 2 fall residential sites, and 2 winter residences (Binford 1978, 76, 78, 176, 180, 270, 294, 307, 314, 351, 353, 356-7, 380, 430, 436 & Tables 2.8, 2.9, 5.1, 5.3, 6.6, 6.13, 6.17-8, 7.1-4, 7.13, 8.1, 8.4).

5.5 Sex and age distributions

Although sex and age do not enter the MNI calculations they remain an important part of paleoeconomic studies in general, not least for the assessment of hunting strategies, season of kill and time of occupation (see also Seasonality, Section 5.6).

The Maglemosian material is well documented as far as sex and age determinations go. Yet we are faced with a basic, but overriding, issue of representation. As shown in Table 4, the species frequencies (MNIs) are generally low (and would have remained low even if sex and age had entered into the MNI calculations). Then, for example, if we were to work with the two sexes and say three age-groups (neonatal, young and adult), we would expect a division of the MNIs into six groups, which again would seem to yield statistically too small numbers for a reliable, comparative analysis.

Consequently, considerations pertaining to sex and age must remain general.

5.6 Seasonality

Several aspects go into the determination of season of occupation. For instance, tooth eruption, fusion of articular ends of bones, antler development, presence of migrating birds and fish, hibernating animals, availability of fruits and seeds, and so on.

Traditionally it has been thought that there are more indicators for spring, summer and autumn than there are for winter. However, with the techniques available today, the demonstration of winter occupation is not a problem (e.g. Rowley-Conwy 1993, n.d., and personal communication). It should always be borne in mind, however, that just because a certain season is not visible in the material, this does not necessarily mean lack of occupation.

As to the Maglemosian it is commonly possible to make a broad seasonal determination of sites. However, a precise placing of a site into just one or two months for a more nuanced elucidation of the settlement pattern is deemed premature given the present state of knowledge.

5.7 Butchery, marrow processing and tool manufacture

As shown by Noe-Nygaard (1973, 1988), Legge & Rowley-Conwy (1988) and

Richter (1982) information is generally available on aspects of butchering, marrow processing and tool manufacture techniques.

As this study is concerned with the general patterns of exploitation only broader aspects will be dealt with. It is argued that all three tasks are related and anticipated in a single strategy. This is supported by the fact that apart from some specifics, there is no separate set of techniques associated with each one of the tasks. For example, the articular ends of cylindrical bones are removed both for marrow extraction and to get rid of them before the shaft is split or worked into tool components. If the bone was of no immediate interest it was probably treated in a more careless fashion.

5.8 Spatial analysis

Spatial analysis of stone and bone/antler material respectively, generally follows the guiding principles laid down by Blankholm (1991) with particular emphasis on the method Presab (Blankholm 1991, 151f, 174f, 199f). Two sets of analysis will be made for each site; one for flint artifacts and another for species representation.

Because of the differing preservation potentials and conditions, the two materials cannot be grouped into a single analysis. It should also be mentioned that because there are too many interdependent variables conditioned by the original composition of the anatomy of the various species (rather than human behaviour), more detailed spatial analysis of elements has been omitted.

6 The relationship between zoological material and basic residential analytical units

As in previous investigations of various aspects of the Maglemosian, e.g. hut floors, socio-styles, and so forth (Blankholm 1980, 1981, 1984, 1987a), it is important to base studies on analytical, spatially segregated units.

The differing preservation potentials and conditions for the two categories of material, flint and bone/antler, make it almost impossible to achieve even approximate spatial congruency between flint-based analytical units and concentrations of bone and antler. For this reason two sets of analyses will be made; one for the flint and bone material (see also Section 5.8).

Only in a limited number of cases is it possible to indicate a possible spatial relationship between main concentrations of zoological data and certain flint-based units (see Table 5).

6.1 The spatial relationship between tools, waste products and bone/antler

A number of formation processes militate against the use of formal spatial analytical methods for the investigation of relationships between tools and waste products of flint, and bone/antler, respectively.

First, tools, pre-forms and waste products of bone and antler are broadly correlated in space among themselves and with other zoological data because of the prevailing preservation conditions.

Generally it is not possible to carry out a fully integrated spatial analysis for both flint and bone for the higher and drier parts of sites simply because bones are not preserved or are too sparsely represented in those areas. Basically, we can investigate only those parts of sites containing preserved bone material and this might very well bias the picture. For instance, even if we found that certain tool types of flint were positively associated with certain kinds of bone tools or waste (or even if the flint tools were absent from the higher parts of the site), this relationship could be spurious since we would not know whether the pertinent bone artifacts originally spread over the entire site. In fact, what could be seen as strong positive associations could turn out to have been just local or marginal phenomena of probably low behavioural relevance.

On several sites it is furthermore uncertain whether the zoological material was in the first place discarded on dry land where tools may have been used, or whether most of the material may be characterized as tossed out debris of mixed origin.

**Table 5. The relationship between zoological units and hut floors
(Blankholm 1980, 1984, 1987a).**

Zoological unit	Hut floor
Mullerup Syd	Mullerup South 2
Mullerup Nord	–
Ulkestrup I	Ulkestrup I
Ulkestrup II	Ulkestrup II
Sværdborg I	
1917-18	–
1923	–
Area A (1943)	
NE	Central
S	Southern
Areal B	United
Areal C	
NE	Northeastern
SE	–
SW	Southwest, north and south
Sværdborg II	Sværdborg II
Lundby I (1929)	–
Lundby II	Lundby II?
Skottemarke	–
Ageröd I:B	–
Ageröd I:D	Ageröd I:D
Ageröd V	–
Segebro	–

Moreover, as mentioned in Section 5.8, there are too many inter-dependent variables conditioned by the original composition of the anatomy of the various species (rather than human behaviour) to make detailed spatial analysis of elements feasible.

Several other potential and real sources of error are obvious. Firstly, bone and antler tools generally are too few in number for reliable spatial analysis. Secondly, the function of the tools can only be assumed. Thirdly, several tool types and by-products were not recognised at the time of excavation and were discarded on site with the debitage (see also Blankholm 1991).

Thus, the general procedure adopted has been to make two sets of analyses: the flint material is investigated first, and a tentative match is then made with the bone material. Accordingly, the spatial analytical results below (using Presab, Blankholm 1991) must be taken with some reservation. All measurements of spatial extent in the analyses below are approximate.

Mullerup Syd

The contoured distribution of flint debitage and the analytically defined hut floor are shown in Figure 4a.

Omitting 8 axes from the central part of the site and lumping flake and blade scrapers, a Presab analysis (unsmoothed, gridded data) of the flint tools resulted in 7 groups (Fig. 4b). The data base is listed in Appendix C.

Group 1. Scrapers only; 20 cases, except for one, with a peripheral distribution (13 single occurrences) relative to the indicated dwelling (Fig. 4a and Blankholm 1980). At the southern and western edge of the floor area there are 2 and 4 contiguous squares respectively.

Group 2. Burins only; 6 single occurrences, also with a peripheral distribution, but generally closer to the analytically defined floor.

Group 3. Unilaterally and bilaterally retouched blades only; 15 cases, generally with a peripheral distribution (11 single squares) relative to the indicated floor, but with two concentrations of 2 x 1 m each near its southern margin.

Group 4. A single case of a scraper and burin together near the eastern edge of the floor.

Group 5. Scrapers and laterally retouched blades; 11 cases centrally positioned on or near the floor. Two coherent areas of 3 m² each are located on the northeastern and southern part of the floor respectively.

Group 6. Burins and laterally retouched blades; 4 cases with 2 located on the floor and another two in the periphery of the site.

Group 7. Scrapers, burins and laterally retouched blades; 3 cases located on the floor.

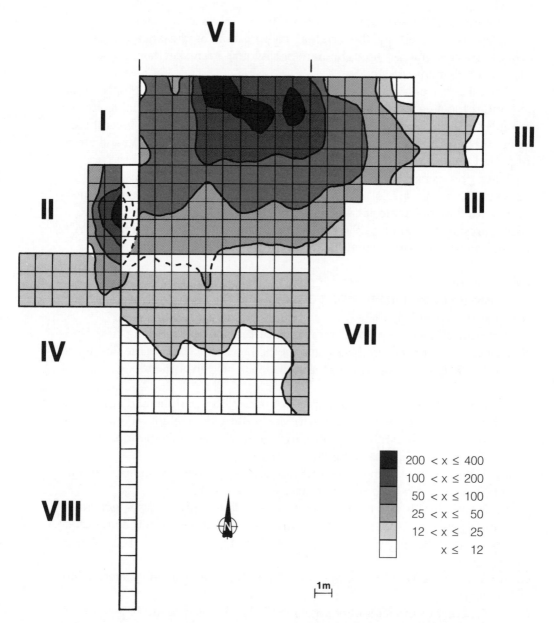

Fig. 4a. Mullerup Syd. Contoured distribution of debitage. $\Sigma = 13727$, $\bar{X} = 50$.

No particular flint tool type is restricted to a particular part of the site. Rather, it is in the association of types that some patterning is found.

We can perceive a central area (the analytically defined dwelling area) with all three major classes (scrapers, burins and laterally retouched blades) present

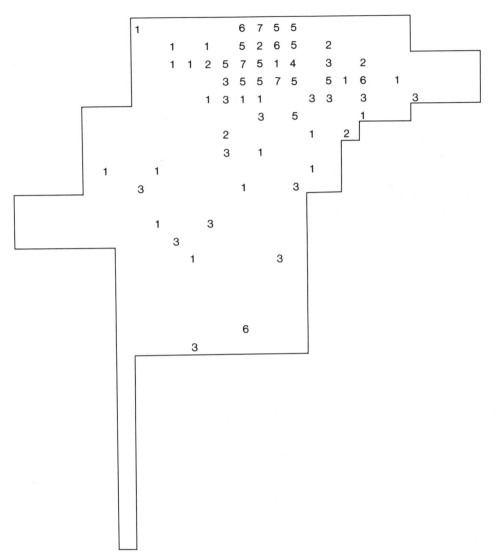

Fig. 4b. Mullerup Syd. Presab. Flint tools.

in various combinations, but without any consistent internal patterning. This probably was a multitask work area.

In addition to this is a broad fan extending all the way from the east to the southwest of largely isolated, single occurrences of any of the three classes in the low-lying part of the excavated area. This may be interpreted as a discard and toss zone.

Unfortunately, the original records do not indicate the location of any

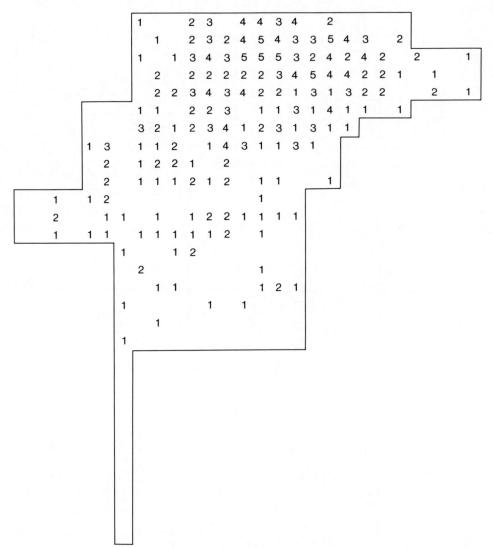

Fig. 4c. Mullerup Syd. Presab. Bones.

hearths, nor can these be reconstructed. Consequently reconstruction of hearth related activities must be omitted.

A Presab analysis of the distribution of the five major species converted from 26 groups into a simpler representation of number of species present, shows the following (Fig. 4c):

1.   1 species present; 69 cases, almost exclusively found on the periphery of the faunal distribution.

2. 2 species present; 44 cases, also generally peripherally distributed, but mostly closer to the centre of the faunal distribution than Group 1.
3. 3 species present; 23 cases, generally closer to the centre of the faunal distribution than Groups 1 and 2 above.
4. 4 species present; 17 cases with a general distribution fairly similar to Group 3.
5. 5 species present; 5 cases, all within the limits of the floor and re-presenting the centre of the faunal distribution.

The spatial layout of the numerical distribution of flint waste is congruent with that of worked and unworked bone and antler (Fig. 4c), showing that in this particular case bone and antler is preserved over the entire site.

At this coarse level of resolution bone tools do not add much to the picture. The following example will suffice. Barbed bone points associate with the stone tool groups as follows: 1 x Group 1, 2 x Group 3, 2 x Group 5; i.e. altogether 5 points out of 31 were found in association with stone tools. The dissociation with burins should be noted. Generally barbed points are peripherally distributed relative to the floor.

Unbarbed points and bodkins associate as follows: 2 x Group 1, 2 x Group 2, 3 x Group 3, 4 x Group 5 and 1 x Group 7. Altogether 12 out of 37 were found in association with flint tools. Generally the distribution is more even than that of the barbed points, with several both on the floor and in the periphery.

Tusk-knives associate as follows: 2 x Group 2, 1 x Group 5 and twice with plain bone points. Thus 5 out of 11 tools are associated with the floor, the remainder are found in isolation on the periphery.

Antler axes: 4 out of 6 are associated centrally with Group 1, 5, 6, and 7, respectively.

Thus particular bone tools are not generally associated with particular flint tools in any consistent way, and only occasionally associated among themselves.

No specific activity areas can be discerned from what is left from the original records. Larger articulated sections of animals are missing. The IPD distribution in Figure 4d (the distribution of *Intact* bones and *Proximal* and *Distal* ends of limb bones, except for AST, CAL & PHAL) is interesting with its high proportion of intact bones. These are densely packed in the dwelling area, from which a more mixed discard area extends towards the periphery. This is not consistent with, say, Binford's (1978) toss pattern around open air hearths; yet it is not to be expected either if food consumption and bone-working primarily were indoor phenomena on the site.

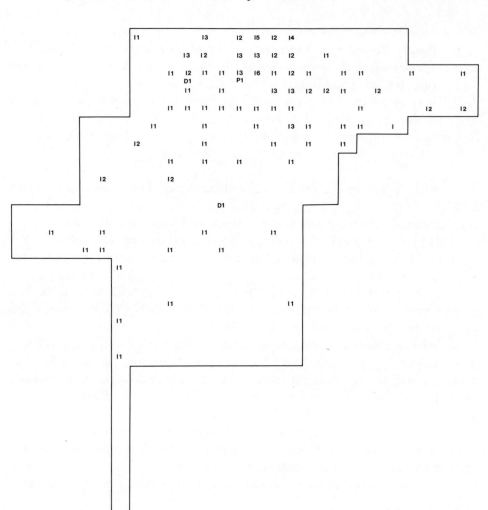

Fig. 4d. Mullerup Syd. IPD-distribution.

The general impression of the pattern is a largely undifferentiated multi-task hut floor, surrounded by a peripheral, submerged discard and toss zone.

Ulkestrup I

A spatial analysis of the flint tools (K. Andersen *et al.* 1982, Figs. 13-16) using Presab (Blankholm 1991) on smoothed, gridded data reveals 6 groups, see Figures 5a and b.

Group 1. Burins and cores; 4 cases in the eastern periphery of the refuse layer.

Group 2. Scrapers, burins and cores; 4 cases in the outmost periphery of the refuse layer.

Group 3. Burins, triangular microliths and cores; 2 cases in the northeastern part of the refuse layer.

Group 4. Scrapers, burins, triangular microliths and cores; 12 cases. This combination characterizes the immediate entrance area at the southestern end of the hut floor.

Group 5. Burins, lanceolate and triangular microliths, and cores; 3 cases at the northwestern end of the floor.

Group 6. Scrapers, burins, lanceolate and triangular microliths, and cores; with 35 cases this is the standard tool set characterizing the actual floor area.

Since cores are an element in all 6 groups, variability is essentially created only by scrapers, burins, lanceolate and triangular microliths. While flint tools extend all over the site, bone and antler is almost only preserved in the waterlogged refuse area to the east and south (Fig. 5c). Since the latter was below the water table at the time of occupation (K. Andersen *et al.* 1982) there is no need to attempt to integrate both flint and bones in a formal spatial analysis. This is a genuine discard/refuse area with no major articulated sections of animals and no activity areas whatsoever. Thus, the Presab analysis (Blankholm 1991) of the species distributions only serves to illustrate associations in a discard area. The configuration shows 6 groups (Fig. 5c):

1. Red deer, pig and aurochs; 3 cases in the northeastern and southeastern periphery.
2. Red deer, elk and aurochs; 1 case in the northern part of the site.
3. Red deer, roe deer, pig and aurochs; 3 cases in the northwestern and southeastern periphery.
4. Roe deer, pig, elk and aurochs; 1 case in the southwestern periphery.
5. Red deer, pig, elk and aurochs; 8 cases of which 6 are contiguous in the northern part of the faunal distribution.
6. All five species; 11 contiguous cases covering the central and southern part of the faunal distribution.

If toss or discard behaviour was haphazard, this pattern is only to be expected (no species is restricted to a particular area by itself, and the further one gets to the periphery from the centre or point of emergence of the distribution the fewer species are found in association). The almost complete absence of roe deer bones from the northern part is interesting, but should not be overrated. In essence, Group 5 equals Group 6 (less roe deer) in composition, and the

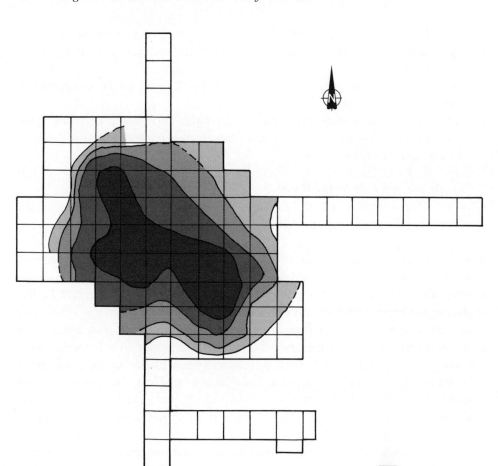

Fig. 5a. Ulkestrup I. Contoured distribution of debitage. Σ = 10557, $\bar{X}$ = 143.

only thing one can say for sure is that for one or another reason roe deer
bones were not thrown in this direction.

The IPD distribution of limb bones (save for AST, CAL & PHAL) in Figure
5d largely reflects the situation around the presumed entrance area, but does
not allow firm behavioural conclusions. The concentration of proximal ends
at the centre of the distribution is interesting, but not readily explicable,

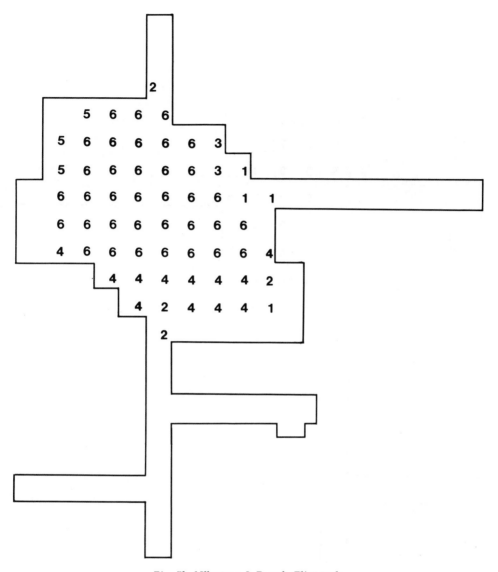

Fig. 5b. Ulkestrup I. Presab. Flint tools.

whereas the more marginal distribution of intact bones is in line with expectations for toss out patterns in a discard zone.

The homogeneity of the floor area proper is striking. This may be termed a multitask area (including consumption) situated around an internal hearth. The opposing layout of Group 4 and 5 may indicate some internal division of space. A perusal of the actual frequencies of the tool types would also seem to indicate a division of the hearth area into a southern and northwestern

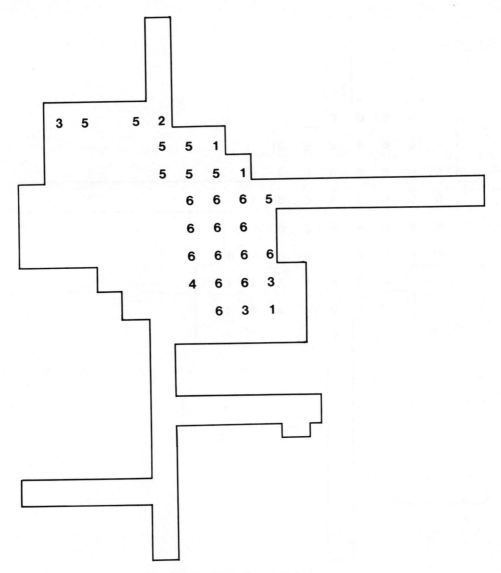

Fig. 5c. Ulkestrup I. Presab. Bones.

working/consumption area respectively (see K. Andersen *et al.* 1982, Blank-holm 1980, 1984). However, this division may prove spurious since the divi sion line is equivalent to a pre-excavation drainage ditch (Section S/9 -10, K. Andersen *et al.* 1982). Also, contrary to Grøn (1983) a stylistic analysis of the microliths does not lend statistical support for a division into 'personal space' or motor habits (Blankholm 1980, 1985, 1990).

What is most clearly evident is on the one hand a multitask floor area with

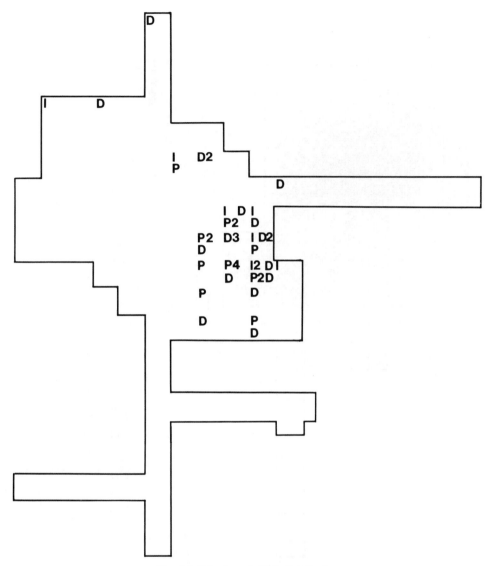

Fig. 5d. Ulkestrup I. IPD-distribution.

an internal hearth, and on the other a connecting refuse layer without activity areas.

Ulkestrup II

A spatial analysis of the flint artifacts (K. Andersen *et al.* 1982, Figs. 19-22) using Presab (Blankholm 1991) on smoothed, gridded data reveals 8 groups (Figs. 6a & b).

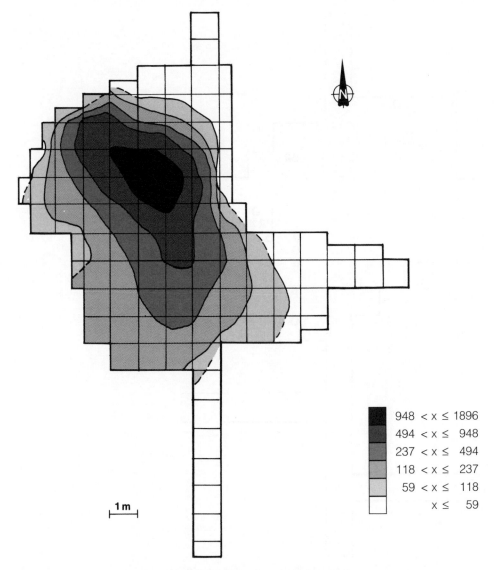

Fig. 6a. Ulkestrup II. Contoured distribution of debitage. Σ = 22793, X̄ = 237.

1. Scrapers and cores; one case in the western periphery of the site.
2. Burins and triangular microliths; one case in the northeastern corner of the site.
3. Burins and cores; two cases in two locations in the northern and eastern perimeter.

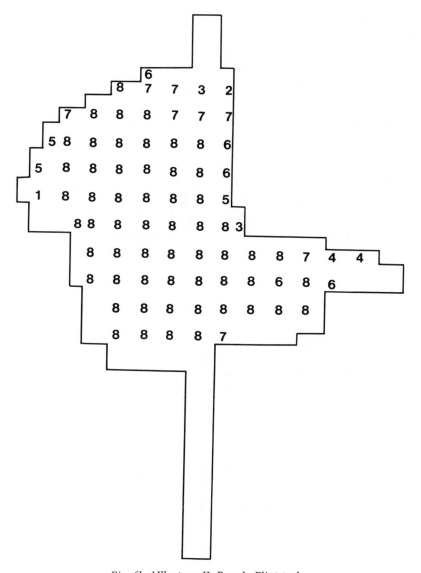

Fig. 6b. Ulkestrup II. Presab. Flint tools.

4. Triangular microliths and cores; two contiguous cases in the easternmost periphery of the site.
5. Scrapers, burins and cores; three cases of which two are contiguous on the western periphery, and one is on the eastern perimeter.
6. Scrapers, microliths and cores; four cases, all on the periphery. Two are

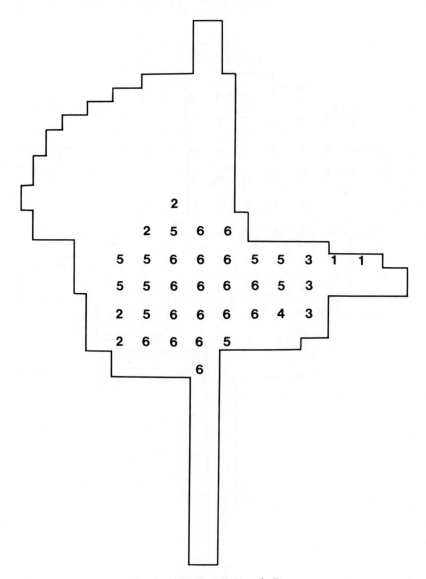

Fig. 6c. Ulkestrup II. Presab. Bones.

contiguous in the eastern margin, whereas the others are situated in the northwest and southeast corners.

7. Burins, microliths and cores; eight cases of which five are contiguous in the northern part of the site, the rest are found in isolation in various places along the periphery.

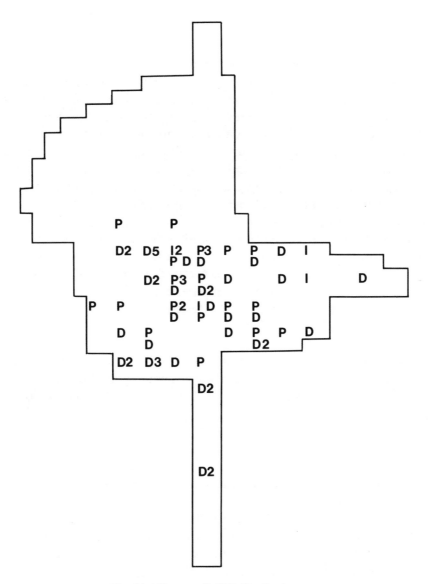

Fig. 6d. Ulkestrup II. IPD-distribution.

8. Scrapers, burins, triangular microliths and cores; 58 cases, all contiguous, the combination characterizing the entire central area of the site.

As at least two occupations seem to be responsible for the assemblage, the above must be taken with some reservation. However, the configuration seems homogeneous enough to indicate that the layout did not change dramatically over time.

Again, it is evident that cores enter all groups (except for Group 2), which may indicate that manufacture of blades and flakes was an essential activity.

From Figure 6b the only probable trend is a dominance of groups containing burins around the northern periphery, and of groups containing scrapers on either side of the centre. Otherwise, the picture is essentially the same as that of Ulkestrup I; a hut floor area with a single hearth surrounded by a consumption and multitask work area covering the floor and extending towards the lakeshore to the east. In this context probably Groups 1-7 may be seen more as accidental combinations in the water covered waste zone than indicators of possible activity areas.

As for Ulkestrup I a division of inside space is seemingly apparent from the actual numerical distribution of tools (burins, scrapers, microliths). At least there seem to be two opposing concentrations to the north and south of the hearth. Again a stylistic analysis of the microliths does not support any notions of social division of space manifested in motor habits. Probably a more likely explanation is simply that there were two preferred seating areas, which may or may not have been used by several persons.

The faunal assemblage generally derives from the southern and southeastern part of the site, which largely was submerged at the time of occupation (see K. Andersen *et al.* 1982). Thus there is no need to attempt to integrate flint and bones in spatial analysis.

A Presab analysis (Blankholm 1991) of the faunal distributions (smoothed, gridded data) consequently only serves to illustrate the composition and associations in a discard area and has no behavioural bearing on actual activity areas (Fig. 6c). The configuration is made up by 6 groups:

1. Red deer and aurochs; 2 cases in the eastern periphery of the site.
2. Red deer, roe deer and pig; 4 cases in 2 contiguous areas in the northwestern and southwestern periphery of the faunal distribution.
3. Red deer, roe deer and aurochs; 3 contiguous cases in the eastern periphery of the site.
4. Red deer, roe deer, elk and aurochs; a single case in the southeastern periphery of the site.
5. Red deer, roe deer, pig and aurochs; 10 cases almost encircling Group 6 below.
6. Red deer, roe deer, pig, elk and aurochs; 17 cases in one contiguous area covering the centre of the faunal distribution.

Red deer and roe deer are both members of all groups (except for Group 1), and variation is thus essentially caused by the presence or absence of pig, elk and aurochs. It is also conspicuous for the configuration that the farther one gets from the centre (or point of emergence) of the distribution towards the periphery of the site (or the distribution), the fewer species are generally present. This is a common picture on most sites. In essence, most variability is found in the marginal areas, as is only to be expected if toss or discard behaviour was haphazard with no particular differentiation between species being followed.

Large, articulated sections of animals are absent and the IPD-distribution of long bones (Fig. 6d) only confirms the above comments on species distribution.

Again, the general impression of Ulkestrup II is a multitask floor area with a connecting submerged discard area.

Sværdborg I, 1917-18

Due to various circumstances, more detailed spatial analysis of the flint and bone tools from this part of Sværdborg I has been omitted (a general plan of Sværdborg I is shown in Fig. 7). Instead a general assessment of the various industries will be made.

Friis-Johansen (1919, 118) made it clear early on that the manufacture of blades and flint artifacts was restricted to a number of areas characterized by high densities of flint waste. He also mentioned a possible hearth in Section XIX, square F1 (Friis-Johansen 1919, 120 & Fig. 1). However, as seen in Figure 8a, the excavation cross-cuts 3 of the major flint concentrations, and apparently no attempt was made by the excavator to plan the excavation so as to reveal any particular aspect of the site in its entirety. Most certainly the layout does not permit a detailed assessment of hut floors etc.

Not uncommonly, bone and antler is found outside the flint-knapping areas, although there is some overlap. It also needs emphasizing that bone and antler within the major flint concentrations was highly fragmented. Again this may be interpreted to suggest major, multipurpose work and consumption areas with extended discard zones, but no detailed analysis or interpretation can be made since both bone fragments and flint waste was discarded on site after completion of excavation.

A Presab analysis on smoothed, gridded data (Fig. 8b) of the presence or absence of the five major animal species reveals the common picture of all species found together in the major concentrations with perhaps more accidential associations in the periphery.

The 12 Presab groups are:

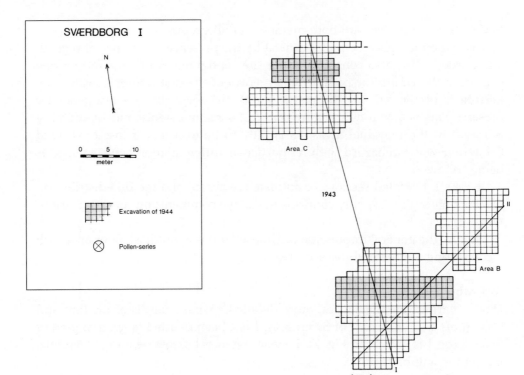

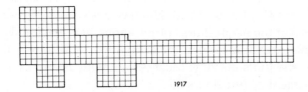

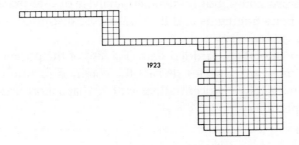

Fig. 7. General layout for Sværdborg I.

1. Roe deer only; 3 cases in the southern periphery of the faunal distribution in Section XVII.
2. Elk only; 2 cases in the southern periphery of the faunal distribution in Section X.
3. Roe deer and elk; 6 cases, of which 3 are contiguous in the southern periphery of the faunal distribution in Section X; the remaining 3 being isolated points on the periphery of the distribution in Sections XVII and XX.
4. Red deer, roe deer and pig; 8 cases, all marginally distributed in Sections I, XI, XVIII and XIX.
5. Red deer, pig and elk; 4 cases with 3 forming a contiguous area on the border between Sections I and XI, and with a single occurrence in the southern margin in Section I.
6. Roe deer, pig and elk; 5 cases of which 2 are contiguous in the southern part of the faunal distribution (in Section X), the rest being isolated occurrences in the southern part of the distribution, in Section XVII (1 case), and in the eastern periphery of the site, in Section XX (2 cases).
7. Red deer, roe deer, pig and elk; 35 cases in 4 coherent areas (3 cases in the southwestern periphery of Section I, 22 cases partly circumscribing and partly separating Group 12 areas in Section XI, 2 cases in the western half of Section XVIII, and 7 cases in the eastern periphery of the site, in Section XX) and in a single location in the western periphery of Section I.
8. Red deer, roe deer, pig and aurochs; 8 cases in two contiguous areas of two cases each in the western and southwestern periphery of Section I, and in 4 single occurrences (1 in the eastern part of Section I, the remainder in peripheral locations in Sections XVIII and XIX).
9. Red deer, roe deer, elk and aurochs; 4 cases in one contiguous area of 3 cases on the border of Sections XI and XVII, and in a single occurrence in the northeastern periphery of Section I.
10. Red deer, pig, elk and aurochs; 13 cases of which 9 form a contiguous band running north-south in the eastern part of Section I, the remaining 4 generally being more marginally located in Sections I and XI.
11. Roe deer, pig, elk and aurochs; 11 cases in 4 concentrations (2 cases on the Section I/X border in the southern periphery of the faunal distribution, 2 cases, also in the southern periphery of the faunal distribution in Section XVII, 2 cases close to the Section XI/XVII border, and 3 cases on the Section XVIII/XIX border) and in 3 isolated locations: in the northeastern and eastern part of Section I, and in the southern part of Section XX. The close proximity everywhere to Group 12 cases is interesting.
12. Red deer, roe deer, pig, elk and aurochs; 118 cases, and the most numerous type of association on the site, in 7 concentrations (55 cases essentially characterizing the central part and northern periphery of Section I, 3 cases

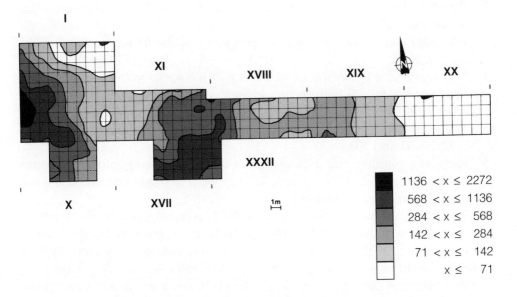

Fig. 8a. Sværdborg I, 1917-18. Contoured distribution of debitage. $\Sigma = 89273$, $\bar{X} = 284$.

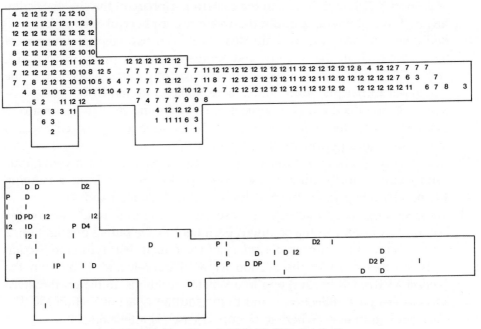

Fig. 8c. Sværdborg I, 1917-18. IPD-distribution.

on the Section I/XI border, 6 cases in the northern periphery of Section XI, 4 cases in the central part of the distribution in Sections XI and XVII, 3 distribution in Section XVIII, and 26 cases covering most of the distribution in Section XIX).

It is interesting that what characterizes the central areas of the faunal distribution is the presence of all five major species. Save for a few odd and marginal occurrences, no area is entirely dominated by a single species or just a couple of species. The Group 12 concentrations are partly overlapping with, partly complementary to, the major flint concentrations in Figure 8a. In essence the pattern is just what one would expect from haphazard toss and discard behaviour.

No major articulated sections of animals were found.

The IPD-distribution of the major limb bones (Fig. 8c) is partly complementary to the major flint concentrations, partly peripheral to the major Group 12 concentrations, which may suggest that larger bones, or sections of bones, were to some extent cleared from more intensively used areas.

Four major concentrations are apparent in Figure 8b. However, since the borders between them seem to match conspicuously with the divisions between the main excavation sections, they are perhaps more likely to reflect a systematic recording error. Thus, for this reason, for reasons of statistical representation, and because there is seemingly no real difference in character between the assemblages from the various areas, the zoological material will be treated as a single assemblage in subsequent analyses (Chapter 7 and forwards).

Sværdborg I, 1923

As with Sværdborg I, 1917-18 and most other pre-World War II excavations, analysis of this site is somewhat marred by the fact that a number of formal tool classes were not recognized at the time of excavation. Moreover, those classes (e.g. burins, notched and denticulated blades and flakes, microburins and core rejuvenation flakes) cannot be considered even today because blades and flakes were regarded merely as waste and were discarded on site after excavation and counting. Consequently the number of tool types available for analysis is relatively small.

A tentative Presab analysis on smoothed, gridded data of the four classes flake scrapers, microliths, axes, and cores reveals 6 groups (Fig. 9b); the contoured distribution of debitage is shown in Figure 9a.

1. Microliths only; three cases, all in marginal positions.
2. Cores only; 55 cases, all in marginal positions except for a large cohesive

area (39 cases) covering most (approx. 4 x 11 m) of the southern part of main section XXXVI.

3. Scrapers and cores; 38 cases, partly marginally distributed, partly forming three coherent, but separate, areas in the eastern and southern part of the site (5 x 2 m in northeastern Section XXXVI, 5 x 2 m in eastern Section XXXVI, and 7 x 3 m on the border between Sections XXXVI and XL).

4. Microliths and cores; 18 cases, partly marginally distributed, partly forming smaller coherent areas (1 x 2, 2 x 2, and 3 x 1 m) in various parts of Section XXXVI.

5. Scrapers, microliths and cores; with 84 cases, the most frequent combination. This is the dominant characteristic of the long trench through Sections XXXIV and XXIII and also forms a large, coherent but irregularly shaped area in the northern, central and western part of Section XXXVI and the eastern part of Section XXIV.

6. Scrapers, microliths, axes and cores; 13 cases in 4 concentrations: one at either end of the long trench through sections XXXIV and XXIII (2 x 1 and 2 x 2 m, respectively), and another two a little further towards the periphery from either two above (2 x 3, and 2 x 1 m, respectively).

Again cores are an element in all groups except for Group 1. The occurrence of cores on the periphery is a common feature on Maglemosian sites. They are among the heaviest artifacts and may often have been cleared or thrown away from the active half of Main Section XXXVI, which may denote a more extensive flint-knapping area. This also is corroborated by the relatively high density of flint debris in the area (see Fig. 9a). It is also apparent that Groups 3 and 4 do not by themselves make functional sense. One would not normally assume functional relationships between scrapers and cores on the one hand and microliths and cores on the other (except when the latter denote micro-blade production for microliths). Consequently, there is no need to attempt the definition of activity areas from these groups alone.

In fact considering Groups 5 and 6, which only are distinguished by the presence of axes in Group 6, much points towards the usual general or multi-purpose use of space.

The long trench through sections XXXIV and XXIII is interesting. Apparently, this cross-cut the hearth already discussed by Friis-Johansen (1919, 119-20) in his discription of the test-squares XXIII/A1-B1 and XXIV/A10-B10. The cultural layer here was up to 15 cm thick and very rich in contents. The four squares alone yielded 5949 pieces of flint waste and 4001 bits of bone. About 25% of the flint was burnt and the soil matrix was greyish, sandy and contained charcoal with an abundance of charred bone debris and fish scales (Friis-Johansen 1919, 119-20). Figure 9a shows that the hearth area also

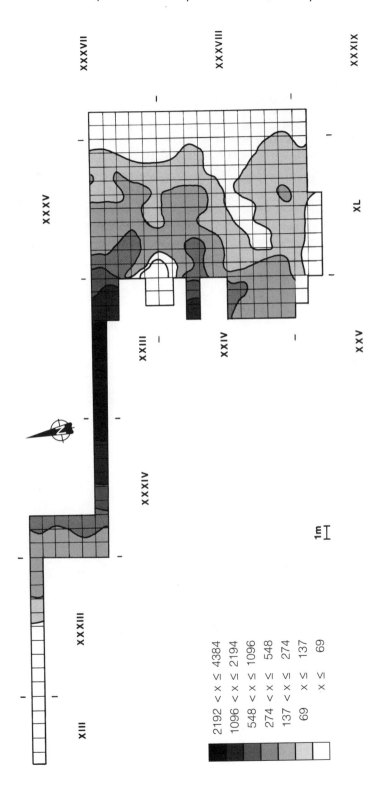

Fig. 9a. Sværdborg I, 1922-23. Contoured distribution of debitage. Σ 71749, x̄ = 174.

2192 < x ≤ 4384
1096 < x ≤ 2194
548 < x ≤ 1096
274 < x ≤ 548
137 < x ≤ 274
 69 < x ≤ 137
      x ≤ 69

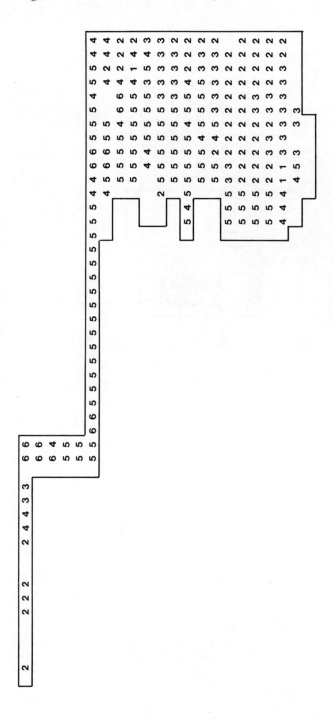

Fig. 9b. Sværdborg I, 1922-23. Presab. Flint tools.

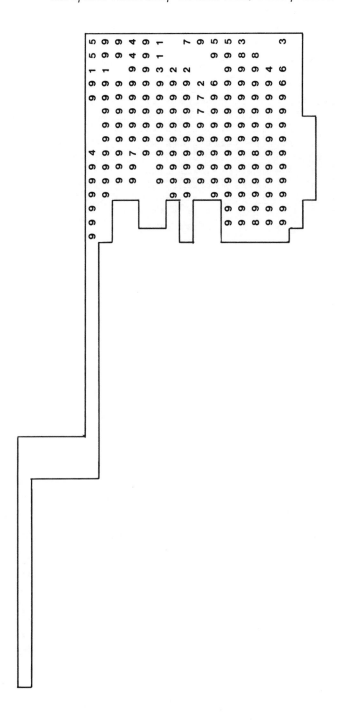

Fig. 9c. Sværdborg I, 1922-23. Presab. Bones.

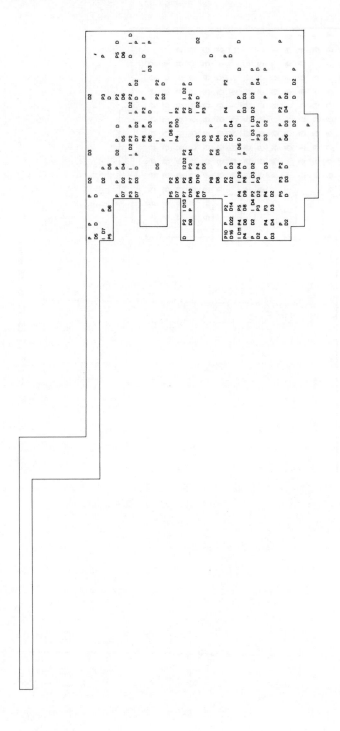

Fig. 9d. Sværdborg I, 1922-23. IPD-distribution.

contains by far the largest concentration of flint debris of which a conspicuous amount was burnt (Broholm 1924, 90). Specific flint-knapping areas at the hearth were discovered by Broholm. Two large, flat stones measuring 77 x 65 and 80 x 75 cm, respectively, were found in squares XXIII/H5 and XXXIV/G5.

On top of and immediately around each of them, respectively 2911 and 585 pieces of flint waste were found, as well as innumerable smaller fragments (Broholm 1924, 91). No doubt this large fireplace was a major center for consumption and activity, probably measuring about 10 m in diameter.

Unfortunately, the excavation layout in this part of the site precludes the search for a hut floor in the standard way (Blankholm 1984, 1987a). In fact, the purpose of the excavation was to provide bone and antler artifacts (Broholm 1924). However, the sheer extent and magnitude of the most likely area for a hut site, namely the hearth area, may in fact indicate that this part of the site was used for some other purpose, although the exact meaning remains obscure. Cores, scrapers and microliths are most abundant (i.e. have the highest frequencies) in the hearth area, as is debitage. Axes, however, are clearly found not within, but around the hearth. In fact there may be some kind of symmetry in artifact composition around the hearth, although this can only be judged from the single trench. The hearth proper is characterized by Group 5 followed in close proximity by Group 6 (see above). Unfortunately, model seating plans cannot be imposed on or inferred from the site, but certainly both flint-knapping and food consumption and possibly also the manufacture of tools were part of the activities.

As noted, the major purpose of Broholm's excavation was to uncover a large number of bone and antler artifacts in order to more fully elucidate this component of the Maglemosian toolkit. Unfortunately, he almost only excavated to the east of the hearth area and consequently it is impossible to obtain a full picture of the distribution of the zoological material relative to the fireplace. That is, it is impossible to determine whether or not the apparently standard pattern of an extended discard zone formed a full circle. It also is impossible to decide where the lake margin was at the time of occupation.

The Presab analysis on smoothed, gridded data (Fig. 8c) shows the now familiar composition of species. Excluding groups with cases less than two, the configuration shows that Group 9 (all five species present) covers almost the entire area of preserved bone material except for the eastern periphery where as expected more random variation is found. The latter is thus apparently without behavioural significance. In fact, the evidence points towards a typical extended and mixed discard and toss zone without any signs of major articulated sections of animals. The distribution of intact bones and proximal and distal ends (Fig. 8d) does not seem to indicate the stereotypic Binfordian model seating plan (Binford 1978). Save for one intact bone each of elk and aurochs, only pig shows a large number of intact bones. This is among the smallest and also among the least exploited of the animals and thus no surprise. However, the intact bones of pig are mostly situated closer to the fireplace than would be expected from the standard model. The distal ends generally outnumber the proximal, which is a common trend reflecting consumption and manufacture patterns, particularly for humerus and tibia. Moreover, there is no obvious behavioural trend to be observed in their respective or relative distributions, save for the fact that they are also most frequent in the immediate vicinity of the hearth. However, because only the area to the east of the hearth has been excavated general conclusions cannot be arrived at for the entire distribution.

Sværdborg I, 1943-44, Area A
The contoured distribution of flint debitage and the outline of analytically defined hut floors is shown in Figure 10a. A Presab analysis of the flint tools (smoothed, gridded data) reveals 12 groups (Fig. 10b).

1. Triangular microliths only; 10 cases, of which all except for two (at gridcorners LV, H2 and LV, H8) are along the periphery in smaller coherent areas (5 cases extending in a band on either side of gridcorner LIV, A2, 2 cases (2 x 1 m) in western Section LII) and in a single location at gridcorner LVI/K3.
2. Cores only; 4 cases, all except for one (at gridcorner LV, F4) marginally distributed in a 4 x 1 m band in the northern part of Section LVI.
3. Scrapers and triangular microliths; 3 contiguous cases (3 x 1.5 m) in the central part of the area around grid-corner LV, F-G/2.
4. Triangular microliths and cores; 64 cases and the most frequent combination. The distribution generally is peripheral, sometimes covering large areas around the margin. However, two internal band-shaped concentrations are apparent. One measuring roughly 4 x 2 m is situated in the southwest corner of Section LV, while the other is about 2 m wide and runs curvilinearly from the south-central part of Section LVIII through the northeastern part of Section LV.
5. Triangular microliths and axes; 5 cases in two separate areas in the western part of the site. One in the south measures approximately 2 x 1 m, while the other measuring roughly 3 x 1 m is in the northeastern part of Section LIV.
6. Scrapers, triangular microliths and cores; 22 cases in 5 separate areas: 1) 2 x 2 m in the central part of Section LII; 2) an angular area of roughly 8 m^2

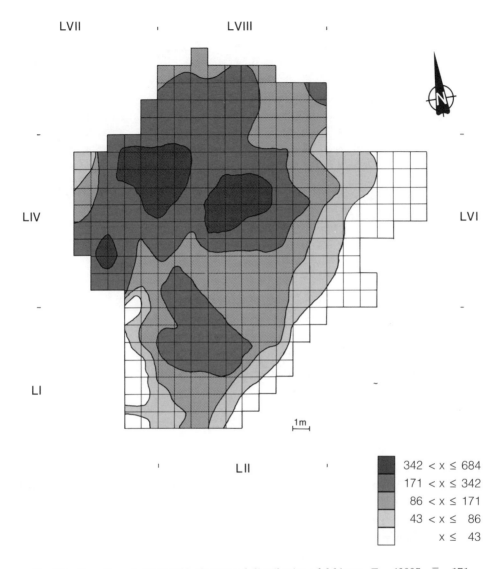

Fig. 10a. Sværdborg I, 1943-44A. Contoured distribution of debitage. $\Sigma = 49005$, $\bar{X} = 171$.

in the southern part of Section LV; 3) approximately 3 x 1 m in the western part of Section LV; 4) roughly 3 x 1 m on the border between Sections LIV and LV; and 5) approximately 2 x 2 m in the southern part of Section LVIII.

7. Burins, triangular microliths and cores; 35 cases in 7 areas: 1) approximately 2 x 2 m in the western part; 2) roughly 3 x 2 m in the eastern part of Section LVIII; 3) approximately 3 x 1 m in the western periphery

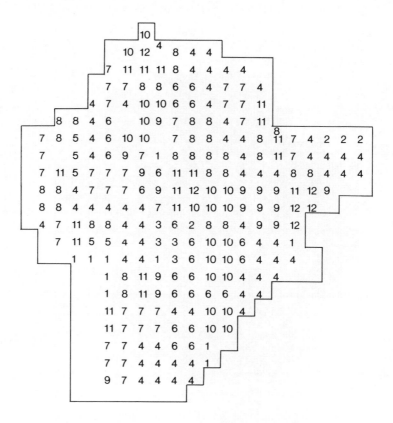

Fig. 10b. Sværdborg I, 1943-44A. Presab. Flint tools.

of Section LIV; 4) approximately 3 x 2 m on the border between Sections
LIV and LV; 5) approximately 1 x 1 m centrally in Section LV; 6) roughly
2 x 1 m in the southeast part of Section LIV; and 7) roughly 5 x 3 m in the
southwestern part of Section LII.

8. Triangular microliths, axes and cores; 33 cases in 7 areas: 1) a curved,
   roughly 4 x 1 m area in the southwestern part of Section LVIII; 2) a 2 x 1
   m area in the northeastern part of Section LVII; 3) a 4 x 4 m area in the
   northern part of Section LV; 4) a 2 x 1 m area in the western part of
   Section LVI; 5) a 2 x 2 m area in central Section LIV; 6) a 2 x 1 m area in
   the southeastern part of Section LIV; and 7) a 2 x 1 m area in the
   southeastern part of Section LV.

9. Scrapers, burins, triangular microliths and cores; 16 cases in 4 areas: 1) a
   1 x 1 m area in northern Section LV; 2) a roughly 4 x 1 m area in western
   Section LV; 3) approximately 3 x 3 m in eastern Section LV; and 4) a 2 x
   1 m area on the Section LII/LV border.

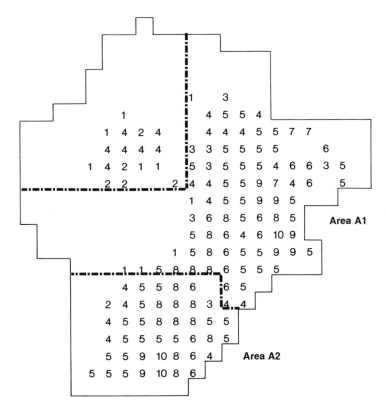

Fig. 10c. Sværdborg I, 1943-44A. Presab. Bones.

10. Scrapers, triangular microliths, axes and cores; 22 cases in 5 areas: 1) 3 x 1 m in western Section LVIII; 2) 3 x 2 m on the Section LVIII/LV border; 3) 2 x 2 m in eastern Section LV; 4) 3 x 2 m in southeastern Section LV; and 5) 2 x 2 m in eastern Section LII.

11. Burins, triangular microliths, axes and cores; 19 cases in 8 areas (all measures approximate): 1) 3 x 1 m in western Section LVIII; 2) 6 x 1 m in a band running from southeast Section LVIII through northeast Section LV and into northwest Section LVI; 3) 1 x 1 m in eastern Section LIV; 4) 3 x 1 m in central Section LV; 5) 1 x 1 m in western Section LVI; 6) 2 x 1 m in southeast Section LIV; 7) 2 x 1 m on the Section LII/LV border; and 8) 2 x 1 m on the Section LI/LII border.

12. All five classes; 6 cases in 3 areas (all measures approximate): 1) 1 x 1 m in northwest Section LVIII; 2) 1 x 1 m in central Section LV; and 3) 3 x 2 m in western Section LVI.

Again it is evident that triangular microliths and cores make up the common elements in the groups; triangular microliths and cores are members of 11 and 9 groups respectively, being both together in 8 groups. In essence this means that most of the variability is created by the presence or absence of scrapers, burins and axes. Moreover, taking other contextual information into account, no group would seem to be functionally homogeneous or to indicate specialized activity sets or areas. In fact, the picture is the common one. Triangular microliths and cores (both occuring in great numbers) form the underlying carpet and are naturally also found in isolation in the periphery. The actual activity centres seem to be multifunctional manufacture and consumption areas denoted by the groups with the largest number of tool classes (Groups 9-12), which also match well with locations close to or on the delineated hut floors (Fig. 10a).

As to the faunal assemblage, roe deer and pig are numerically the dominant species, whereas red deer and notably elk and aurochs are sparsely represented. This is also reflected in the Presab analysis revealing a 10 group configuration in which the former two species co-occur in 8 groups (Fig. 10c):

1. Roe deer only; 10 cases, mostly in single occurrences along the periphery of the faunal distribution in Section LV.
2. Pig only; 6 cases peripheral to the faunal distribution in Section LV.
3. Red deer and roe deer; 7 cases peripheral to the major distribution of faunal remains in Area A.
4. Roe deer and pig; 26 cases. 7 cases characterize the smaller of the faunal distributions in Section LV; the remainder mostly occur in smaller areas along the periphery of the major faunal distribution of Area A.
5. Red deer, roe deer and pig; 49 cases in 6 concentrations generally characterize the central parts of the major faunal distribution in Area A: 1) 15 cases (roughly 7 x 4 m) in an irregular concentration in Sections LI, LII and LV, 3 cases (3 x 1.5 m) in central Section LII, 5 cases (4.5 x 4.5 m) on the Section LII/LV border, 2 cases (2 x 1 m) in south-central Section LV, 4 cases (4 x 1 m) along the periphery in Section LVI, 16 cases (7 x 4 m) in an irregularly shaped area in eastern Section LV, and 2 cases (2 x 1 m) on the periphery in Section LVI.
6. Roe deer, pig and elk; 14 cases in 4 coherent areas: 1) 3 x 3 m in western Section LVI; 2) 2 x 1 m in southeastern Section LV; 3) a 6 x 1 m band extending from LV, E4 down to LII, D10; and 4) 3 x 1 m in the south-central part of Section LII.
7. Roe deer, pig and aurochs; 3 cases of which two are contiguous (2 x 1 m) in the northern periphery of the faunal distribution in Section LVI, and one

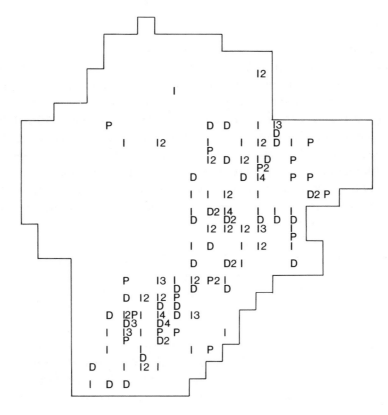

Fig. 10d. Sværdborg I, 1943-44A. IPD-distribution.

case is a single occurrence on the center of the border between Sections LV and LVI.

8. Red deer, roe deer, pig and elk; 15 cases in a single location (LV, A4) and 2 coherent areas: a large (6 x 3 m) irregular area extending from the center of Section LII up to the central part of Section LV, and a small (2 x 1 m) area in the southern periphery of the faunal distribution in Section LII.

9. Red deer, roe deer, pig and aurochs; 8 cases in 3 coherent areas: 1) 3 x 1.5 m in the central part of the faunal distribution, in Section LV; 2) 3 x 1.5 m in the periphery of the faunal distribution, in the southwestern corner of Section LVI; and 3) 2 x 1 m in the southern periphery of the distribution, in Section LII.

10. All five species; 3 cases in 1 single occurrence at LV, A3, and in a small area (2 x 1 m) in the southern periphery of the distribution, in Section LII.

The most frequent combination is red deer, roe deer and pig (Group 5), which in spatial terms characterizes the assemblage. No major articulated sections of animals were found in Area A.

Two features set Area A apart from the rest of Sværdborg I: Firstly, the northeastern part of Area A is characterized almost entirely by elements from front legs (Area A1), whereas the southern part (Area A2) is dominated by elements from rear legs. Such sorting is rare, however. Secondly, the area covered by the northwestern floor (Fig. 10a, Blankholm 1987a, Table 9.1) is characterized by elements from roe deer and pig only. There is no surprise in that the numerically most dominant species also characterize the periphery of the settlement (as is also evident for the larger part of Area A), but this approximately 5 x 5 m area in the northwestern part of the settlement is clearly set apart from the general refuse areas to the east and may either denote a small temporary butchering/manufacturing or consumption area or, less likely, a short occupation concentrating on the exploitation of only these two species.

The distribution of intact bones and proximal and distal ends of limb bones from red deer, roe deer and pig (Fig. 10d) compared to that of calcined flint (Henriksen 1976, Fig. 18) does not resemble the basic Binfordian model seating plan (Binford 1978). Possibly the level of resolution (1 x 1 m gridded data) is too gross for this kind of assessment. Yet considering Area A in general, the faunal evidence may be suggested to represent the refuse from at least two and possibly three households, probably corresponding to Hut floors 1, 2 and 4, respectively (Fig 10a). In this particular case, however, it would seem impossible to separate multipurpose work areas from general discard areas.

Sværdborg I, 1943-44, Area B

The spatial distribution of debitage (Fig. 11a) indicates the presence of three hut floors labelled central, northwest and northeast, respectively (Blankholm 1984, 1987a, Table 9.1).

A Presab analysis (smoothed, gridded data) of the flint tool classes reveals 12 groups (Fig. 11b):

1. Triangular microliths only; 6 cases in 3 concentrations (all measurements approximate): 1) 3 x 1 m on the Section LXVII/LXVIII border, i.e. between the northwestern and northeastern hut floors; 2) 3 x 1 m on the border between Sections LXV and LXVII, southwest of the northwestern hut floor; and 3) 2 x 1 m on the southern periphery of Area B.
2. Cores only; 4 cases in a 3 x 1 m concentration on the southern periphery, and in an isolated area in the southeastern part of Area B.

    As evidenced from other places (see above), triangular microliths and cores are not only the numerically most common tool classes on the site;

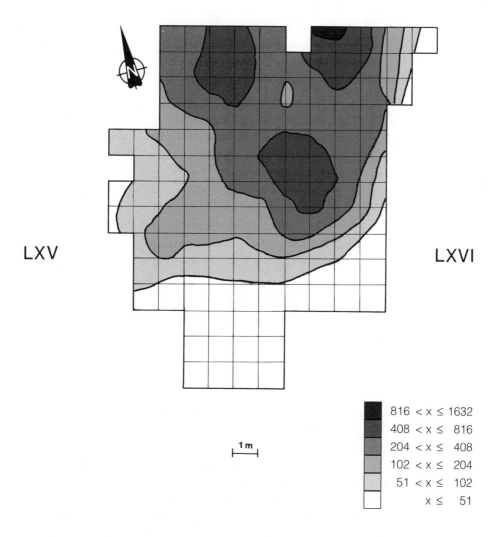

LXV

LXVI

1 m

	816 < x ≤ 1632
	408 < x ≤ 816
	204 < x ≤ 408
	102 < x ≤ 204
	51 < x ≤ 102
	x ≤ 51

Fig. 11a. Sværdborg I, 1943-44B. Contoured distribution of debitage. Σ = 25315, X̄ = 204.

they also form the common elements among the Presab groups, and it is no surprise that they characterize the site margins and marginal areas between hut floors. Thus, in essence, most variation is caused by the remaining classes.

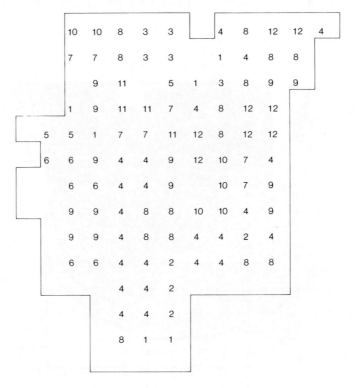

Fig. 11b. Sværdborg I, 1943-44B. Presab. Flint tools.

3. Burins and triangular microliths; 5 cases, all in one concentration (4.5 x 3 m) between the northwestern and northeastern hut floors.
4. Triangular microliths and cores; 23 cases and the most frequently occurring combination. It generally circumscribes the central and northeastern floor.The highest frequencies of both microliths and cores coincide with the floors, which may merely suggest that this combination is in fact only a basic refuse/general work area characteristic.
5. Scrapers and triangular microliths; 3 cases in one 2 x 1 m concentration in the northern part of section LXV, and a single case in the low frequency border area between the two northern floors. Both the smoothed and unsmoothed (not shown) data on scrapers would suggest outside use, probably hide or bone working.
6. Axes and cores; 6 cases in two concentrations in the western part of the site: 1) an approximately 4.5 x 3 m large area in the northern part; and 2) a 2 x 1 m area in the central part of section LXV. There is no direct functional correlation between axes and cores, and the latter may be disregarded as an underlying variable. Thus the situation is similar to many

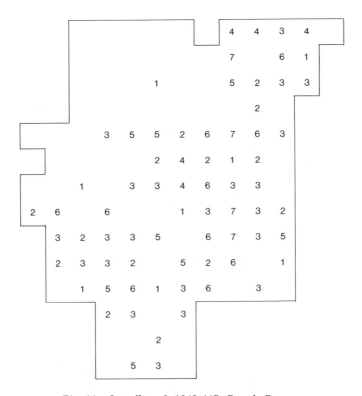

Fig. 11c. Sværdborg I, 1943-44B. Presab. Bones.

other sites. Apparently some heavy-duty activities requiring axes were re-legated to areas at some distance from the central habitation areas, although the floors proper are not completely devoid of axes.

7. Scrapers, triangular microliths and cores; 7 cases in 3 concentrations: 1) 2 x 1 m immediately west of the northwestern floor; 2) a curvilinear band in the zone between the central and northwestern floor; and 3) 2 x 1 m immediately east of the central floor. This group is functionally hetero geneous. The evidence suggests that the use of scrapers generally, but not exclusively, was an outdoor phenomenon, probably for hide or bone-working (see also Group 5 above).

8. Burins, triangular microliths and cores; 15 cases in 6 areas: 1) 2 x 1 m within the central floor; 2) 3 x 1.5 m adjacent to the northeastern floor; 3) 2 x 1 m in the northern part of the central floor; 4) 2 x 2 m in the south-western part of Section LXV; 5) 2 x 1 m in the southeastern part of the site (Section LXVI); and 6) 1 x 1 m in the southwestern periphery (Section LXV).

9. Triangular microliths, axes and cores; 13 cases in 6 areas: 1) 2 x 1 m south-

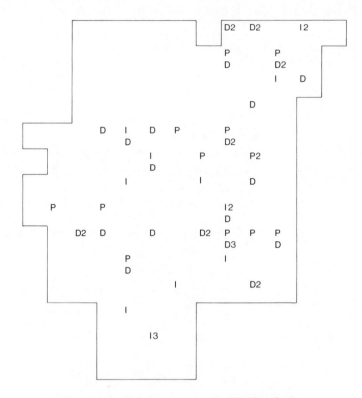

Fig. 11d. Sværdborg I, 1943-44B. IPD-distribution.

west of the northwestern floor; 2) 2 x 1 m southeast of the northeastern floor; 3) 2 x 1 m adjacent to the central floor; 4) 2 x 2 m in Section LXV in the western part of the site; 5) 2 x 1 m east of the central floor; and 6) an isolated location at LXV, E9.

10. Scrapers, burins, triangular microliths and cores; 6 cases in 2 concentrations: 1) 2 x 1 m adjacent to the west side of the northwestern floor; and 2) 3 x 1-2 m overlapping with the central floor.

11. Scrapers, triangular microliths, axes and cores; 4 cases in a single concentration measuring approximately 4.5 x 1.5 m extending across the zone between the central and northwestern floors.

12. Burins, triangular microliths, axes and cores; 8 cases in 3 concentrations: 1) 2 x 1 m on the central floor in Section LXVIII; 2) 2 x 1 m on the central floor 1 in Section LXV/LXVI; and 3) 2 x 2 m in the eastern periphery between the central and northeastern floors (Section LXVI/LXVIII).

There is almost no consistency in pattern across the site. However, again the hut floors proper may be interpreted as multipurpose consumption and work areas surrounded by extended discard zones without conspicuous activity areas. Yet the general trend for scrapers and axes to be found outside the floors may suggest that activities such as hideworking that require some space, and heavy-duty activities requiring axes, were generally performed in the open.

A Presab analysis of the distribution of red deer, roe deer and pig (unsmoothed, gridded data) reveals 7 groups (Fig. 11c):

1. Red deer only; 8 cases, all single occurrences in the periphery of the faunal distribution, except for one case within the central floor.
2. Roe deer only; 14 cases of which 7 are peripheral to the faunal distribution and the remaining 7, except for one on the central floor, are found just outside this floor and between the central and northeastern floors.
3. Pig only; 22 cases, all peripheral to the faunal distribution, except for one in LXVI, K7 and a concentration of 4 squares in the southwestern part of the site in Section LXV.
4. Red deer and roe deer; 5 cases, of which 3 are associated with the northeastern and 2 with the central floor.
5. Red deer and pig; 8 cases in 3 areas: 1) 2 x 1 m west of the central floor; 2) 3 x 1 m southwest of the central floor; and 1 x 1 m southeast of the central floor, i.e. all intermediate between the central floor and the periphery of the site.
6. Roe deer and pig; 10 cases, of which 8 are single occurrences without systematic patterning, and 2 are found adjacent to one another on the southern periphery of the faunal distribution.
7. Red deer, roe deer and pig; 4 cases, of which one is located in Section LXVIII, J3, and the rest at the northern and southern ends of the central floor.

The distribution of species is somewhat different from the usual picture as there is a relatively high number of 'single species occurrences' in apparently no consistent order. On the other hand, the actual frequencies of skeletal elements are low for this part of Sværdborg I, and the above results may probably be due to chance. Yet groups containing two or more species (e.g. Group 4, 6 and 7) are generally associated with the floor areas and thus the general consumption/work areas described for the flint tools.

Unfortunately the positions of hearths cannot be firmly assessed, and the distribution of intact bones and proximal and distal ends (the IPD-distribution, Fig. 11d) does not invite the imposition of model seating plans. The majority of the intact limb bones is found on the periphery, which probably indicates clearing of the site rather than the rudiments of a discard pattern from a consumption area. Clearing is also suggested by the find of an almost complete wolf skeleton in the southeast corner of Area B. Apart from this, however, larger articulated sections of animals are missing.

Sværdborg I, 1943-44, Area C

The contoured distribution of flint debitage and analytically defined hut floors are shown in Figure 12a. A Presab analysis of the flint tool classes (smoothed, gridded data) reveals 9 groups (Fig. 12b):

1. Burins and cores; 5 cases in 5 isolated locations at gridcorners LX, B10, LXII, B10, LXIII, D2, LXIII, K3, and LXIII, J9.
2. Triangular microliths and cores; 40 cases most of which are located at the margin of the excavation. However 3 larger coherent areas exist: 1) 6 x 4.5 m in the western part of the excavation in Section LXII; 2) 6 x 4.5 m in the southwestern corner of the site in Section LIX; and 3) an approximately 9 x 1.5 m curved band stretching from LX, F9 up to LXIII, H2.

    As in many other parts of Sværdborg I triangular microliths and cores form the common elements through the groups (triangular microliths are members of 8 groups, cores of all 9 groups). Consequently they are found over the entire site and generally only contribute to the spatial variation by their frequencies. In this respect they are clearly dominant within the 3 floor areas (Fig. 12a), while the coherent areas described above are not directly associated with these. The coherent areas are in fact characteristic of the marginal zones of the site and also of the low density zone between the northern and southern occupation areas.
3. Scrapers, triangular microliths and cores. This is simply Group 2 with scrapers added. 8 cases, with a single exception marginally distributed in one isolated location and 4 smaller, coherent areas: 1) gridpoints LX, F8 and LXII, D2; 2) 3 x 1.5 m on the southern periphery in Section LIX at the edge of Hut floor 3; 3) 2 x 1 m on the southwestern periphery in Section LIX; and 4) 2 x 1 m on Hut floor 3 in Section LIX.
4. Burins, triangular microliths and cores, essentially Group 2 with burins added; with 32 cases the dominant combination after Group 2. Apart from a number of isolated, peripheral occurrences, there are 7 coherent concentrations, all of which are outside the floor areas. However, since burins are also part of the larger floor associated groups (Group 8 and 9), we cannot suggest that activities requiring burins were solely an outdoor phenomenon. 1) 4.5 x 1.5 m in the northwestern part of Section LXIII to the east of Hut 1; 2) 3 x 1.5 m in the northeastern part of Section LXIII, due east of Hut 1; 3) 4.5 x 3 m in the southeastern part of Section LX, east of Hut 2; 4) a curvilinear band, approximately 9 x 1.5 m across the border between the western parts of Sections LX and LXIII, east of Hut 2; 5) Another band,

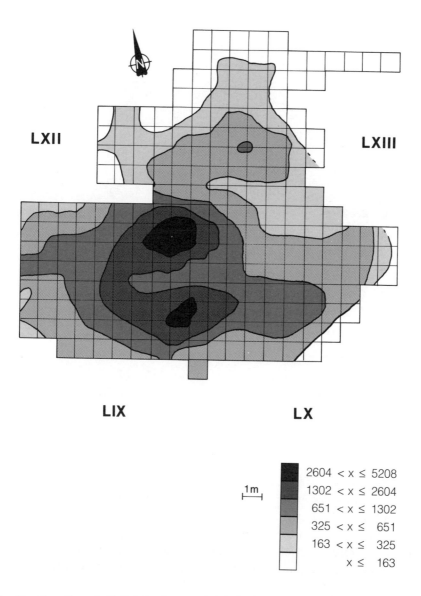

LXII

LXIII

LIX

LX

	2604 < x ≤ 5208
	1302 < x ≤ 2604
	651 < x ≤ 1302
	325 < x ≤ 651
	163 < x ≤ 325
	x ≤ 163

1m

Fig. 12a. Sværdborg I, 1943-44C. Contoured distribution of debitage. Σ = 149762, X̄ = 651

approximately 6 x 1.5 m across the LX/LXIII border further east of Hut 1; 6) 2 x 1 m in the central part of Section LIX between Huts 1 and 2; and 7) 3 x 1 m in the western periphery of the site in Section LIX.

5. Triangular microliths, axes and cores; 18 cases in 2 isolated, peripheral locations and 4 areas: 1) 2 x 1 m in the northern part of Section LXIII, northeast of Hut 1; 2) 3.5 x 3 m in the eastern part of Section LXII,

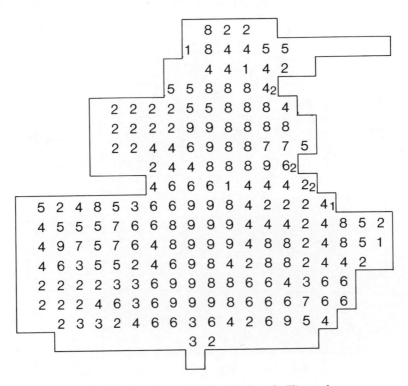

Fig. 12b. Sværdborg I, 1943-44C. Presab. Flint tools.

southwest of Hut 1; 3) a large irregular area of approximately 8 m² on the western LIX/LXII border, west of Hut 2; and 4) 2 x 1 m on the eastern LX/LXIII border.

6. Scrapers, burins, triangular microliths and cores; 28 cases in 5 marginal locations and 4 coherent areas: 1) a 6 x 3 m band extending from Section LXII, A3 down to LIX, E10, almost circumscribing the western end of Hut 2; 2) another 6 x 1 m band extending from Section LIX, C9 down to LIX, D6, almost circumscribing the western end of Hut 3; 3) 3 x 2 m in the western part of Section LX, east of Hut 3; and 4) 2 x 2 m in the southeast corner of the site.

7. Scrapers, triangular microliths, axes and cores; 6 cases in 2 marginal locations and 2 coherent areas: 1) 2 x 1 m in central Section LXIII; and 2) 2 x 1 m in north-central Section LIX, west of Hut 2.

8. Burins, triangular microliths, axes and cores; 27 cases in 2 separate marginal locations and 6 coherent areas: 1) 2 x 1 m on the northern LXII/LXIII border, northwest of Hut 1; 2) a large irregular area of 7.5 x 4 m in the western part of Section LXIII, covering part of Hut 1 and the adjacent area to the east; 3) 2 x 1 m in Hut 2; 4) 2 x 2 m in the northern part of Section

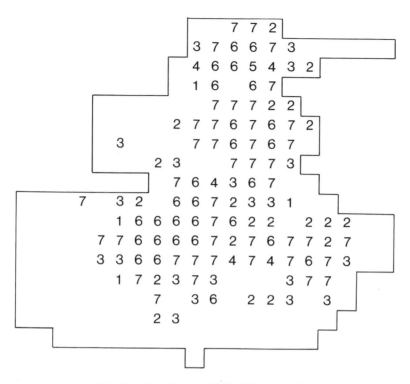

Fig. 12c. Sværdborg I, 1943-44C. Presab. Bones.

LX, east of Huts 2 and 3; 5) 2 x 1 m on the LX/LXIII border; and 6) 4.5 x 3 m in the eastern part of Hut 3.
9. All five classes; 18 cases in 3 individual locations and 2 major concentrations: 1) 3 x 1.5 m on the LXII/LXIII border in connection with Hut 1; and 2) a 6 x 2 m band running north-south around the LIX/LX border and cross-cutting Huts 2 and 3.

Again the general trend is that the more artifact classes a group contains, the closer it is to the hut floors. In fact, as in the other cases, the configuration suggests a number of multifunctional working and consumption areas on, or very close to, the floors and with very extended refuse areas with only slight hints of space divisions. For instance, as far as 'outside space' goes, scrapers are generally found at some distance from the floors in various combinations, which may suggest that activities such as hide-working that require space took place towards the periphery. Axes also seem to be found at some distance from the floors, again possibly indicative of heavy-duty work being carried out towards the periphery.

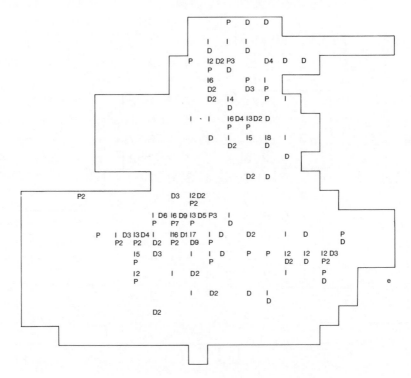

Fig. 12d. Sværdborg I, 1943-44C. IPD-distribution.

A Presab analysis (gridded data) of the skeletal elements of red deer, roe deer and pig (Fig. 12c) reveals 7 groups:

1. Red deer only; 3 marginal cases.
2. Roe deer only; 20 cases, almost exclusively marginal.
3. Pig only; 20 cases, almost all marginal or in the intermediate area between Huts 1 and 2.
4. Red and roe deer; 5 cases in no particular pattern.
5. Red deer and pig; 1 case in the northern part of the site.
6. All three species; 28 cases and the second most common combination. Generally, but not exclusively, associated with the floor areas and immediate surroundings, and to a large extent surrounded by units with the most common combination — roe deer and pig (Group 7).

No species or skeletal element is anywhere exclusively confined to one particular part of Area C. To the contrary, there is a high degree of overlap that increases as one approaches the floors. Towards the periphery and in the zones between the occupation areas proper it is only natural to find isolated spots and even larger areas characterized by only one or two of the dominant species (see Group 2 and 3 above). This is not the same as mutual exclusion at the general level, however. Although not included in the analysis for reasons of representation, elk and aurochs generally correspond with Group 6 (all three species).

No larger articulated sections of animals were found.

The distribution of proximal and distal ends and intact limb bones of roe deer and pig is interesting (Fig. 12d). In the northern sector there is a clear diagonal band of intact bones mixed with some distal ends running northwest-southeast across Section LXIII, i.e. in the area of Hut 1. Unfortunately, the position of hearth(s) is difficult to assess in this area, but in general terms the above distribution would not seem to match the standard Binfordian toss zone model (Binford 1978). In fact it generally runs along the longest dimension of the highest concentration of bone debris in Area C and may more correctly suggest a simpler phenomenon such as butchering or manufacturing processes. In the southeastern part of Area C, in Section LX, there is another limited concentration of intact bones and distal ends correlating with a large concentration of bone debris, perhaps reflecting manufacture rather than consumption. Finally there is a marked and limited concentration of intact bones and distal ends (but also a good number of proximal ends) in the area of Hut 2 on the border between Sections LIX and LXII. This correlates with the highest concentration of bone debris and also matches one of the areas characterized by the presence of all five flint tool classes. As such it is suggestive of a mixed consumption and manufacture area, but there is no apparent or real similarity to the standard model seating plan.

Sværdborg II

The contoured distribution of flint debitage and the analytically defined hut floor is shown in Figure 13a. A Presab analysis of the flint tool classes (smoothed, gridded data) reveals 13 groups and is shown in Figure 13b.

1. Cores only; 4 cases on the northern and western periphery.
2. Burins and cores; 2 cases on the western periphery.
3. Microliths and cores; 7 cases in 3 separate, coherent areas in the north-eastern, southeastern and southwestern peripheries.
4. Burins, microliths and cores; 2 contiguous cases on the eastern periphery.
5. Notched and denticulated pieces, axes and cores; 1 case in the south-western part of the site.
6. Scrapers, microliths, notched and denticulated pieces and cores; 7 cases in two coherent areas: 1) 3 x 2 m in the northeastern area; and 2) 2 x 1 m in the northwestern part of the excavation.

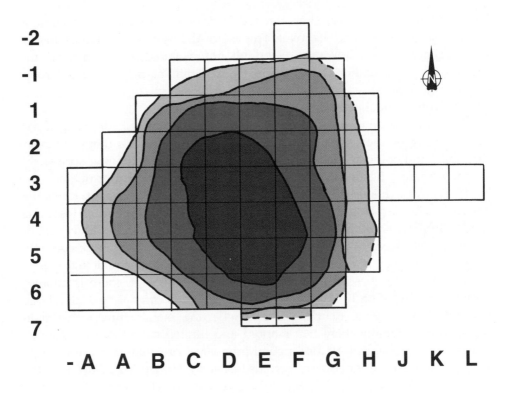

Fig. 13a. Sværdborg II. Contoured distribution of debitage. Σ = 19630, $\overline{X}$ = 322.

7. Burins, microliths, notched and denticulated pieces and cores; 3 cases of which 2 are contiguous in the eastern part of the excavation.
8. Scrapers, microliths, notched and denticulated pieces, laterally retouched pieces and cores; 3 cases in 1 coherent area across the central part of the excavation.
9. Burins, microliths, notched and denticulated pieces, axes and cores; 2 cases in 1 coherent area in the southwestern part of the excavation.
10. Burins, microliths, laterally retouched pieces, axes and cores; 1 case in the northern periphery.

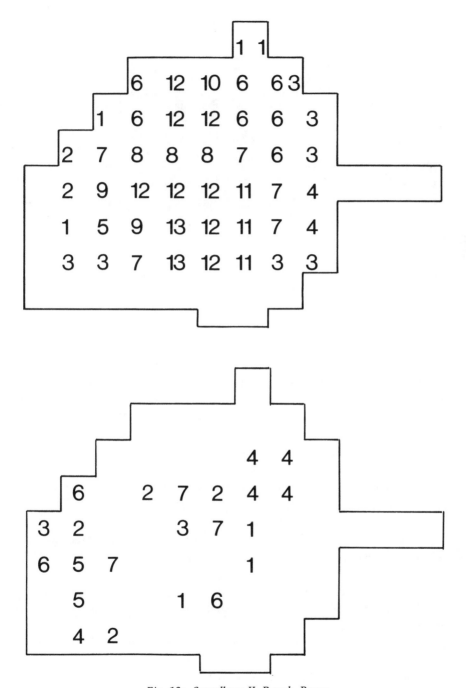

Fig. 13c. Sværdborg II. Presab. Bones.

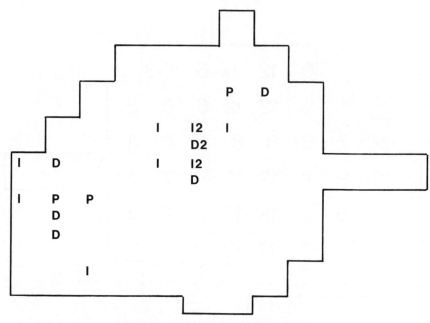

Fig. 13d. Sværdborg II. IPD-distribution.

11. Scrapers, burins, microliths, notched and denticulated pieces, laterally retouched pieces and cores; 3 cases in 1 coherent area in the east-central part of the excavation.
12. All classes; 8 cases and the most frequent combination found in 2 areas: 1) a 5 x 1 m angular area in the south-central; and 2) another 3 x 1 m angular area in the northern part of the excavation.
13. All classes except for scrapers; 2 cases adjacent to the southern Group 12 area.

A tentative Presab analysis of the relatively scant and fragmented antler and bone material reveals 7 groups (Fig. 13c):

1. Red deer only; 3 cases, all within the floor (Fig. 13a): Two contiguous cases adjacent to the east side of the hearth, and a single occurrence in the southwestern corner.
2. Roe deer only; 4 cases in no consistent pattern: 1 on the floor adjacent to the north side of the hearth, and 3 in the refuse area west of the floor.
3. Pig only; 3 cases. 1 adjacent to the northwest side of the hearth, the other two in the periphery of the site at either side of the floor.
4. Red deer and roe deer; 5 cases of which 4 form a coherent (2 x 2 m) area

adjacent to the northeast corner of the floor, and the last is found on the southwestern periphery of the refuse area.

5.   Red deer and pig; 2 contiguous cases in the centre of the refuse area west of the floor.
6.   Roe deer and pig; 3 cases: 1 on the southern part of the floor, and 2 on the western periphery of the refuse area.
7.   Red deer, roe deer and pig; 3 cases: 2 contiguous squares adjacent to and extending northwest from the hearth, and a single occurrence near the centre of the refuse area.

Evidently all three species occur more frequently in association with other species than by themselves.

No larger articulated sections of animals were found.

The IPD-distribution (Fig. 13d) does not support firm conclusions. What can be seen is that there is no differentiation between species, and perhaps a weak tendency for intact bones to be found in the northwest corner of the floor. However, since we are dealing with inside space, the latter may not be readily interpreted as a reflection of toss behaviour around the hearth.

As indicated, the bone industry falls nicely into two separate areas (E.B. Petersen 1972, 48 & Fig. 8.1; Blankholm 1980, Pl. 155). The largest concentration of tools and waste (notably bone points) also contains the highest densities and corresponds to the extent of the hut floor, whereas the other concentration with lower densities but with the largest tools is found in the western and southwestern part of the settlement. This fits expectations. Most work requiring lighter tools apparently took place around the hearth in the hut, while heavy-duty activities and work requiring more space and involving large flint and bone tools (flint axes and bone adzes) took place in the open. However, clearance of used heavy tools to the periphery may also have taken place.

As at Ulkestrup I and II, cores form an element common to all groups. Certainly blade and flake production took place at the site and generally the distribution of cores matches those of highest debitage density and of core rejuvenation flakes. Otherwise the composition of the groups is not readily functionally obvious. For instance, the two cases of burins and cores (Group 2) may be purely accidental, while the combination of microliths and cores (Group 3) does not make sense since microburins (usually a good indicator of microlith production) are absent from the site.

By and large the presumed living area — the hut floor — is characterized by Groups 8, 11 and 12, that is to a maximum of 5-7 tools. Compared to Group 12 (all tool classes), Group 8 in the vicinity of the hearth lacks burins and axes, while Group 11 only lacks axes.

Again we are dealing with a fairly homogeneous tool spectrum around a hearth on a presumed hut floor — a multifunctional consumption and work area — with an extended work and discard area towards one side (the west).

6.2. Conclusions

The overall impressions from the above analyses are:

Hut floors were multifunctional work and consumption areas (in the clear-cut cases around a single hearth) with extensive adjacent butchering, toss and discard zones. Internal and external division of space into more specific activity areas is possible in some cases, but with no consistent pattern between sites.

Discard behaviour for bones was haphazard. Generally no species is restricted to specific, or larger, areas, and the further one gets towards the periphery from the center or point of emergence of the faunal distribution, the fewer species are found in association, and then characteristically those species dominating the assemblage. Moreover, except for a few odd cases, no particular element(s) seems restricted to particular parts of a site.

Larger articulated sections (at least 2 joints) are absent.

The IPD-distributions of the large limb bones generally show no consistent differentiation between species. This corroborates the above suggestion of haphazard discard behaviour. The occasional tendency for intact bones (or the entire IPD-distribution) to occupy peripheral areas is only to be expected from the tossing or clearence of heavier elements from the active parts of the settlements (the same is often seen for cores). Generally there is no fit with Binford's (1978) model seating plan for outdoor hearths.

7 Sex, age and season

7.1 Sex and age

As mentioned (Section 5.5), there is no basis for detailed assessments of sex and age. The low MNI frequencies in Table 4 simply do not permit a statistically reliable division into the two sexes and the customary three age groups: newborn, juvenile and adult. Consequently the following statements are of a general nature.

Commonly newborns, juveniles and adults of both sexes were hunted through the summer season (see below). It is possible, but far from certain, that a 'conserving' strategy was employed for red deer in some places (Bay-Petersen 1978, 135). However, most of the evidence seems to indicate a strategy which, based on several species, made it possible to make up for temporarily unbalanced culls of any single species' local population (see also Section 1.3).

In fact, given the low MNI's, assuming low human population and site density, and considering the various species turn-over rates, culls may never have been too heavy. This has a bearing on the long standing notion of Degerbøl (1933) and Aaris-Sørensen (1988) that elk and aurochs apparently disappeared from the Danish islands during the Atlantic period because of over-exploitation. Is this a reality or a myth based on a mixture of paradigmatic bias and sampling error? First, let us consider the MNI's for elk and aurochs in the 20 Scandinavian, Maglemosian units. For elk only 6 units contain more than 2 individuals, while for aurochs the corresponding figure is 4. Thus the actual number of animals killed among the two species generally was low and only rarely matched any of the other three species. This must be taken into account when comparing figures from later periods.

At any rate, the aurochs was already only sparsely represented in the Maglemosian. When it occurs in greater numbers this may be attributed to greater sample size and/or particular strategic significance of the sites. It should also be emphasized that Aaris-Sørensen's comparison is one of mainly Maglemosian inland sites on the one hand, and largely coastal sites from later periods on the other, which by itself may introduce economic, behavioural and cultural bias in the equation (see also Newell 1990).

7.2 Season

As noted in Section 5.6, it is rarely possible to determine season of occupation within the margin of just a couple of months. Yet broader seasonal parameters

Site	Month												
	01	02	03	04	05	06	07	08	09	10	11	12
Mullerup Syd	?	——————————————————————									?	?
Ulkestrup I			— ———————————————									
Ulkestrup I			—————————————————									
Lundby I	—	————————————————————————————										
Lundby II			———————————————									
Sværdborg 1917-18			—————————————————									
Sværdborg 1923			—————————————————									
Sværdborg I:A NE			—————————————————									
Sværdborg I:A S			—————————————————									
Sværdborg I:A Total			—————————————————									
Sværdborg I:B		—————————————————————										
Sværdborg I:C NE			——————————————————————									
Sværdborg I:C SW			———————————————									
Sværdborg I:C SE			—————————————————									
Sværdborg I:C Total			——————————————————————									
Skottemarke	—											—
Holmegård I		—————————————————————————										
Holmegård V			——————————————————————									
Ageröd I:B			—————————————————									
Ageröd I:D					——————							
Ageröd V			—————————————————									
Segebro			—————————————————									
Star Carr				— —————————								

Fig. 14. Seasonality in overview.

for the occupation may be given as long as it is recognized that activities need not have been continuous over the seasonal bracket. It must also be emphasised that it is impossible to resolve use/disuse for seasons for which there are no indications.

A summary of the evidence (notably P. Rowley-Conwy's data on tooth-eruption; 1993, and data from Sværdborg I, 1923, Lundby I, Holmegård I and V kindly placed at my disposal) and of the published literature and other sources on antlers, epiphysical fusion, migratory birds, nuts, etc. (Winge 1903, 1919, Rosenlund 1972, 1979, Aaris-Sørensen 1976 and private files kindly placed at my disposal, and Richter 1982 and private files kindly placed at my disposal) is given in Figure 14. Only non-shed antlers are considered as shed antlers are an easily collected raw-material, and have in some cases been shown to be overrepresented compared to the site-specific material (see also Legge & Rowley-Conwy 1988).

The details for the various sites are enumerated below with the indicated months for occupation in parantheses. Estimated season denotes maximum period for occupation.

Mullerup Syd

Red deer: Juvenile maxilla (06-?), juvenile with deciduous teeth erupting (06-07).

Roe deer: Juvenile mandible with M1 erupting (less than 6 months; 06-11), juvenile antler in velvet (12-01).

Pig: 2 right maxillas with deciduous teeth and M1 unerupted (less than 4 months, 04-07), several mandibles with M1 erupting (07-10) and one mandible with M2 erupting (12-03), 1 juvenile tibia (05-06).

Elk: 1 juvenile maxilla (05-?), 1 juvenile mandible, deciduous teeth not fully erupted (05-06), and 1 juvenile mandible with worn deciduous teeth, their successors ready to erupt (ca. 1 year+, possibly killed 06-10).

Birds by presence of adults or young: whooper or mute swan (03-09), crane (04-10), cormorant (04-08).

Reptiles: European tortoise (summer).

Hazelnuts: 09-10.

Estimated season: 03-10.

Ulkestrup I

Pig: 1 maxilla fragment, ca. 6 weeks (05-06), 1 mandible, ca. 2 months (05-06), 1 mandible, less than 2 months (04-06), 1 scapula, foetus (04), 1 scapula, foetus/newborn (04), 1 scapula, newborn (04), 1 distal humerus, foetus/newborn (04), 1 distal radius, newborn (04), 1 metacarpal, newborn (04), 1 distal metacarpal, newborn/juvenile (04-05), 1 pelvis fragment, newborn/juvenile (04-05), 2 tibia fragments, newborn (04), 1 tibia fragment, foetus/newborn, less 6 weeks (04-05), 1 atlas, 6 weeks (05), 1 lumbar vertebra fragment, foetus/ newborn (04), 1 rib fragment, newborn (04).

Elk: 3 phalanges, very juvenile (07-08).

Aurochs: 3 maxilla fragments, newborn (05-06), 2 mandibles, newborn/juvenile (05-07), 2 distal humeri, newborn (05-06), 3 pelvis fragments, newborn (05-06), 1 rib fragment, newborn (05-06).

Birds (young/juvenile): bittern (05-08), black stork (05-07), garganey (04-08), white-tailed eagle (05-08), coot (05-09), corncrake (06-09).

Hazelnuts: 09-10.

Estimated season: 04-10.

Ulkestrup II

Red deer: 1 radius, juvenile, ca. 2 months (06-08).
Roe deer: 1 frontlet with antlers (04-10).
Pig: 1 skull fragment, newborn/juvenile (04-05), 2 humerus fragments, newborn (04), 1 distal humerus, newborn (04), 1 radius fragment, newborn (04), 1 pelvis fragment, foetus/newborn (04), 1 femur fragment, newborn (04), 1 vertebra, newborn (04), 1 lumbar vertebra, foetus/newborn (04).
Aurochs: 3 maxilla, newborn (05-06), 2 mandible fragments, newborn (05-06), 1 mandible fragment, 3-6 months (07-10), 1 scapula, foetus (05-06), 3 scapuli, newborn (05-06), 1 ulna fragment, ca. 3 months (07-08), 1 proximal tibia, newborn (05-06), 2 atlas, newborn (05-06), 1 thorax vertebra, newborn (05-06), 1 rib fragment, foetus/newborn (05-06), 4 rib fragments, newborn (05-06).
Birds (young/juvenile): Bittern (05-08), Black stork (05-07), Garganey (04-08), White-tailed eagle (05-08), Coot (05-09), Corncrake (06-09).
Hazelnuts: 09-10.
Estimated season: 04-10.

Sværdborg I, 1917-18

Red deer: 1 frontlet with antlers attached (10-03), 2 skull fragments with burrs attached (04-?), 1 metacarpal, newborn/juvenile (06-08).
Roe deer: 1 antler with burr attached (04-10).
Crane: 04-10.
European tortoise: 5 lower shells (summer).
Estimated season: 03-10.

Sværdborg I, 1923

Red deer: 1 skull fragment with antlers (10-03), 1 skull fragment with burr (05-08).
Roe deer: Numerous frontlets with antlers (04-10).
Estimated season: 04-10.

Sværdborg I, 1943-44, Area A, Northeast

Roe deer: 1 frontlet with antlers (04-10).

Sværdborg I, 1943-44, Area A, South

Roe deer: 2 frontlets with antlers (04-10).

Sværdborg I, 1943-44, Area A, Total: 04-10.

Sværdborg I:B

Roe deer: 1 juvenile humerus and 1 juvenile fragment of humerus (07-?).

Pig: 1 juvenile mandible, 1 juvenile scapula (05-08).
Estimated season: 05-?

Sværdborg I, 1943-44, Area C, Northeast
Roe deer: 4 frontlets with antlers (04-10).
Elk: 1 mandible, ca. 16-18 months (09-11).
Estimated season: 04-11.

Sværdborg I, 1943-44, Area C, Southeast
Roe deer: 3 frontlets with antlers (04-10).
Estimated season: 04-10.

Sværdborg I, 1943-44, Area C, Southwest
Roe deer: 4 frontlets with burrs (04-10).
Estimated season: 04-10.

Sværdborg I, 1943-44, Area C, Total: 04-11

Sværdborg II. No direct indicators.

Lundby I
Determination after Peter Rowley-Conwy's (1993, Fig. 1) data on wild pig jaws.
6 juvenile jaws aged 2-8 months (06-11), 11 juvenile jaws aged 11-16 months (02-08), 2 juvenile jaws aged 16-22 months (08-01), 3 juvenile jaws aged 23-26 months (03-06), 7 juvenile jaws aged 25-27 months (05-07).
Estimated season: Year round, but see text below.

Lundby II
Determination after Rosenlund (1979, 133 & Fig. 3).
Red deer: 1 metatarsal, newborn, 1-2 weeks (05-07).
Roe deer: 1 metatarsal, newborn, 3-4 weeks (06-07), a jaw and several limb bones from a 3-4 week old individual (06-07).
Pig: 1 mandible, juvenile, ca. 3 months (07-08), 1 humerus, juvenile, ca. 1-2 months (06-07), 1 radius, newborn, ca. 0-1 weeks (04-05).
Elk: Several bones from a ca. 4 months old individual (09-10).
Badger: Several bones from ca. 6 months old individuals (08-09).
Swan: Several bones from ca. 2-3 and ca. 4 months old individuals (08-10).
Estimated season: 04-10.

Holmegård I

Data on pig jaws after Rowley-Conwy (1993, Fig. 1).
3 jaws aged 2-3 months (06), 10 jaws aged 2-5 months (06-08),
1 jaw aged 4-6 months (07-09), 2 jaws aged 12-17 months (04-08), 2 jaws aged 14-16 months (06-07), 1 jaw aged 16-18 months (08-09), 1 jaw aged 16-20 months (08-11), 1 jaw aged 19-22 months (11-01), 1 jaw aged 21-24 months (01-03), 2 jaws aged 25-27 months (05-07).
Crane: 04-10.
Hazelnuts: 09-10.
Estimated season: Year round, but see text below.

Holmegård V

Roe deer: 3 frontlets with antlers (04-10)
Pig: 1 jaw aged 2-7 months (06-11)
Crane: 04-10.
Estimated season: 04-11.

Skottemarke

Elk: femurs and tibias with unfused epiphyses, approximately 20 months (Møhl 1978, 7) (12-01).
Estimated season: 12-01.

The result is a very homogeneous picture, even if the smaller analytical units are considered. Throughout, the season of occupation is March/April to September/October, i.e. the summer or warmer half of the year. (In any event we cannot expect prehistoric people to have used our contemporary 4-fold division of the year into Spring, Summer, Autumn, and Winter of three months each; rather time was organized around subsistence and work-related schedules). Only Skottemarke sets itself apart with occupation in December/January.

This is in accordance with earlier notions (e.g. E.B. Petersen 1973, Møhl 1980, Blankholm 1980, S.H. Andersen 1981), but this also is the first time that season is determined down to the level of individual units on the larger sites as, for instance, for Sværdborg I, 1943-44. In other words, the evidence is now conclusive for entire individual sites, whereas it was previously uncertain for which part(s) of sites the determinations were valid.

Some hints of winter activity also is present at, for example, Lundby I and Holmegård I. It may well be that less intensive or occasional use was made of those sites in the winter, but seasonal determination in this particular case must be considered with some caution (Rowley-Conwy 1993). It is based on tooth-eruption in mostly older pigs, and the older pigs (and other animals) grow, the more difficult it is to determine their age and thus the month or season for their kill.

8 On the track of a prehistoric economy

When an archaeo-zoological assemblage is screened for usable and discarded tools, preforms, and by-products from tool manufacture (at times it may be difficult to tell traces from butchering and tool manufacture apart (Henriksen 1976)) one is left with a residue, which in the broadest sense may be interpreted as the leftovers from butchering, consumption and treatment for other purposes, e.g. storage or caching. It is the latter evidence that will be used to elucidate the exploitation of the large game.

Of course, to infer human behaviour from such a 'minimal' material may involve methodological problems (e.g., Noe-Nygaard 1988, Aaris-Sørensen 1988). However, as in the present case, consistency in data representation between or among several sites with differing preservation conditions helps to eliminate or alleviate such problems. It also should be remembered that taphonomic flow-charts (e.g. Aaris-Sørensen 1988, 36) are theoretical constructs only, which may or may not reflect the line of processes in a real case. In addition taphonomic charts sometimes tacitly assume that whole animals were introduced onto the sites, regardless of species. This, of course, may render calculations about taphonomic loss spurious. As is well evidenced in the ethno-archaeological literature,

...meat is not normally transported, shared, stored, cooked, or otherwise treated in whole animal units..., butchering is a dismemberment strategy, and the resulting segments of the anatomy are what are transported, processed and cooked. (Binford 1978b, 70)

In the following we will look in detail on how large game was exploited. The methodology is outlined in Section 5.4. For ease of comprehension the Correspondence Analysis plot is split into an element, species, and site configuration.

8.1 Configuration of elements

The configuration of elements shows 5 groups (Fig. 15a):

1. Maxilla (MAX) and mandibles (MAN).
2. The axial skeleton; vertebrae (VERT) save for 1st and 2nd cervicals, ribs (R), sternum (ST), sacrum (SAC), and pelvis (PELV).
3. Scapulae (SC), and the upper and middle limb bones: proximal and distal

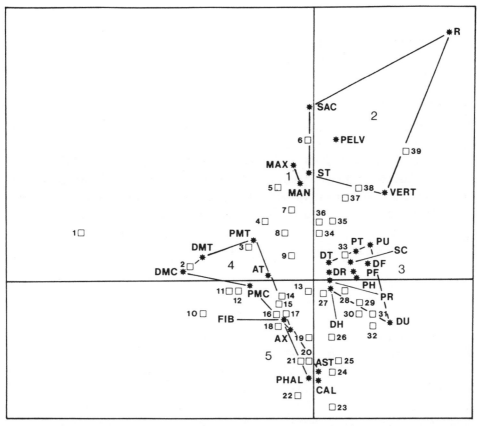

*Fig. 15a. Configuration of elements. * and boldface abbreviations = skeletal elements according to Table 3. Squares and lower case numbers: 1) Sværdborg I, 1943-44, Area C, red deer, 2) Star Carr, aurochs, 3) Star Carr, red deer, 4) Mullerup Syd, red deer, 5) Star Carr, roe deer, 6) Meiendorf, reindeer, 7) Mullerup Syd, roe deer, 8) Segebro, red deer, 9) Segebro, roe deer, 10) Sværdborg I, 1943-44, Area A, red deer, 11) Ulkestrup II, red deer, 12) Sværdborg I, 1917-18, red deer, 13) Sværdborg I, 1943-44, Area A, roe deer, 14) Ageröd V, red deer, 15) Sværdborg I, 1943-44, Area C, roe deer, 16) Star Carr, elk, 17) Mullerup Syd, elk, 18) Sværdborg I, 1943-44, Area C, pig, 19) Lundby I, aurochs, 20) Sværdborg I, 1917-18, roe deer, 21) Sværdborg I, 1917-18, aurochs, 22) Sværdborg I, 1917-18, elk, 23) Sværdborg I, 1917-18, pig, 24) Sværdborg I, 1923, elk, 25) Sværdborg I, 1923, aurochs, 26) Sværdborg I, 1923, red deer, 27) Lundby I, red deer, 28) Lundby I, roe deer, 29) Sværdborg I, 1923, roe deer, 30) Lundby I, elk, 31) Sværdborg I, 1923, pig, 32) Lundby I, pig, 33) Segebro, pig, 34) Lundby II, elk, 35) Lundby II, pig, 36) Lundby II, roe deer, 37) Mullerup Syd, pig, 38) Stellmoor A, reindeer, 39) Skottemarke, elk. Element groups are marked with upper case numbers (see text for description).*

humerus (PH, DH), proximal and distal radius (PR, DR), proximal and distal ulna (PU, DU), proximal and distal femur (PF, DF), and proximal and distal tibia (PT, DT).

4. 1st and 2nd cervical vertebrae (AT, AX), proximal and distal metacarpals (PMC, DMC), and proximal and distal metatarsals (PMT, DMT).
5. Lower parts of rear legs; fibulae (FIB), astragalus (AST), calcaneus (CAL), plus front and rear phalanges (PHAL).

8.2 Configuration of species

There is no exact qualitative or quantitative scale for representation. Consequently, it is possible only to speak in terms of patterns or trends. It should also be noted that the elements closest to the intersection of axes 1 & 2 on the Correspondence Analysis plot (Fig. 15b) may be regarded as the 'commonwealth' representation for the species. For clarity, the most extreme case relative to its group cluster has been removed, except for elk.

The impression from the species configuration in Figure 15b is one of general, but divergent, trends in the exploitation of red deer, roe deer, pig, elk and aurochs.

Red deer

Red deer generally is well represented in all elements, except for the axial skeleton (Element Group 2 above) and maxilla (MAX, Element Group 1 above), which are poorly represented.

The emphasis clearly was placed on antlers plus front and rear legs (save for femurs). Both are obvious seen in terms of tool manufacture and food supply. As indicated, the head proper (save for mandibles) and the axial skeleton are generally underrepresented. While the lack of heads most likely reflects that these were left at the kill site, the lack of axial parts remains an interpretative problem. The frequent presence of AT and AX may indicate that the rest of the spinal column with ribs (R) and pelvis (PELV) was often brought in as well. If this were the case it must have been for the purpose of meat consumption, because an investigation of all tools from bone and antler from all finds (Table 2) clearly shows that of the axial skeleton only ribs were used as raw material for tools (notably barbed and unbarbed bone points). Yet the axial elements *are* generally missing and thus they must have been lost in the process of consumption, in the poorer preservation conditions on dry land (though the even softer pig vertebrae are often numerous; see below), abandoned in the field, or perhaps removed from the settlements (possibly with preserved meat) for use in other locations. It is at present impossible to decide which was the case.

In relation to roe deer and pig, the relatively higher dominance of red deer, elk and aurochs phalanges could result from the Schlepp effect. This would fit well with the suggestion of field-butchering and perhaps even selective transport, since apparently only the most sought-after parts of the largest

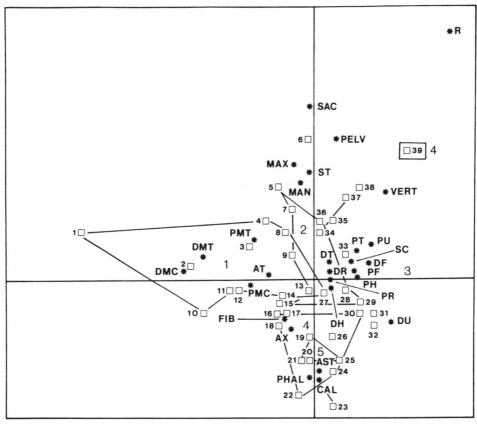

Fig. 15b. *Configuration of species. Base map and symbols as for Figure 15a. Species in boldface numbers: 1) red deer, 2) roe deer, 3) pig, 4) elk & 5) aurochs.*

animals were carried back in the hides with the phalanges attached as 'riders' or handles.

Roe deer

Roe deer shows a more uniform representation of elements, although, as for red deer, ribs (R) are notably generally underrepresented (these may, as for the limb bones, have been selected for tools in greater quantities, see Table 2). The same applies to some extent to the rest of the axial skeleton. The latter may have been caused by the same factor(s) as for red deer, but otherwise the evidence may be interpreted to suggest that roe deer, and particularly the young animals, were carried back to the habitation sites complete or in sections amounting to complete animals.

Pig

Pig generally is well represented for all elements inclusive parts of the axial skeleton (Element Group 2 above), notably ribs (R) and pelvis (PELV), and maxilla (MAX) from the head region (Element Group 1 above).

In fact, pig shows the most uniform representation of elements altogether. Bones from the head (in excess of maxilla and mandibles) occur very frequently and much suggests that the animals generally were brought in complete, or in sections amounting to complete animals. The pig is a valuable meat source and the middle limb bones (RA, UL, MC, T, FIB, and MT) were frequently used for tools (see Table 2).

Although pig bones are reckoned among the least resistant in terms of preservation, it is in fact vertebrae and sterna (the least resistant bones) that are most frequently preserved compared to the other species. This puts the underrepresentation of vertebrae and ribs, in fact the entire axial skeleton, of red deer and roe deer in perspective! In other words, had these bones from red deer and roe deer in general been brought home, we would most certainly have found them in much greater numbers. Thus their absence cannot be explained by preservation bias.

Elk

Elk falls in a large group characterized in particular by Element Group 5, i.e. lower parts of rear legs and phalanges (fibula (FIB), astragalus (AST), calcaneus (CAL), and phalanges (PHAL)), and in a conspicuous single occurence that aside from the 'commonwealth' also is characterized by a strong representation of the axial skeleton (Element Group 2).

Clearly, the exploitation of elk depended on whether it was exploited as a single, or as one among several, species.

At Skottemarke it was exploited as a single species and essentially the whole skeleton (except for metapodials) is well represented. This will be discussed below.

When hunted as one of several species, the use pattern is in some respects similar to that of red deer. In comparison, heads (represented by jaws) seem to have been brought home more frequently, but then again both the axial skeleton and legs are more poorly represented. This may indicate that the latter elements either were discarded at the kill site, which together with the conspicuous lack of femurs may indicate selective transport, or it may suggest that the elements were more frequently transferred to other locations in one or another state of preservation, or used for tools.

As noted for red deer, the Schlepp-effect is visible.

Aurochs

Aurochs shows a pattern very similar to the larger group of elk with a strong representation of Element Group 5, i.e. fibula (FIB), astragalus (AST), calcaneus (CAL), and phalanges (PHAL).

The exploitation pattern for aurochs is most similar to that of elk as exploited as one of several species. It is a huge animal with the same meat and raw material potential as elk. However, probably its very size is suggestive of an apparently greater selectivity on the kill sites.

8.3 Configuration of sites

In addition to the South Scandinavian Maglemosian sites, the Correspondence Analysis plot (Fig. 15c) also shows the position of the Atlantic settlements of Segebro and Ageröd V (red deer only; Larsson 1983) in Sweden (Larsson 1982), the Preboreal Maglemosian site of Star Carr, England (Legge & Rowley-Conwy 1988), and the Late Glacial sites of Meiendorf and Stellmoor A, Germany (reindeer only; Grønnow 1987).

Red deer, pig, elk and aurochs set themselves apart and thus may serve to differentiate between sites, although it is possible only to speak of tendencies. It should be emphasized that the site comparison is not by species, but is generalized and gives an allover picture based on all species with MNI > 4 and elements per species per site > 50. Consequently, the following sites or units have been omitted: Mullerup Nord, Ulkestrup I, Sværdborg II, Ageröd I:B and I:D. Also, occasionally some species have had to be omitted from (or are not present at) other sites; e.g. roe deer, pig and aurochs from Ulkestrup II and Ageröd V. A check with MNI ≥ 2, however, generally shows the same trends as the analysis with MNI > 4.

Despite some variation, the site configuration is fairly homogeneous. Only four sites set themselves apart: Skottemarke, which aligns itself with Meiendorf and Stellmoor A (see below), Sværdborg I, 1917-18 and Sværdborg I, 1943-44 Area C with their marked domination of metapodials, and Sværdborg I, 1923 which is similar to Lundby I.

A more detailed study of Mullerup Syd, Sværdborg I, 1923 and Star Carr, however, shows a high level of agreement. These sites also belong among the richest and may reflect a higher degree of selective transport, perhaps (but not necessarily) based on larger animal populations, although the inhabitants never went as far as to leave larger sections of animals articulated in the refuse. The same may pertain to Skottemarke, Meiendorf and Stellmoor A, although in a different way (see below).

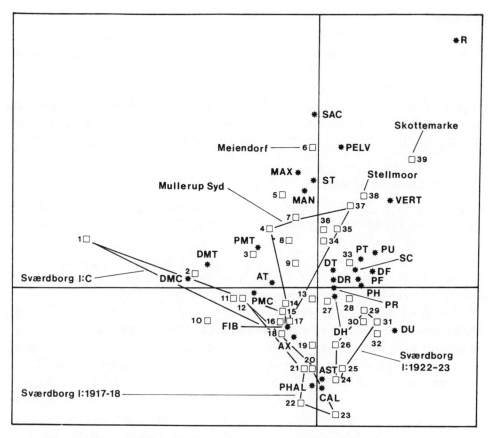

Fig. 15c. Configuration of sites. Base map and symbols as for Figure 15a.

8.4 The settlement pattern

Judging only from locations with preserved bone and antler material there are two categories of sites.

The first comprises sites that for nearly 100% is characterized by exploitation of a single species, e.g. Skottemarke (elk), Meiendorf and Stellmoor A (reindeer), of which, of course, only Skottemarke is Maglemosian. These sites are not identical, but may be interpreted as a hunting station/kill site, a seasonal hunting camp (Grønnow 1987), and a 'multiple kill-butchering location' or more precisely 'a base camp for seasonal reindeer hunting' (Grønnow 1987), respectively.

The other category is made up by the rest of the sites. Despite some minor discrepancies, they show similar exploitation patterns species by species. Moreover, taking into account the topographical setting, the great intensity in tool production and use, the consumption of flint, bone and antler, the

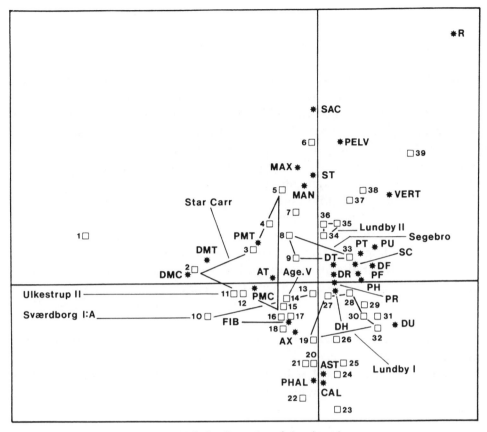

Fig. 15d. Configuration of sites (cont.).

presence of hut floors — in every respect what may be termed the result of many and various activities — plus the seasonal determinations, these sites may best be interpreted as summer base camps. A more narrow interpretation, e.g. hunting stations or the like, as has been proposed for Star Carr (Legge & Rowley-Conwy 1988), would not seem appropriate.

There are no conclusive chronological trends in exploitation patterns, nor in any other cultural or behavioural domain, in the Maglemosian. Of course, it may be argued that some intensification occurred over time (fragmentation of skeletal elements is very marked on some late Maglemosian sites, e.g. Ulkestrup I and II, Sværdborg II, Ageröd I:B and I:D). However, other agents may be responsible for this, such as heavy traffic by peat-extraction equipment and/or trampling by the original inhabitants. In any case this phenomenon would not seem to fit into Noe-Nygaard's (1977) scheme of two culturally distinct ways of butchering and marrow fracturing in the Mesolithic. She states:

...the marrow fracturing technique employed at Star Carr...and Kongemosen...is very similar while it differs in nearly all respects from the pattern found in the material from Præstelyngen...and Muldbjerg I...(Noe-Nygaard 1977, 229)

In the first place, I doubt the validity of a scheme built only on four sites from what are usually considered to be four different cultural contexts. Moreover, her argument is at variance with more recent findings, which do not corroborate differential butchering and marrow fracturing processes through the Mesolithic, but which suggest that a high degree of fragmentation, among other things, is generally either situational or caused by traffic on more solid ground. For instance, fragmentation is very notable in the active parts of Ertebølle shellmiddens (Bratlund pers. comm.).

Furthermore, it is impossible to discuss matters in terms of inland and coastal exploitation. So far there are no coastal settlements documented from the South Scandinavian Maglemosian proper, and for the ensuing Kongemose Culture the material still awaits full recording and analysis. The only indicators of some sort of contact with the sea are two bones of grey seal from Sværdborg I, 1917-18 and another from Ageröd I:HC (Friis-Johansen 1919, Althin 1954).

However, the Late Glacial sites (based on a single species of animal) differ from those of the Postglacial (based on several species of animals). The Late Glacial sites Meiendorf and Stellmoor A group themselves conspicuously on the plot in Figure 15c, showing a relatively high representation of the axial skeleton, which means that substantial parts of the animals (at Stellmoor often complete) were brought into the actual sites, or indeed killed at, or very close to, them. Moreover, compared to the Maglemosian, the Late Glacial sites (notably Stellmoor) are characterized by a high degree of articulation, which means that larger sections of the animals (again particularly at Stellmoor) were simply discarded without further processing. In fact, at these early stages we are dealing with entirely different economic practices. At the Ahrensburgian site of Stellmoor it was based on drives and bulk kills of a single species (reindeer), creating a huge surplus for storage (particularly at Stellmoor) (Grønnow 1987) and probably also resulting in temporary outbursts of extreme gluttony. At the Hamburgian site Meiendorf,

The hunting method was rather 'small-scale' drives...or maybe most frequently *individual stalking*. (Grønnow 1987, 154)

Further,

...exploitation of both the complete animals and the butchered segments brought home from elsewhere was very intensive. (*ibid.*)

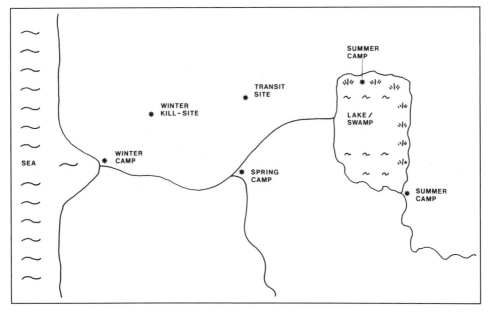

Fig. 16. The settlement pattern.

This should be seen in contrast to the Maglemosian sites at which major articulated sections of animals are virtually absent among the large species, and where the representation of the axial skeleton, even among the larger species, is generally low (see Sections 8.1-3 above).

The Maglemosian economy thus differs from that of the Late Glacial. Moreover, when selective transport occurred within the former, this generally did not result in large articulated sections being thrown out. Rather *ad hoc* selections were made on more distant hunting stations or at kill sites away from the base camps.

Sites with only flint preserved are more difficult to assess. Detail and extent of excavations and level of documentation vary considerably, and functional differentiation in terms of variation in tool composition would seem premature. A number of hut floors have been delineated (Blankholm 1984, 1987a), which closely resemble their counterparts with preserved organic remains. It still remains an open question, however, whether or not multiple floors or units in larger settlement areas (e.g. Klosterlund and Sværdborg I) were occupied simultaneously.

In Jutland, however, there is some variation in topographical location. Most commonly, as on the Danish islands, sites are located on low-lying sandy riverbanks, on peninsulas, or on former islands in the river and lake systems.

However, a small but increasing number of sites is found on higher ground at some distance from major courses or bodies of water (E.B. Petersen 1973, 1986, 1989, 1993). Some have been termed transit camps (E.B. Petersen 1973), but equally fitting labels may be kill sites or hunting stands.

The Maglemosian settlement pattern may thus be modelled as in Figure 16 with summer base camps involving a broad range of activities on the one hand, and hunting stations or kill sites used in the middle of the winter on the other, but with both lying inland. These two categories of sites are manifest in the material, and the interpretation is in accordance with earlier but largely intuitive notions (e.g. E.B. Petersen 1973, S.H. Andersen 1981, Blankholm 1980, 1981, 1987a). We can only guess at activities in other places at other times in the resource use cycle. It is possible that winter camps, probably aggregation camps, were located on the coasts for the exploitation of both marine and terrestial resources, while spring sites for the exploitation of migrating fish may be indicated by the virtually hundreds of smaller sites along the major river systems and their tributaries. Sites on higher ground, away from major bodies of water, may as noted be transit camps, kill sites, or hunting stands.

However, group composition among the larger, non-migratory and small-herd animals does not by itself require seasonal migration by their human predators. In fact, human movements should rather be seen as a combination of an economic strategy to counteract overexploitation and a social strategy permitting the operation of communication and mating networks.

Because we lack solid details of the year round settlement and exploitation pattern, it is difficult to assess whether the Maglemosians in general followed a logistical or a foraging strategy (Binford 1978).

The presence of kill-butchering sites and some aspects of the exploitation of particularly red deer could suggest a more long-sighted and anticipating (logistical) strategy: That is, certain parts of the animals were probably not consumed or used directly after killing and butchering, but were stored. Also, as indicated, the very fact of seasonal movement could be taken to point in this direction. However, as also emphasized, there is nothing in the general ecology or behaviour of the animals that would necessitate large-scale movement. Moreover, we cannot speak of widely differing butchering processes or exploitation patterns among the social units on the larger sites, which we would expect if a logistic strategy were practiced (Binford 1978). Further, there is nothing in the Maglemosian context heterogeneous enough to indicate social differentiation without food sharing. To the contrary, the generally very homogeneous picture of the Maglemosian may be interpreted to suggest an egalitarian society, perhaps involving immediate or *ad hoc* food sharing and consumption of game.

In conclusion, what we have found is a series of new aspects of the exploitation of the large mammalian fauna. Of course, these only formed a part of the entire Maglemosian economy. However, I believe that not only are we on the track of this prehistoric economy: we are on the right track!

9 A multicausal model for hunter-gatherer development in South Scandinavia from the Late Paleolithic to the introduction of farming

Some years ago I presented a multicausal model for the transition from hunting and gathering to farming, from the Ertebølle Culture to the Early Neolithic TRB (Funnelbeaker) Culture (Blankholm 1987b). Despite obvious biases in the record, an attempt will be made below to tentatively expand the time perspective of the model by approximately 5000 years — back to the end of the Upper Paleolithic.

According to Gamble (1986, 38-40), most of the variability in the Upper Paleolithic and the Mesolithic in Europe was probably rooted in, and began to become evident with, the appearance here of anatomically modern *Homo sapiens* around 35,000 BC. It is also apparent that global development from then on was neither unidirectional nor rigorously ecologically determined in its details.

Gamble is to be commended for a fresh and global perspective. From a general point of view there may be a good deal of truth to his arguments. However, changes leaving less significant impact on the archaeological record may be just as important in their own right as part of a regional or even global development or trajectory.

Turning to the South Scandinavian case, views on the Mesolithic/Neolithic transition have changed considerably over time (Blankholm 1987b, 155). Generally, however, only a single, and most often external, agent coupled with a triggering factor has been emphasized as the dominant cause of change: Migration (Brøndsted 1957, 143f, Becker 1947, 285f), diffusion/migration (Troels-Smith 1953, 42f), demographic pressure (Jensen 1982), or ecological and environmental change (Andersen 1973, Paludan Müller 1978, Rowley-Conwy 1983, 1984, Zvelebil & Rowley-Conwy 1984). In fact, what has been offered is a variety of largely monocausal, if not deterministic, explanations only occasionally showing greater concern with internal, dynamic agents and social variables (Jennbert 1984, Mahler *et al.* 1983). Apparently only a few people seem to realize that environmental change and the presence or absence of various resources only sets a new stage and does not in itself determine the future structure of a society (Blankholm 1987b).

Clearly what is needed for properly resolving the past is an integrative, multicausal approach, which for any time and place permits the most essential variables and parameters to be elucidated and explained (Section 1.1).

Unfortunately, there is no exact or quantitative scale for assessing the above phenomena. In fact we lack standardization of concepts such as technological innovation, territoriality, economic intensification and social complexity (to mention but a few). Consequently, it needs emphasizing that comparisons must remain general and basically qualitative.

9.1 A multicausal model

Combining the apparent and real 5000 year megatrends of environmental development, technological innovation (S.H. Andersen 1973, 1981, Clark 1975, Blankholm 1987b), population growth and demographic stress (S.H. Andersen 1973, E.B. Petersen 1973, David 1973, Newell 1973, Wobst 1976, Meiklejohn 1978, Jensen 1982, Madsen 1982, Constandse-Westermann *et al.* 1984, Constandse-Westermann & Newell 1987, Blankholm 1987b), territories (S.H. Andersen 1973, 1981, P.V. Petersen 1984, Madsen & J.E. Petersen 1984, Blankholm 1987b, 1990, Price 1985), sedentism (Blankholm 1987b, Rowley-Conwy 1983), economic intensification (S.H. Andersen 1981, Rowley-Conwy 1983, Blankholm 1987b), storage and exchange (Fisher 1981, Blankholm 1987b, Price 1985), and social complexity (e.g. Newell 1984, Price 1985, Clark 1975, Meiklejohn 1978, Constandse-Westermann & Newell 1987, Blankholm 1978, 1984, 1987a and b, 1990, S.H. Andersen 1983, Albrethsen & E.B. Petersen 1976, Larsson 1984, 1987, Madsen 1982, Jennbert 1984), we may tentatively outline the following model. In the event it will be shown that the transition to farming was indeed the result of long term and complex processes.

With the onset of the Holocene, the environment became considerably more diversified and affluent. That Late Glacial ambulatory store of necessities, the long-range migratory reindeer, disappeared and was replaced by small-herd, non-migratory cervids, wild boar and aurochs, besides a wide range of carnivores, fish and fowl.

Demographically, the long-term population increase through the Upper Paleolithic began to make an impact after the first expansion into the ice-free areas and most likely was slowly amplified by contingents retreating from the encroaching North Sea. Moreover, the replacement of the migratory reindeer with largely stationary species rendered neccessary the restructuring of the annual resource use cycles into smaller territories. If sea mammals were exploited along the former North Sea coast, the gradual reduction of available land area would in itself have caused long-term contraction of resource use areas.

Concurrent with these processes there are conspicuous signs of technological innovation and economic intensification in the Maglemosian; but why?

In a previous context (Blankholm 1987b and above) I have argued that environmental change sets a new stage and provides a new framework, but does not in itself determine the structure or organisation of the ongoing society. In most cases options are left open for the selection of appropriate short and long term strategies.

In my view, in the Early Mesolithic new strategies were needed to take account of the ecological setting, economic prospects, social relations, history and traditions, and several viable options were open. It is, perhaps, hardly surprising that people opted to maintain a mobile settlement pattern and a resource use schedule making use of a variety of resource spectra. This safeguarded against the potential for over-exploitation of important, but stationary resources. Yet if this were the only reason, settlement patterns probably could have been arranged in a variety of ways. What is interesting is the apparent economic intensification, not least the exploitation of resource spectra to which not much attention had apparently hitherto been paid, such as fishing and fowling and probably sea mammal hunting, which seems to go beyond a mere ecological or trivial economic explanation. More likely a greater part of the explanation is rooted in increasing population and spatial contraction of mating networks, coupled with the ecologically induced reduction of resource use areas. The society remains egalitarian, at most with charismatic or acquired status and some personal gear, but with a widely open communication network and no stylistically distinct boundaries (Blankholm 1990).

Once begun, the various trends continue. Technological innovation and diversity increases along with economic intensification and population growth. Territories and the spatial range of higher order social groups or relations diminish. These trends were probably causally related so that increase in population led to increasingly tighter clustering of mating networks and diminishing spatial range of the participating social units, and in turn led to the formation of gradually smaller territories for the regulation of access to resources. This again caused increasing economic intensification and technological innovation. Sedentism and social diversification, however, apparently did not develop until the Ertebølle Culture.

For the latter period high economic intensification and bulk kills or bulk collection of natural resources at certain times of the year probably led to the development of storage as part of a more logistically oriented economy (Blankholm 1987b). Concomitantly, risk was reduced by the development of a social storage and exchange system based on the existing social structure and possibly reflected in durable goods such as, for instance, shoe-last axes. Such a system could easily have led to skewed accumulation of wealth among those already possessing earned or ascribed status, and in turn could have led to social pressure to boost the economy even further for the accumulation of ever more wealth and enforcement of control. Concurrently, we see in the skeletal material (Constandse-Westerman & Newell 1987) an increasing number of lethal conflicts among the members of this sedentary, highly territorial and now rapidly growing population. Eventually, it would all have led to diminishing returns caused by over-exploitation, and:

If some resources declined, as seems to be evident in some areas, a situation would have arisen where the social storage system could no longer fulfil its initial obligations and purpose, that is to deliver food to groups at risk. In this situation people began to use an alternative, namely farming or food production; but what mechanisms were the most responsible or prominent in this strategic turn-over? (Blankholm 1987b, 160)

It may be argued that the Ertebølle diversified social system did not break down just because a few, but important, resources like the oyster declined or disappeared, but rather steadily developed into the full hierarchisation of the Neolithic. Most likely,

...those accumulating wealth, facing the possibility of losing power and status, would have urged rapid change to a mode of production that was both at hand and through which surplus and thus wealth could continue to be accumulated and redistributed, and status reassured. (Blankholm 1987b, 160)

In short, the transition to farming most likely originated in properties of the developing social structure. At first, intensification, storage and farming resulted in increasing, but unequal, accumulation of wealth through social storage and exchange, and in that event to the ritualised reinforcement of power and the construction of megaliths as territorial and status markers. This trend temporarily culminated in the Early Middle Neolithic social structure in which rank was expressed in battleaxes, copper ornaments and monuments, and where the polished flint axe played a central role as the primary medium and link between subsistence, exchange and commercial and ritual hoarding (Kristiansen 1984, Blankholm 1987b).

Viable alternatives to the introduction of farming were available, however. Efficient population control, for one, could have ensured the Ertebølle way of life and would not have increased production or created surpluses that could be seized. They could also have opted fully for stock-rearing, which could take place anywhere, which would have inhibited the system of landrights, land allocation and territoriality from eventually emerging, and which would have provided better for direct storage in cattle and stock and less for social storage (Blankholm 1987b, 160).

In any event, none of this happened, most likely because a solution more favourable to people in power was available.

To conclude, the above model attempts to outline the long-term development over 5000 years of South Scandinavian hunter-gatherers from the end of the Paleolithic to the introduction of farming. This development was complex in nature and multicausal in character and shows the gradually accumulating effect of both natural and social forces in operation, but in which the social dimension played a more prominent and decisive role than previously acknowledged.

It is no more than a tentative model. Clearly much more research needs to be done in order to investigate more fully the trends we perceive and the feasibility of the above or any combination of existing models. If the above stimulates such research, it has served its purpose.

10 Conclusions

Briefly summarized, the above analysis of the Maglemosian subsistence data and economy has led at least to the following:

1. There is a basis for the investigation of faunal exploitation patterns at the level of identifiable skeletal elements (Section 5).
2. There is a basis for the calculation of a mininum number of individuals (MNI) per species per site, or analytical unit, for red deer, roe deer, pig, elk and aurochs following Binford's (1978) method (Section 5 and Appendix B).
3. The number of animals killed was generally small.
4. A partition of the MNI data into sex and age groups would yield too small numbers for reliable, comparative analysis.
5. Because the study investigates the actual, rather than the theoretical, exploitation of species, site catchment analysis and calculation of biomass is not feasible (Section 5.3).
6. Because of inherent theoretical and methodological problems, utility indices and representation graphs (Binford 1978) cannot be used in the present context (Section 5.4).
7. Spatial analysis using Presab (Blankholm 1991) shows that hut floors (or basic analytical units) denote multifunctional work and consumption areas with adjacent, extensive butchering, toss and discard zones. Internal and external division of space is visible in some cases, but not in any consistent pattern among sites (Section 6).
8. Discard behaviour with regard to bones is haphazard. Generally no species or skeletal element is restricted to specific, or larger, areas. Larger articulated sections of animals are absent.
9. The distributions of intact bones and of proximal and distal ends of large limb bones generally show no consistent differentiation between species.
10. Basically, there is no fit with Binford's (1978) model seating plan for outdoor hearths.
11. Generally, newborns, juveniles and adults of both sexes within the five major species were hunted following a strategy that made it possible to temporarily remedy unbalanced culls of any single species' local population.
12. The season of occupation is March/April to September/October. Only one site (Skottemarke) unambiguously shows use in the winter in December/January.

13. A Correspondence Analysis based on %MNI for skeletal elements per species per site shows the configuration of elements, species, and sites respectively (Section 8).

The configuration of elements shows 5 groups:

a) Maxilla and mandibles.
b) The axial skeleton; vertebrae (except 1st and 2nd cervicals), ribs, sternum, sacrum, and pelvis.
c) Scapulae, and the upper and middle limb bones: proximal and distal humerus, proximal and distal radius, proximal and distal ulna, proximal and distal femur, and proximal and distal tibia.
d) 1st and 2nd cervicals, proximal and distal metacarpals, and proximal and distal metatarsals.
e) Lower parts of rear legs; fibula, astragalus, calcaneus, plus front and rear phalanges.

The species configuration shows that the exploitation of the large game followed general, but divergent, trends among the species, and for elk even within the species. All 5 species were hunted for their meat and for raw materials for tool manufacture. Field butchering seems evident for the largest species: red deer, elk and aurochs. For these animals the Schlepp-effect is visible. Apparently only the most highly required necessities were carried back in the hides with the phalanges attached as 'riders', whereas roe deer and pig generally were brought back complete, or in sections amounting to complete animals.

The site configuration lends support to conclusions about the Maglemosian settlement pattern. This included on the one hand summer base camps on lakes, involving a broad range of activities, and on the other hunting stations or kill sites, with both being inland. It is suggested that winter aggregation camps were located on the coast, while spring sites for the exploitation of migratory fish were located along the major river systems.

Group composition among the larger non-migratory, small-herd animals did not by itself require seasonal migration on the part of their human predators. Rather, human movements must be seen as a combination of an economic strategy to counteract overexploitation, and of a social strategy to facilitate the operation of communication and mating networks.

The generally very homogeneous picture of the Maglemosian suggests an egalitarian society, perhaps involved with immediate or *ad hoc* food sharing and consumption of game (Section 8.4).

14. A multicausal model for the 5000-year development of hunter-gatherers in South Scandinavia from the Late Paleolithic to the introduction of farming shows that the development was complex in nature, and shows the gradually accumulating effects of both natural and social forces in operation. However, among these the social dimension played a more prominent and decisive role than has previously been acknowledged.

Appendix A

Zoological database

This appendix contains the raw database of skeletal elements per site organized into species, excavational sections, and units. Only sites used in the spatial analyses are included. Data on sex, age, articulation, refits, indeterminate pieces, and teeth are excluded. Abbreviations largely follow the system of Binford (1978), Grønnow (1986) and Legge & Rowley-Conwy (1988) and are listed in Table 3.

Mullerup Syd

Red deer

Section I

Unit		Unit		Unit	
A7	1T	F7	1MAX, 1PHAL	H4	1MAN
A10	1ANT(shed)	F8	1PHAL	I1	1PELV
D1	1ANT	G1	1MC, 1CARP	I2	1SC, 1 CERV
E1	1MT	G2	1CARP	I3	1PHAL
E2	1MT	G3	1MT, 1SC	K1	1MAN, 1R
E3	1MT, 1PHAL	G5	1AST, 1TARS	K4	2PHAL
E7	1VERT	G8	1R	K8	1PHAL
E8	1MT	H1	1SC, 1MT, 1CAL		
F3	1MT	H2	1T, 1MT		
F6	1MAN, 1PHAL	H3	1MAN, 1MT, 1CARP		

Section II

Unit		Unit	
H8	1AST	H9	1ANT

Section III

Unit		Unit		Unit	
A2	1MAN	A3	1MAX	A4	1MAN
B2	1SC, 1MT, 1PHAL	B3	1PELV	B4	1R
B6	1AST	C4	1SK(f), 1PHAL	C7	1F
D5	1F	E4	1MT	E5	1PHAL
F6	1T				

Section VII

Unit	
D3	1CAL
D4	1R
F2	1ANT(f)

Roe deer

Section I

Unit		Unit		Unit	
A3	1CARP	E1	1ANT(f), 2MT	F7	1SK(f)
A7	1F	E2	1MT	F8	1SK(f)
B4	1MAN	E3	1U	G1	1MT
C3	1MT	E4	1SK+ANT	G2	1MAN, 1SC, 1MT
C5	1SK(f), 1MT	E5	1MAX, 1AT, 1PELV	G3	1SK(f), 1R, 1VERT
D2	1T, 1MT	E6	1RIB, 1R, 1 PELV	G4	1MAN, 1CAL
D3	1R, 1MT	F2	1SK(f)	G5	1AT
D5	1F	F3	1SC	G7	1SC
D6	1CAL	F4	1U	G8	1MAN
D7	1SK(f)	F5	1MAN	H1	1R, 1MT

Unit		Unit	
H2	1MC, 1CAL	K2	1SK(f), 1 MAN, 1MT
H3	1SK+ANT, 1SK(f), 1U, 1MT	K3	1MAN, 2SC, 1MT
H10	1CAL	K4	1AT, 1 CERV, 1SC 1F, 1MT
I1	1AX, 1MAN, 2T	K6	1R, 1T, 1CAL
I2	1U, 1T, 1AST		
I3	1SK(f)		
I4	1MAN, 1F		
I7	1MT		
I8	1SC		
K1	1MC, 1MT		

Section II

Unit		Unit	
I8	1CERV	I10	1SC

Section III

Unit		Unit	
A2	1SC	C5	1PELV
A4	1MAN	D2	1MAN
A5	1MAN	D3	1SC, 1T
A7	1PELV, 1T	D5	1MAN
B2	1SK(f), 1TARS	G3	1T
B3	1SK(f), 1MAX		
B6	1MAN		
C2	1MAN, 1PELV		

C3   1MT
C4   2SC

Section IV

Unit
F2   1T

Section VII

Unit		*Unit*		*Unit*	
A5	1 SC	D2	1PELV	I2	1R
B9	1TARS	F3	1MT	K2	1AST, 1CAL

Pig

Section I

Unit		*Unit*		*Unit*	
A1	1T	C5	1MT	E6	1MAN
A6	1MAN, 1TARS	C9	1F, 1T	E7	1MT
A7	1SC, 1MT	D2	1R	E10	1PELV
A8	1MAX, 1CERV,	D4	1T, 1CAL, 1TARS	F5	1MT
	1MT	D5	1F	F7	1PHAL
A9	1MAN	D7	1SK(f)	F8	1SK(f), 1CAL
B4	1MAX	D10	1CARP	F9	1MAX
B5	1AST	E1	1T, 1CAL	F10	1TARS
B6	1R	E2	1H	G1	1VERT, 1CAL
B7	1SK(f)	E4	1MAN, 1VERT	G2	1MT, 1CAL
B9	1SK(f)	E5	1SK(f), 1MAX,		
			1U, 1PHAL		

Unit		*Unit*	
G3	1PELV, 1FIB,	K1	1MT
	1MT	K2	1MAN, 1PELV
G5	1T	K3	1U, 1TARS
H1	1T	K6	1MAX
H2	1CARP	K8	1T
H3	2T		
H5	1MT		
I2	2VERT, 1CAL		
I3	1MAX		
I4	1U		
I7	1SK(f)		

Section II

Unit		*Unit*	
I8	1PHAL	I9	1R, 1MT

Section III

Unit		Unit	
A4	1MAN, 1SC	C5	1CARP
A6	1T	D2	1CARP
A7	1MAN, 1U	D3	1MAN
B2	1VERT, 1SC	E3	1PHAL
B4	1MAX	F2	1SC
B5	1MAX	F4	1TARS
B6	1AX	H5	1T
B7	1MAN, 1VERT	K5	1R, 1U
C2	1PELV(f)		
C4	1MAX, 1T		

Section IV

Unit		Unit		Unit	
F1	1 PHAL	I1	1SK(f)	K4	1U(f)
H1	1AST	I2	1T, 1CARP	K9	1F
H3	1R, 1CARP	I3	1R, 1MT	K10	1T

Section VII

Unit	
A3	1VERT
B2	1AST
C3	1PELV, 1U
C4	1MAN
C6	1T
E2	1R
E7	1MAN
F2	1MAN
F3	1T
I6	1MAX

Elk

Section I

Unit		Unit		Unit	
B10	1PHAL	E4	1CARP, 1AST, 1PHAL	H2	1RIB, 1PHAL
C7	1MAX	E7	1PHAL	H3	1PAT, 1CARP, 1CAL, 3PHAL
C8	1MC	F2	1CARP	H4	1CARP, 1PHAL
C9	1TARS, 1PHAL	F6	1PHAL	H6	1RIB, 1U
C10	1PHAL	F9	1TARS	H7	1CAL
D3	1DR, 1ANT	F10	1DMC	H8	1PHAL
D4	1ANT, 1PHAL	G1	1ANT, 1PHAL	I1	1PAT
D9	1PHAL	G3	1CARP, 1PHAL	I2	1RIB
E1	1MT	G8	1RIB, 1PHAL	I3	1MAN, 1F, 1PHAL
E3	1CARP, 1TARS, 1PHAL	H1	1ANT, 1MT, 1PHAL	I4	1R

Unit		Unit	
I5	1MT	K8	1AST
I6	1AST, 1PHAL	K10	1PHAL
I7	1AST		
K1	2PHAL		
K2	1MT, 2AST		
K3	1AX, 1PHAL		
K4	1SK(f), 2RIB, 1R, 1PHAL		
K5	1MT, 6PHAL		
K6	1RIB, 1PELV, 1F, 1PHAL		
K7	1PHAL		

Section III

Unit		Unit		Unit	
A2	1MAN, 1PHAL	B6	1PHAL	G3	1SK(f), 1PHAL
A3	1FIB, 1PHAL	C2	1PHAL	H4	1PHAL
A4	1SK(f), 1R, 2PHAL	C4	1PHAL	H5	1MT, 1PHAL
A5	1SC, 1PHAL	C6	1F, 1PHAL		
A7	1AST	D2	3CARP		
A8	1SK(f)	D3	1ANT		
B1	1ANT, 1PHAL	D4	2CARP		
B2	1ANT, 1SC, 1PHAL	D6	1F, 1PHAL		
B3	1SK(f), 2PHAL	E5	1PELV, 1CARP, 1PHAL		
B4	1MT, 1PHAL	F2	1CAL, 1PHAL		

Section IV

Unit		Unit	
F2	1TARS	F3	1CAL

Section VII

Unit		Unit		Unit	
A5	1PHAL	H2	1PHAL	K6	1F
G7	1PELV	H5	1PHAL		

Aurochs

Section I

Unit		Unit		Unit	
B5	1PHAL	F8	1PHAL	I10	1RIB
B7	1TARS, 1CAL, 1PHAL	G2	1SC, 1MT		
B8	2AST	G3	1PT, 1LUM		
B9	2TARS	G4	1TARS, 1PHAL		
C8	1PHAL	H2	1LUM, 1PELV		
		H3	1PELV, 1F		

D5	1VERT		H5	1CARP
D10	1PHAL		H7	1CAL
F5	1VERT		I3	1PELV
F6	1RIB		I5	1CERV
F7	1CARP			

Section II

Unit		*Unit*		*Unit*	
I8	1PHAL	I9	1SK(f)	I10	1LUM

Section III

Unit		*Unit*	
A4	1MT	D4	1PHAL
B1	1SC	E3	1PAT
B2	1PHAL	E5	1CARP, 1MC
B3	1PHAL		
B4	1TARS		
B10	1PHAL		
C2	1ST		
C3	1VERT, 1PAT		
C5	1PHAL		
D3	1VERT, 1PHAL		

Section IV

Unit	
I1	1PAT

Section VII

Unit	
B3	1PHAL
B7	1SK(f)
D4	1PHAL
E2	1PELV
E3	1CARP
F5	1PHAL
G2	1PHAL
H3	1PHAL
H6	1PELV
I6	1CARP

Ulkestrup I

Red deer

Unit	
Ø02,S09	1CERV
Ø00,S09	1RIB(f)
V01,S09	1RIB(f)
V02,S09	1SC(f), 1CERV(f)
V02,S12	1ANT(f), 1CAL
V02,S13	1PHAL
V02,S14	1RIB, 1F(f)
V03,S09	1MAN(f), 1SC(f)
V03,S10	1MAN(f), 1CERV(f), 6LUM(f), 1SC(f)
V03,S11	2LUM, 1RIB(f), 1DH

Unit	
V03,S12	1PH, 1PF, 1AST 1THOR(f), 1LUM
V03,S13	1THOR(f)
V03,S14	1THOR, 1LUM
V04,S09	2CERV(f), 1THOR(f)
V04,S10	1THOR(f), 1LUM(F), 2PELV(f), 3RIB(f), 1PH, 1PHAL
V04,S11	1ANT(f), 1SK(f), 1AX, 1CERV(f), 4LUM(f), 1SAC, 4PELV(f), 2RIB(f), 3DH, 1PHAL
V04,S12	2LUM, 1RIB(f), 1PF, 1AST
V04,S13	1ANT(f), 1SAC, 1RIB(f)
V05,S08	1RIB(f)
V05,S09	1CERV(f), 1LUM(f), 2PHAL

Unit	
V05,S10	1LUM(f)
V05,S11	2CERV(f), 1LUM(f), 1THOR(f), 1RIB(f), 1DMT, 1PHAL
V06,S07	1H(f)
V06,S08	1RIB(f)
V07,S06	1PELV(f)

Unit	
V07,S07	1CERV, 1THOR
V09,S06	1RIB(f)
V10,S06	1AX
V11,S06	1AT, 2SC

Roe deer

Unit	
V02,S12	1MC
V03,S11	1CERV(f), 1RIB(f), 1MC
V03,S12	1DMC
V04,S10	1ANT, 1ST
V04,S11	2SK(f), 1RIB(f), 1PHAL
V04,S12	1PELV(f), 1DH, 1PMC, 1MT(f)
V04,S13	1MAN(f)
V04,S14	1MT(f)
V05,S11	1PMC
V05,S12	1LUM(f)

Unit	
V05,S13	1PELV(f), 1PMT
V07,S03	1DT
V08,S10	1AST
V11,S06	1MC

Pig

Unit	
V02,S09	1DRA, 1U(f)
V02,S14	1RIB(f)

Unit	
V04,S12	1PELV(f), 1PR, 1PMT, 3PHAL

V03,S09	1LUM(f)
V03,S10	1MAX(f), 1PELV(f), 1SC
V03,S11	1SK(f), 5RIB(f), 1DH, 1CARP, 1DMC, 2F(f), 1PHAL
V03,S12	2SK(f), 1H(f), 2MP, 1DF, 1PHAL
V03,S13	1T(f), 1CARP
V04,S09	1MAN, 1MAN(f)
V04,S10	1AT, 1SAC, 1PELV(f), 2RIB(f), 1SC, 1DH, 1PR, 1U(f), 1MC, 1T(f), 4PHAL
V04,S11	2SK(f), 2MAX, 1AT, 1THOR(f), 1DH, 1F(f), 7PHAL

V04,S13	1THOR(f), 1RIB(f), 1H(f), 1CAL, 2PHAL
V05,S07	1THOR
V05,S08	1DF, 1DMT
V05,S09	1MAN, 1MAN(f), 1SC
V05,S10	1CERV(f), 2PHAL
V05,S11	2RIB(f), 1PMT, 1PHAL
V05,S12	1PF, 1T(f)
V05,S13	1CERV(f), 1PHAL
V05,S14	1AX, 1DT

Unit	
V06,S08	1PH
V07,S15	1H(f)
V08,S06	1DT

Unit	
V09,S06	1MAN, 1SC, 1PHAL
V10,S07	1PHAL

Elk

Unit	
V03,S10	1MC
V03,S11	1RIB(f)
V04,S11	1SK(f)
V04,S12	1PELV(f)
V05,S09	2RIB(f), 1PHAL
V05,S10	1MAX, 1MAN, 1PHAL
V05,S11	1PAT
V06,S08	1R
V07,S07	1PELV(f), 1RIB(f)
V09,S06	1RIB(f), 2PHAL

Aurochs

Unit	
E05,S09	1PHAL
E00,S09	1CERV(f)
V02,S09	1MAN(f)
V03,S10	1DH
V03,S11	1PHAL
V03,S12	1SK(f), 1MAX(f), 1PELV(f) 1DRA
V03,S13	1DH, 1PHAL
V03,S14	1MAX, 1PH, 1DH, 1R(f)
V04,S08	1CERV(f)
V04,S09	1CERV(f)

Unit	
V04,S10	2SK(f), 1AX, 3CERV(f), 2THOR(f) 1SAC, 1RIB(f)
V04,S11	1AT, 1CERV(f), 1PHAL
V04,S12	2PELV(f), 4RIB(f), 1PHAL
V04,S14	2RIB(f)
V05,S09	1CERV(f), 1PHAL
V05,S10	1CERV(f), 1PELV(f), 1SESAM
V05,S11	1MAN(f), 1CERV(f), 1SESAM
V05,S12	1RIB(f)

Aurochs continued

	V05,S13	1CERV(f), 1AST
	V05,S14	1THOR(f), 1PHAL

Unit

V06,S08	1MAN(f)
V07,S07	1RIB(f)
V10,S06	1RIB(f)

Ulkestrup II

Red deer

Unit	
V17,S32	1MAX(f), 1THOR(f)
V17,S33	1MAN(f), 2RIB(f)
V18,S32	1THOR(f), 4RIB(f)
V18,S35	1SC(f), 1DT
V19,S33	1PELV(f), 1RIB(f), 1DR
V19,S34	2RIB, 1RIB(f), 1SC(f) 2PHAL
V20,S32	1DT
V20,S33	1LUM(f), 1PHAL
V20,S34	1CERV(f), 2THOR(f), 1LUM(f), 1RIB, 1RIB(f) 1PR, 1DMP, 1DMC, 1F(f), 1CAL, 4PHAL
V20,S35	1CERV(f), 1DT, 1PHAL
V21,S32	1CERV(f), 2LUM(f)

Unit	
V21,S33	1MAN(f), 3RIB(f), 1DH, 2PHAL
V21,S34	1ST, 1U(f), 1DMP, 2PHAL
V21,S35	2CERV(f), 1R(f), 1DMC, 1PHAL
V22,S32	1ANT, 1MAN(f), 1LUM(f), 1RIB(f), 1DH, 1PR, 2MP, 1PT, 1FIB, 5PHAL
V22,S33	1ANT(f), 1SK(f), 1SK+ANT, 1CERV, 1THOR(f), 4RIB(f), 2DH, 1DR, 1CARP, 3PT, 1DT, 1DMT, 2PHAL
V22,S34	1SK(f), 1MAX(f), 1AX, 1CERV(f), 6THOR(f), 4RIB(f), 1DR, 1CARP, 1DF, 1DMT, 1PHAL
V22,S35	1ANT, 1AT, 1CERV(f), 1THOR(f), 3RIB
V22,S36	1MAN(f), 1AX, 1CERV, 1RIB, 1PAT
V22,S37	1DT
V22,S38	2RIB(f)

Unit	
V22,S40	1DH, 1PHAL
V22,S41	1PAT
V23,S31	1THOR(f), 1PF, 1PHAL
V23,S32	1AX, 1THOR(f), 1RIB(f), 1R, 11PHAL
V23,S33	1SK(f), 1AT, 1CERV(f), 3THOR(f), 2RIB(f), 1SC(f),1DR, 1PU, 2CARP, 1DT, 6PHAL
V23,S34	1MAN(f), 1CERV(f), 1PELV(f), 1DMP
V23,S35	4CERV
V23,S36	4SK(f), 1MAX(f), 1RIB(f), 1T(f), 2TARS 2AST
V24,S32	1DMC, 1DT, 2PHAL
V24,S33	1AT, 2PHAL
V24,S35	1MAN(f), 1THOR(f), 1RIB(f)

Unit	
V24,S36	1MAN(f), 1SC
V25,S32	1PHAL
V25,S33	1AST
V25,S35	1DT
V25,S36	1DH
V26,S33	1R(f)
V26,S34	1PMC

Roe deer

Unit		Unit	
V15,S33	1PMT	V21,S35	2SK(f), 2PELV(f), 1RIB(f)
V19,S32	1DH	V22,S32	1SK(f), 1MAX(f), 1RIB(f), 1MC(f), 1F, 1T(f), 1MP, 1TARS, 1AST
V19,S33	1PF		
V19,S34	1MC(f)		
V19,S35	1PF, 1MT(f)		
V20,S33	1RIB(f)		
V20,S34	1MT(f)	V22,S33	1MAX(f), 1PELV(f), 1RIB(f), 1F(f), 1DT
V20,S35	1SK(f), 1PMC, 1DT	V22,S34	4RIB(f), 1U(f),1MC, 2PF, 1PMT, 1TARS, 5PHAL
V21,S33	2RIB(f), 1F(f)		
V21,S34	1RIB(f)		
		V22,S35	1RIB(f), 1SC
		V22,S36	1PELV(f), 1PF
		V22,S37	1CERV(f), 1DF, 1CAL
		V22,S38	1CERV(f), 1F(f)
		V22,S39	1F(f)
		V22,S40	1PH, 1DH

Unit		Unit	
V23,S31	1PMP	V25,S32	MAN(f), 1DR, 1DU, 1DF
V23,S32	1MAX(f), 1T, 1AST	V25,S34	1PR
V23,S33	1ANT(f), 2RIB(f), 1PMT, 1PHAL	V25,S35	1AT, 1AX, 1H(f), 3F(f)
V23,S34	3MAN(f), 1SAC, 1PELV (f), 3RIB(f), 1DR, 1DU 3PHAL	V25,S36	1DF
V23,S35	1MAN(f), 1CERV(f), 1LUM(f), 1PELV(f), 2RIB(f)		
V23,S36	1PELV(f), 3RIB(f), 2SC, 1PT, 1CAL, 1PHAL		
V24,S32	1DR, 1DF, 1CAL, 1PHAL		
V24,S33	1MAN(f), 1RIB(f), 1DF, 1DMT		
V24,S35	1LUM(f), 1DH, 1PU, 1MC (f), 1PHAL		
V24,S36	1RIB(f), 2DMC, 1DF, 2AST		

Pig

Unit		Unit	
V20,S33	1MT(f)	V23,S32	1DR, 1PMT
V21,S32	1LUM(f)	V23,S33	1RIB(f)
V21,S33	1RIB(f)	V23,S34	1PT
V21,S34	1MAN(f), 1RIB(f), 1H(f)	V23,S35	1MAN(f)
V21,S35	1SK(f), 1LUM(f)	V23,S36	1MAN(f), 1DH, 1F(f)
V22,S32	1PELV(f)		
V22,S33	1VERT, 1H(f), 1PAT	V24,S30	1VERT(f)
V22,S34	1SK(f), 1MAX(f),	V24,S32	1DH, 1R(f)

	2PELV(f)		
V22,S35	1RIB(f), 1T(f)	V24,S33	1H(f)
V22,S37	1PELV(f)	V24,S36	1MAX(f), 1SC
		V25,S31	1DF

Unit	
V25,S33	1RIB(f)
V25,S35	1SK(f)
V25,S36	1AST, 2CAL
V26,S34	1H(f), 1F(f)

Elk

Unit		*Unit*	
V20,S35	1DR	V23,S35	1CAL
V21,S34	1PR	V23,S36	1CAL
V22,S32	1PR	V24,S36	1DMT
V23,S33	1SK(f)		

Aurochs

Unit		*Unit*	
V16,S33	1DH	V20,S33	1SC, 1PHAL
V17,S32	1MAX(f), 2RIB(f)	V20,S34	2MAX(f), 1RIB(f)
V17,S33	2MAN, 1MAX(f)	V20,S35	1MAN, 1RIB(f)
V18,S32	1SK(f), 1SAC, 1MT	V21,S32	1DMC, 1PHAL
V18,S33	1U	V21,S33	1AT, 1RIB(f)
V19,S32	1SESAM	V21,S34	2SK(f), 3SESAM
V19,S33	1MAN(f), 1RIB(f), 1PHAL		3RIB(f)
V19,S34	2CERV(f)	V21,S35	1SK(f), 1MAX,
V19,S35	1RIB(f)		1RIB(f)
V20,S32	1PU	V22,S32	2SK(f), 1RIB(f),
			1PU
		V22,S33	2SK(f), 1CERV(f),
			2RIB(f), 1SC, 1PU, 1T(f)
		V22,S34	1CERV(f), 1THOR(f),
			3RIB(f), 1SC, 1PR,
			1PAT

Unit		*Unit*	
V22,S35	1THOR(f), 1AST, 1PHAL	V24,S35	1THOR(f)
V22,S36	1SC(f), 1PHAL	V24,S36	1RIB(f), 1H(f)
V22,S37	1PHAL	V25,S33	1PHAL
V22,S38	1SESAM		
V22,S39	1SC(f)		
V23,S32	1MAN(f)		
V23,S33	1MAX(f), 1THOR(f),		
	1RIB(f), 1PT, 2TARS		
V23,S34	1AT, 1PHAL		
V23,S35	1SK(f), 1CERV(f),		
	THOR(f)		
V23,S36	1SK(f), 1CERV(f), 1RIB(f)		

Sværdborg I, 1917-18

Red deer

Section I

Unit		Unit		Unit	
A2	1PHAL	C3	1ANT, 1MAN(f)	E3	1CARP
A4	1TARS	C4	1ANT	E4	1ANT
A5	1MT(f)	C5	1F	E5	1T(f)
A6	1R(f)	C7	1R(f)	E6	1PHAL
A7	1MAN(f)	D3	1SK+ANT	E7	2TARS, 1PHAL
B6	1ANT, 1PHAL	D4	1AST, 1CAL	E8	1TARS
B7	1SC(f)	D5	2PELV	F2	1SC(f)
B9	1PELV(f), 1T(f)	D6	1ANT, 1T(f)	F3	1R(f), 1MT(f)
B10	1DMT	D10	1CARP	F4	1R(f), 1TARS
C1	1MT(f)	E2	1ANT, 1AST, 1CAL 1MT(f)	F8	1PHAL

Unit		Unit		Unit	
G2	1ANT, 1MAN	H5	1CARP, 1FIB, 1MC 1PHAL	J9	1R(f)
G3	1CARP, 1MT, 1PHAL	H6	1MAN, 1DR	K1	1ANT
G4	1ANT, 1MT, 1PHAL	H7	1SK+ANT, 1U(f), 1CARP, 1F(f), 1PHAL	K5	1ANT, 1CARP, 1PHAL
G5	1F(f), 1T, 1TARS, 2MT, 1PHAL	J2	1ANT	K6	1R(f), 1U(f), 1F, 1MT, 1PHAL
G6	1MT(f), 1PHAL	J3	1PR	K7	1MC, 1PHAL
G7	1SK+ANT, 1SC	J4	1PAT	K8	1MT, 1PHAL
G9	1PHAL	J5	1ANT, 2CARP, 1PHAL		
H1	1ANT, 1SK(f)	J6	1PAT, 1PHAL		
H2	1MT(f)	J7	1AST		
H4	1T(f), 1PHAL	J8	1PHAL		

Section XI

Unit		Unit	
A3	1MT(f)	F3	1ANT, 1MC, 1TARS 1PHAL
B3	1U(f)	G2	1ANT
B5	1MT	G3	1PHAL
C2	2MAN	G4	1ANT, 2PHAL
C4	1CARP	G5	1ANT
D1	1TARS	K2	1AST
D2	1ANT	K3	1AST, 1CAL, 1DMT
E1	1R(f)		
E4	1SC, 1AST		
F1	1ANT, 1MT		

Section XVII

Unit		Unit		Unit	
C10	1CARP	D10	1MAN(f)	F9	1MT(f)

Section XVIII

Unit		Unit	
A1	1ANT	E1	1H(f)
B2	2SC, 1MC	E2	1DT
B4	1ANT, 1MC(f)	F3	1ANT
C1	1MAN(f)	F4	1CAL
C2	1MT(f)	G2	1ANT
C3	1VERT	G3	1SC(f)
C4	1ANT	G4	1MT(f)
D1	1ANT, 1CAL	H3	1MT(f)
D2	1CAL	K1	1ANT
D4	1PHAL		

Section XIX

Unit		Unit	
A1	1ANT	E3	1ANT
A2	1U(f)	E4	1PAT
A4	1CARP	F2	1VERT
B1	1CARP	F3	1MT(f)
C1	1DH	F4	1ANT
C2	1MT(f)	G1	1H(f), 1PAT, 1AST
C3	1SC(f)	G4	1T(f), 1MT(f), 1PHAL
D1	1PHAL	H4	1ANT, 1VERT, 1MT
D3	1ANT	J3	1ANT, 1PELV(f)
E1	1MT(f)	J4	2TARS, 1MT(f)

Section XX

Unit		Unit		Unit	
C4	1T(f)	E1	1AST, 1CAL, 1PHAL	H4	1F(f)
D1	1MAN	F3	1ANT	K4	1SK(f), 1F(f)
D2	1AST	F4	1PHAL		

Roe deer

Section I

Unit		Unit		Unit	
A1	1H(f)	D10	1R(f)	G8	1SC(f)
A4	1U(f)	E3	1SK+ANT, 1MAN,	H4	1AST
A7	1H		1H(f), 1T(f),	H5	1MAN(f), 2PHAL
B7	1T(f)		1AST	H6	1SC(f), 1R(f),
B8	1PELV(f)	E5	1MT(f)		1MT
D1	1SK(f)	E8	1AST	H8	1F(f)
D6	1PHAL	F3	1SK+ANT, 2SC	H9	1T(f)
D7	1MAN(f)	F9	1SC(f)	H10	1TARS

Roe deer continued

D8	1MAN(f), 1AST	G2	1SK+ANT, 1H(f)	J1	1SK+ANT
D9	1MT(f)	G4	1H(f), 1MT(f)	J3	1SK+ANT
		G5	2SK+ANT	J4	1SK+ANT, 1SC(f)
		G6	1PHAL		

Unit

J6	1H(f), 1CAL
J8	1SC(f), 1R(f)
I10	1MAN(f), 1AST
K6	1MT(f)
K8	1SC(f), 1AST
K9	1SK(f), 1TARS

Section X

Unit		*Unit*		*Unit*	
C10	1MAN, 1MT	D10	1MT(f)	F9	1SK+ANT

Section XI

Unit		*Unit*		*Unit*	
A4	1MAN(f)	D5	1H(f)	H4	1MC(f)
A5	1MT(f)	E1	1CAL	H5	1ANT(f), 1MT(f)
B4	1MAN(f), 1MT(f)	E4	1AST, 1CAL	K5	1SK+ANT
B5	1ANT(f)	F1	1H(f)		
C1	1R(f)	F5	1U(f)		
C2	1SK+ANT, 1MAN,	G2	1PHAL		
	1T(f), 1PHAL	G4	1MT(f)		
C4	1F(f), 1MT(f)	G5	1R(f)		
D1	1AST, 3PHAL	H1	1SK+ANT, 1PHAL		
D2	1H(f), 1T(f)	H2	1R(f), 1U(f)		
D4	1ANT(f)				

Section XVII

Unit		*Unit*		*Unit*	
A8	1ANT	C9	1CAL	F10	1CAL
B9	1ANT(f)	D9	1MT(f)		

Section XVIII

Unit		*Unit*	
A2	1H(f)	D3	1MC(f)
A3	1DH	F3	1PELV(f)
A4	1T(f)	F4	1PELV(f)
B1	1MT(f)	G2	1H(f), 1T(f)
B2	1VERT, 1MT(f)	G4	1SK+ANT, 1H
B3	1MT(f)	H3	1T(f)
B4	1VERT, 1MC(f)	J2	1F(f)
C2	1SK+ANT, 1H(f)	K1	1ANT(f)

C3	1ANT(f)	K2	1H(f)
C4	1MT(f)	H2	1PR, 2MT(f)

Section XIX

Unit		*Unit*		*Unit*	
A4	1MAN(f)	E4	1T	J2	1SC(f), 1U(f),
B2	1TARS	F1	1ANT(f), 1MT(f)		1PHAL
B3	1AST	F2	1H(f)	J4	1CAL
B4	1PHAL	F3	2H(f), 1T	K2	1F(f)
C2	1PELV(f), 1MT(f)	F4	1SK+ANT, 1SC(f),	K3	1R, 1T, 1CAL
D1	1R(f), 1U(f)		1H, 1AST		
D2	1SK+ANT, 1H(f)	G1	1SC, 1CAL		
D4	1VERT	G3	1PELV(f)		
E2	1H(f)	G4	1PELV(f)		
E3	1R(f), 1CAL	H2	2H(f)		
		H4	1CAL		

Section XX

Unit		*Unit*	
B2	1SC	J1	1MAN(f), 1CAL
D3	1MT(f), 1PHAL	J2	1F(f)
D4	1PHAL	J4	1VERT
E2	1PHAL	K2	1SK+ANT, 1F(f)
F2	1PHAL	K3	1T(f)
G2	1MAN(f), 1MT	K4	1H(f)
G3	1VERT, 1H(f),		
	1CAL		
G4	1PHAL		
H1	1H(f), 1U(f)		
H2	1VERT		

Section XXXII

Unit		*Unit*	
K9	1H(f), 1CAL	K10	1MT(f)

Pig

Section I

Unit		*Unit*		*Unit*	
A1	1PHAL	C5	1U(f)	E2	1AST, 1MT
A2	1F(f)	C7	1SC(f)	E4	1AST, 2CAL
A4	1PHAL	C9	1H(f)	E5	2PELV, 1TARS
A5	1PELV(f), 1T(f)	C10	1SC, 1PHAL	E6	1R(f), 1U(f),
A6	1R(f), 1AST,	D1	1H(f)		1PHAL
	1PHAL	D3	1H, 1AST, 1CAL	E7	1MAN(f)
A7	1H, 1AST	D5	1MAN(f), 1SC,	E8	1AST
B6	1H(f)		1CAL	E9	1T(f)
B7	1MT(f)	D6	1SC(f)	E10	1H(f)

Pig continued

Unit		Unit		Unit	
C2	1PELV(f)	D7	1SC(f)	F4	1H(f), 2T(f), 3AST
C4	1R(f)	D10	1MAX(f), 1MAN(f)	F5	1U(f), 1CARP, 1PHAL

Unit		Unit		Unit	
F7	2MT, 1CAL	H2	1PHAL	K7	1SC(f), 1R(f), 1PAT
F8	1R(f), 1PHAL	H3	1CARP	K8	1F(f), 1PHAL
F10	1MT(f)	H4	1SC, 1TARS	K9	1PMT
G2	1SC(f), 1AST, 1CAL	H5	1VERT, 1MT		
G3	1H(f)	H7	2PHAL		
G4	1T(f), 1MT(f), 1PHAL	H9	1PHAL		
G5	2SC, 1F, 1AST, 1CAL	J3	1U(f), 1AST, 1CAL		
G7	1PELV, 1F(f), 1T(f), 1MT(f)	J5	1AST, 1PHAL		
		J6	1PELV(f), 1R(f), 1MT(f)		
G9	1T(f)	J7	1MT		
H1	1PELV(f), 2PHAL				

Section X

Unit		Unit	
C10	1R(f)	G9	1CAL

Section XI

Unit		Unit		Unit	
B2	1SK(f), 1MT(f)	E5	1R(f)	H3	1SC(f), 1T(f), 1AST
B3	1SC(f)	F2	1PELV(f)	H4	1SC, 1PHAL
B5	1H(f)	F3	1MAN(f), 1U(f)	J1	1PELV(f)
C2	1CAL	F4	1MAN(f)	J3	1SC(f), 1U(f)
C4	1H(f)	G2	1T(f)		
D3	1R(f)	G3	1F(f)		
D5	1H(f)	G4	1CARP		
E1	1MAN(f), 1H(f), 1PHAL	G5	1U(f)		
		H1	1PHAL		
E3	1PHAL	H2	1VERT		
E4	2CAL				

Section XVII

Unit		Unit		Unit	
B9	1U(f)	C8	1MC(f)	C9	1T(f), 1AST

Section XVIII

Unit		Unit		Unit	
A1	1H	D1	1VERT, 1PHAL	J1	1H(f)

A2	1U(f), 1AST
A4	1MAN(f), 1SC(f), 1PELV(f)
B1	1PELV(f), 1AST
B3	1MAN(f)
B4	1SC(f), 1MT, 1PHAL
C1	1SC(f)
C2	1SC(f)
C3	1AST, 1CAL
C4	1SC(f)

D2	1MAN(f)
D4	1SC, 1CAL
E4	1SC, 1AST
F3	1SC, 1AST
F4	1AST, 1CAL
G2	1VERT
G3	1MAN(f), 1T, 1AST
G4	1MAN(f)
H4	1PMT

J2	1R(f), 1TARS
J3	1U(f), 1CAL
K2	1T(f)
K3	1MAN(f)

Section XIX

Unit

A1	1VERT
A4	1H(f), 1R(f), 4CARP, 1AST
B1	1R(f)
B3	1SK(f), 1VERT
C1	2PHAL
C2	1U(f), 1F(f), 1T(f), 1FIB(f), 1AST
C3	1RIB(f), 1CAL
C4	1F(f), 2PHAL
D1	1RIB(f), 1MT(f)
D2	1PELV(f), 1MT(f)

Unit

D3	1MT(f)
D4	1U(f), 1PHAL
E1	1PELV(F)
E2	1SC(f), 2PELV(f), 1CAL
E3	1CARP, 1PHAL
E4	1SC, 1MT(f)
F1	1SC(f)
F2	1SC, 1R(f)
F3	1SK(f)
F4	1R(f), 1U(f), 1AST

Unit

G2	1H(f), 1MT(f)
G3	1SC, 1TARS
G4	2SC
H1	1RIB(f)
H3	1SC(f), 1T(f), 1MT(f)
H4	1SC(f), 2RIB(f)
J1	3RIB(f)
J2	1RIB(f)
J3	1SC(f), 1R(f), 1T(f)
K1	1H(f), 1CARP, 1AST

Unit

| K2 | 1SC(f), 3RIB(f) |
| K3 | 1SC(f) |

Section XX

Unit

E2	1AST
F1	1MAX(f)
F4	1PELV(f)
G4	1F(f)
H1	1AST, 1CAL, 1MT
H4	1R(f), 1U(f), 1AST
J3	1PHAL
J4	1F(f), 1PHAL
K1	1RIB(f), 1MT(f)
K2	1CARP

Unit

| K4 | 1MT(f) |

Elk

Section I

Unit		Unit		Unit	
A2	1DH	C3	1ANT(f)	E3	1SC(f), 1T(f), 1AST
A5	1PHAL	C7	1H(f), 1R(f)	E4	1ANT(f), 1MAN(f)
A8	1ANT(f), 1PHAL	C8	1F(f)	E5	1SK(f), 1CARP, 1MC(f), 1PAT
B1	1H(f), 1T(f)	C10	1PHAL		
B4	1ANT(f)	D3	1ANT, 1PHAL	E6	2CARP
B5	1R(f), 1PHAL	D5	1PELV(f), 1R(f), 1CARP	E7	1SK+ANT
B6	4DMT			E10	1PHAL
B8	1ANT(f), 1T(f)	D7	1ANT, 1AST, 1CAL	F1	1ANT(f)
B10	1DMT	D8	1PHAL	F2	1PHAL
C2	1ANT(f), 1SK(f)	D9	1R(f), 1U(f)	F3	1ANT(f)
		E2	1R(f), 1U(f)	F4	1MAN(f), 2U(f), 1T(f), 1PHAL

Unit		Unit		Unit	
F5	1U(f)	H4	1SK(f)	K3	1MAN(f), 1T(f)
F6	1SK(f), 1H(f)	H5	2ANT(f), 1MAX(f), 3CARP	K7	1VERT(f), 1R(f) 1CARP, 1PHALF9
F8	1MAN(f), 1R(f) 1R(f)	H6	2CARP, 1AST, 1CAL, 3PHAL	K8	1MAX(f), 1AST
G4	1TARS	H7	2MAX(f), 1DRA, 1PT, 1PHAL		
G5	1PELV(f), 1R(f), 1T(f), 1MT(f), 1PHAL	H8	1MAN(f)		
		H9	3CARP, 1F(f), 1DMT, 1PHAL		
G6	1ANT(f), 1MAN(f), 2CARP	H10	1PHAL		
G7	2ANT(f), 1SK(f), 1MAN(f), 4CARP, 1T(f)	J3	1CARP		
		J7	1MAN(f), 1DH		
		I8	1MT(f)		
G9	1CARP				
G10	1DT				

Section X

Unit		Unit		Unit	
C10	1ANT, 1MAN(f), 1H	E10	1H(f)	G9	1ANT(f)
D10	1AST	F8	1FIB	G10	1CAL

Section XI

Unit		Unit		Unit	
A1	1PAT, 1TARS	D3	1ANT(f)	K3	1R(f), 1U(f)
A4	1PAT	D5	1T(f)	K4	1ANT(f), 1MAN(f), 1R(f)
A5	1T(f)	E4	1DR, 2CARP, 1TARS, 1CAL 1PHAL		
B2	1SC, 1TARS, 1CAL				
B3	2PHAL	E5	1SK+ANT, 1SC, 1TARS, 1AST		
B4	1MAN(f), 1R(f), 2CARP				

B5	1PHAL
C2	1U(f)
D1	2TARS
D2	1TARS

F2	1U(f), 1MT(f)
F4	1SC, 1CAL
G1	1MAN(f)
G3	1MAX(f)
G4	1ANT(f)
K1	1SK+ANT, 1R(f)

Section XVII

Unit		Unit		Unit	
A9	1AST	B9	1PHAL	C9	1MAN(f)
A10	2CAL	B10	1PELV(f)		

Section XVIII

Unit		Unit	
A4	1VERT	E3	1TARS, 1AST
B2	1PHAL	E4	1AST, 1CAL
B3	1PHAL	F1	1H(f), 1PHAL
C2	1SK(f), 1MT(f)	F2	1ANT, 1PHAL
C3	1ANT	F3	1CAL
C4	1SC(f)	G2	1PF
D1	1CARP, 1PHAL	G3	1ANT, 1MAN(f),
D2	1PR, 1DR		1AST, 1PHAL
D3	1DMT	K2	1PHAL
E2	1ANT(f)	K3	2PHAL

Section XIX

Unit		Unit		Unit	
A1	1AST	F4	1SC(f), 1CARP,	K4	1PHAL
A2	1PU		1PHAL		
A3	1DH	G2	1R(f), 1CARP		
B2	1DT	G4	1MAN(f), 2VERT,		
C2	1SK(f), 1CARP,		3CARP, 1MT(f),		
	1PHAL		1PHAL		
D2	1PHAL(f)	H2	1MT(f), 1PHAL(f)		
E2	1R(f), 1U(f),	H3	1PHAL(f)		
	1PHAL	H4	1ANT, 1DR, 1DU		
E4	1CAL(f)	J3	1VERT(f)		
F1	4CARP, 1AST	J4	1TARS, 1PHAL		
F3	1AST	K1	1MC(f)		
		K3	1PAT		

Section XX

Unit		Unit		Unit	
B2	1U(f)	G3	1U(f)	J2	1VERT(f), 1MT(f)
C1	1CARP	G4	1U(f)	J3	1AST
F2	1MT(f), 1PHAL				

Aurochs

Section I

Unit		Unit		Unit	
A4	1MC(f)	C1	1R(f)	E3	3PHAL
A6	1SK(f), 1CERV, 1CAL	C6	1PMC	E5	1CERV
		C7	1PHAL(f)	E6	1F(f)
A7	1THOR	D2	1RIB(f)	F2	1VERT, 1PHAL
B1	1H(f)	D3	1H(f), 1PHAL	F3	1PHAL
B2	1PELV, 1SC(f), 1R	D4	1PELV(f), 1RIB(f)	F4	3PHAL(f)
		D8	1PAT	F6	1VERT
B4	1SC(f), 1PHAL	D10	1RIB(f)	F8	3CERV, 1PHAL
B6	1R(f)	E1	1PHAL	F9	2PHAL
B7	1SC(f)	E2	1H(f), 1PR, 1PHAL	F10	1PHAL(f)
B9	1SK(f)				
B10	1F(f)				

Unit		Unit	
G2	1PHAL(f)	H10	1DT
G5	1MAN(f),1PELV(f), 1PAT, 1PHAL	K5	1TARS
		K8	1PHAL
G6	1PELV(f), 1RIB(f) 1F(f)		
G8	1RIB(f), 1PAT		
G9	1CAL		
G10	1PHAL(f)		
H4	1CARP		
H6	1SC(f), 1VERT, 1F(f), 1PHAL		
H7	1RIB(f), 1PF, 1T(f)		
H8	1MC		

Section X

Unit		Unit	
C9	4CARP	C10	1CARP

Section XI

Unit	
A1	1MC(f), 1PHAL
A5	1PELV(f)
B5	1PHAL
C2	1PHAL
D5	1CAL
E5	1VERT, 1PHAL(f)
G5	1CARP
K1	1PHAL
K5	1LUM(f)

Section XVII

Unit		Unit		Unit	
A10	1DH, 5CARP, 1MT(f)	C9	1PHAL(f)	F9	1RIB(f)

Section XVIII

Unit		Unit	
A1	1VERT	E1	1PHAL
A3	1PELV(f), 1PHAL	E2	1PHAL(f)
A4	1CARP, 1AST	E3	1H(f)
B3	2MAN, 1CAL,	E4	1PHAL
	1PHAL(f)	F2	1CAL
B4	1VERT	F3	1AST
C2	1PHAL	F4	1PELV(f), 1T(f)
C4	1PHAL(f)	H4	1PAT
D2	1PAT	J3	1PAT
D3	1PHAL(f)	J4	1RIB(f)
D4	1CARP, 1PHAL(f)		

Section XIX

Unit		Unit		Unit	
A1	1DF, 1PAT,	F3	1PHAL(f)	J3	1T(f), 1CAL
	1PHAL(f)	F4	1PHAL	J4	1CARP
A3	1PHAL(f)	G1	1PHAL	K3	1TARS, 1CAL,
B2	1DT, 2PHAL(f)	G3	1PAT, 1AST, 1PHAL		1PHAL
C1	1PHAL(f)	G4	1MAN(f), 1PHAL(f)		
D2	1SC(f), 1CARP	H1	1CAL		
D3	1T(f)	H3	1SC(f), 3CARP		
D4	1AST	H4	1TARS		
E2	1PELV(f), 1CARP	J1	1PHAL		
E4	1VERT(f), 1PHAL	J2	1MC(f)		
F1	2MAN, 1PHAL(f)				

Section XX

Unit		Unit		Unit	
B3	1U(f)	D1	1PHAL	H1	1PAT, 1PHAL
B4	1MAN(f)	D4	1MC(f)	J1	1CARP, 1T(f)
C4	1AST				

Section XXXII

Unit	
K10	1MC(f)

Sværdborg I, 1923

Red deer

Section XXIII

Unit		Unit		Unit	
A4	1SC, 1DMC, 1DMC(f)	C5	2TARS, 2AST, 1AST(f)	F5	1AST
	1T(f), 1TARS, 1CAL(f)	D5	1PR	G5	2PHAL
	4PHAL				
B5	1TARS, 1DMC/T, 1PHAL				
C4	1AX				

Section XXIV

Unit		Unit	
A2	1DH, 1DR, 1PHAL	C5	1PELV(f), 1PR,
A4	1AX, 1PELV(f),		2PT, 1DMC/T(f)
	1DMC(f), 1TARS,		
	1PHAL		
A5	1DH, 1DU, 1DMC,		
	1TARS, 2CAL		
A8	1PELV(f), 1PH, 5DH,		
	1DU, 1DF, 1DT, 1CAL		
B1	1PT, 1TARS, 1CAL		
	1PHAL		
B4	1PH, 1DF		
B5	1TARS, 1AST, 1DMT(f)		
B8	1DU, 1PMT, 1PHAL		
C1	1PELV(f)		
C4	1PR, 2DR, 2PHAL		

Section XXXV

Unit		Unit		Unit	
A1	1AST, 1CAL	F1	2PHAL	J4	1TARS
A4	1AT	F2	1PR, 1DF	K2	1VERT, 1SC(f),
B2	1PHAL	F3	1VERT, 1PELV(f),		1DMC, 2DMC(f)
C2	1PT, 1PHAL		1RIB, 1PH, 1PHAL	K3	1PT, 2PHAL
C3	1DH, 1AST, 2CAL	G3	1SK+ANT, 1TARS	K5	1PELV(f),
C5	1AX(f)	G5	1DU		1DMC(f), 1TARS
D1	1PHAL	H2	2VERT		
D2	2PELV(f)	H4	1DMC, 1DMC(f)		
E1	1DU, 1PT, 1PHALf	J2	1PF, 1PT, 1PHAL		
E4	1VERT	J3	1AST, 1CAL, 1DMT		
		J3	2VERT, 1PELV(f),		
			1PHAL		

Section XXXVI

Unit		Unit		Unit	
B1	3RIB	C10	1VERT(f), 1DH	F1	1DR, 1TARS

B3	1DT, 1CAL	D1	2VERT, 1RIB(f)	F2	1DR, 1AST		
B5	1VERT, 1PH	D3	1PELV(f)	F3	2VERT, 1PR,		
B8	1PH(f), 1DU,	D4	1AT(f), 1PELV(f),		1DMC(f), 1TARS,		
	1PHAL		1PT, 1DMT(f),		1PHAL		
C1	1VERT		1PHAL	F5	1DMT(f)		
C2	1PT(f)	D5	1DMC(f)	F6	2VERT, 1DH,		
C4	1PELV(f), 1RIB(f)	D7	2AT(f), 1SC, 1PH,		1PT, 1DMT(f),		
	1DF		1PF		1PHAL		
C5	2VERT(f)	E1	1AX, 1MAN, 1CAL	F7	1ANT, 1VERT,		
C6	1ANT(f)	E2	1DF		1PR(f), 1PHAL		
C8	1ANT(f), 1DMT	E3	1DH	F9	1PELV(f),		
		E8	1CAL, 1PHAL		1DMC(f), 1AST,		
					2PHAL		
				F10	3VERT		
				G4	1PHAL		
				G6	1AX(f), 1DF,		
					1PT, 1PHAL		

Unit		*Unit*		*Unit*	
G8	1MAN, 1PELV(f),	J3	1DMC, 1CAL	K4	1DF, 1PT
	1DT, 1AST,	J4	1AX, 1DMC(f), 2PF	K7	1DMC, 2PF,
	1AST(f), 3PHAL		1DMT, 1DMT(f),		1PHAL
G9	2VERT		1PHAL, 2VERT	K8	10ANT(f),
H1	1AT(f)	J5	1VERT		1VERT, 1RIB,
H4	1TARS(f)	J6	1AT(f), 1DMC(f),		3DMT(f), 1AST,
H5	1VERT		2TARS, 2PHAL		1CAL, 1PHAL
H7	2VERT, 1PF,	J7	1AST, 1PHAL	K9	1SC, 2PR, 1DMC,
	1DMT(f)	J8	1SC, 1PF, 1PT(f),		4PHAL
H8	1PT, 1TARS,		1TARS, 1PHAL		
	1AST(f), 1CAL,	J9	1DU, 1AST, 1CAL,		
	1PHAL		2PHAL		
H10	1AST, 1CAL,	K1	AX(f), 1CAL		
	1PHAL	K2	1PHAL		
J1	1VERT	K3	1AST, 1PHAL		
J2	1AST				

Section XXXVII

Unit		*Unit*		*Unit*	
J1	1PR	K1	1SC, 1TARS	K3	1DMT(f)
J3	1DH	K2	1SC, 1T(f)	K4	1TARS

Section XXXVIII

Unit		*Unit*		*Unit*	
J7	1PHAL	K5	1DH, 1PF	K10	1MAN

Section XL

Unit	
C10	1CAL

Roe deer

Section XXIII

Unit
A4   2SC, 1DH, 1DF, 1PHAL
C4   1SC, 1DF(f), 2AST
C5   1SC, 2DH, 1DH(f), 1PR, 1CAL
D5   1AX, 1DR, 1DT, 2CAL
G5   1PELV(f), 1PT, 1DT, 1DMT(f)

Section XXIV

Unit
A2   1AT, 1PELV(f),
2SC, 1PF, 1DF,
2PT, 1PHAL
A3   1SK(f), 1MAX(f),
3VERT, 1SC, 2PH,
1DH, 1DF, 1PT,
1DT, 1AST, 1PHAL
A4   1AX, 1PELV(f),
2DMC(f), 1PF, 1DF
1PT, 1CAL,
1DMT(f), 1PHAL
A5   1SC, 1PH, 1DH,
1DR, 2DF, 1DF(f),
1AST, 3CAL,
1DMT(f), 1PHAL
B1   2PELV(f), 1SC,
1PH, 1DMC/T, 1DT,
1PMT
B2   2PELV(f), 2SC, 1PH,
1DH, 1PF, 1PT, 1CAL
B3   1AT(f)
B4   1AX(f), 2PELV(f),
2SC, 1DH, 1PR, 1DR,
1PF, 2DF, 1PT, 2AST,
1CAL, 1PHAL
B5   2PELV(f), 2SC, 1DH,
1DT, 1CAL
B8   2PELV(f), 3DH, 1PR,
1DMC/T, 1AST(f),
2CAL, 2PHAL

Unit
C1   1CAL
C2   2PELV(f), 1SC(f)
1CAL
C4   2AT(f), 4PELV(f),
1DH, 2U, 1DMC,
1PF(f), 1DF,
1TARS, 2AST, 1CAL,
2PHAL
C5   1AT(f), 1PELV(f),
2SC, 1PH, 1DH, 1PR,
2DR, 1U, 1U(f), 1PMC,
1DMC, 1DMC(f), 1DF,
1PT, 1AST, 3CAL,
3PHAL

Section XXXV

Unit		*Unit*		*Unit*	
A1	1DH, 1U, 1CAL	E1	1PELV(f), 1DU	H4	1ANT(f),
A4	1PHAL	E2	1PELV(f), 1SC		2SK+ANT
B2	1PELV(f), 1DR	E3	1ANT	J2	1AT(f), 1SC,
C1	1SC, 1CAL	E4	1ANT		1DH, 1PR
C2	1PELV(f), 1PHAL	F1	1AT(f), 1PELV(f),	J3	1SC, 1CAL

C3   3DH, 1PR
C4   2PELV(f), 1PH
D1   1SC, 1DR, 1DMT
D2   1PELV(f), 1DH,
      1AST, 1CAL
D3   1MAN(f)

F2   1SC, 2DH, 1PR,
      1PMC, 1DMC, 1DF,
      1PT, 1AST,
      1CAL(f), 1PHAL
F2   1AT, 1PELV(f),
      1DH, 1PT, 1PMT
F3   3PELV(f), 1SC(f),
      1DH, 2AST
G3   2DF, 1CAL
G5   1DH, 1DR, 1AST
H3   1ANT(f), 1SK+ANT,
      1THOR, 1PELV(f),
      3DH, 1DR, 1U,
      1AST(f), 1CAL

J4   1DH
K2   1PELV(f), 1SC,
      1DMC, 1PHAL
K3   1PELV(f), 1DH,
      1CAL

Section XXXVI

Unit
A2   1PR
A3   1PMT
A4   1DH
B1   1PAT
B2   1PELV(f)
B3   1DH, 1PMT,
      1DMT(f), 1PHAL
B10   1PMC
C1   1DH, 1DU, 1PF
C2   1CAL
C3   1SC, 1DF, 1CAL

Unit
C5   1MAN(f)
C8   2MAN, 1SC, 1PH
C10   1CERV, 1PELV(f),
      1DH, 1PR, 1DF
D1   1PRA
D3   1SC
D4   1PELV(f), 2SC,
      1DR, 1AST
D5   1PR, 1PMC
D8   1DH, 1PR, 1CAL,
      1PHAL
D9   1PELV(f), 1SC,
      1PF, 1PF(f)
E1   1DH, 1DMC, 1DF

Unit
E2   1PELV(f), 1DH,
      2PHAL
E3   1SC(f), 1DR(f),
      1DT, 1PHAL
E5   1PELV(f), 1PF,
      1DF
E9   1AT(f), 1AX,
      2PELV(f), 3DH,
      1PR(f), 1DR,
      1U, 2DT, 1AST,
      3PHAL
F1   1DH, 1DF, 1PMT,
      1CAL
F2   1DH, 1U
F3   2PMC
F5   2SC(f), 1PR,1PT
F6   1PELV(f), 1DH,
      1PF, 1PMT, 1PHAL
F7   3PELV(f), 2SC,
      2DR, 1PHAL

Unit
F9   1ANT(f), 1SK+
      ANT, 1THOR(f),
      3SC,1DU, 1PMC,
      1PF, 1CAL(f), 3PHAL
F10   2MAN, 2CERV
G1   1ANT(f), 1MAN,
      1VERT
G4   1AX(f), 1PELV(f),
      1DF, 1DT
G8   1SK+ANT, 2PELV(f),
      1SC, 1CAL(f)
G10   1SK+ANT, 2SK(f),

Unit
H7   1AX(f), 1MAN,
      2PELV(f), 1SC,
      1DR, 2U, 1DMC(f),
      1PF, 1DF, 1AST(f)
H8   1AX, 1DH, 1CAL
H10   2SC, 3DH, 1TARS,
      1PHAL
J1   1SK+ANT, 1MAN,
      1MAN(f), 1PR, 1DF,
      1CAL, 2PELV(f)
J3   1PELV(f), 1DH, 1U,
      1PMC

Unit
J9   1SC, 1PR, 1DMC,
      1DF, 1PT, 1DT,
      1PHAL
K1   2SC, 1VERT
K2   4PELV(f), 1PMC,
      1PF, 1CAL(f),
      1PHAL
K3   1PELV(f), 1DMC,
      1DF, 1PHAL
K4   1LUM, 1PELV(f),
      1PH, 1DH, 1PR,
      2U, 1DU, 3DF

Section XXXVI continued

	2MAN(f)	J4	1AT, 3PELV(f), 4SC,	K7	2SK+ANT, 2PR,
H1	1SK+ANT		1DH, 2PR, 1DR, 1U,		1U, 2DF, 1PT,
H2	1DH		1PF, 1DF, 1PHAL		1AST
H4	3PELV(f), 1PT	J5	1MAN, 1SC, 1PH,	K8	1MAN, 1SC(f), H5
	2ANT(f), 1MAN,		1DH, 1PF		1DH, 1DR(f),
	1DR, 1U, 1PHAL	J6	1PELV(f), 1PH, 1PR,		1PMC, 1DF,
H5	2ANT(f), 1MAN,		1PF, 1DF, 1PT, 1CAL,		1DMT(f)
	1DR, 1U, 1PHAL		1CAL(f), 3DMT(f),	K9	1PELV(f), 1DH,
			1PHAL		1DF

Section XXXVII

Unit		*Unit*		*Unit*	
J2	1PELV(f)	K3	1DH, 1PR, 2PMC,	K4	1SC, 1PT
K2	2PELV(f), 1DH		1DF, 1DMT		

Section XXXVIII

Unit		*Unit*		*Unit*	
J4	1AST	K6	1U	K10	1THOR(f)
K5	1CAL				

Section XXXIX

Unit	
K10	1AST

Section XL

Unit		*Unit*		*Unit*	
A10	1PMC	E10	1DH	F10	1AST
B10	1DMT	F9	1MT	K9	1SC
E9	1PF				

Pig

Section XXIII

Unit	
A4	1SC, 2DH, 1DMC/T,
	1DT, 1AST, 1PHAL
B5	1PF
C4	1U, 1DF, 2DT,
	1PHAL
C5	1DT
D5	1DH, 1DR, 1PU,
	1DF, 1PMT

Section XXIV

Unit		Unit		Unit
A3	1MAN(f), 1SC, 1DT(f), 1PMC, 1PHAL	C2	2PELV(f), 2DR, 1MC, 1PF(f), 1DF(f), 1CAL, 1CAL(f)	
A4	1PELV(f), 2SC, 1DH, 1PT, 1PT(f), 1DT, 1TARS, 2CAL, 1PHAL, 1PHAL(f)	C4	3PELV(f), 1DH, 1R, 2DF, 1PT, 1TARS, 1AST, 1PHAL, 4PHAL(f)	
A5	1AT, 2SC, 1DR, 1DMC/T, 1PT, 1TARS, 1CAL(f), 2PHAL, 4PHAL(f)	C5	1AX, 1PELV(f), 1SC, 1DH, 1DR, 1DR(f), 3DT, 1TARS, 1PMT, 3PHAL, 2PHAL(f)	
A8	1PELV(f), 1SC, 1U(f), 1DMC/T, 3DT, 1AST, 2CAL			
B1	2SC, 2DH, 1T, 1TARS, 1AST, 3CAL			
B2	1DH, 2DMC/T, 1PHAL 1PHAL(f)			
B4	1PELV(f), 2SC, 1DMC/T, 1DF, 1DT, 1PHAL, 1PHAL(f)			
B5	1SC, 1DH, 1PT			
B8	1U, 2CAL, 2PHAL, 1PHAL(f)			
C1	1AST			

Section XXXIV

Unit		Unit	
A5	1DH	K9	1DU, 1DMC/T, 1AST, 1PHAL

Section XXXV

Unit		Unit		Unit	
A1	1SC, 1U, 1DF, 1DT, 1AST	D5	1MAN(f), 1VERT	H2	2PELV, 1SC, 1T, 1DT
B2	1DU	E1	1AT(f), 1AST	H3	1RIB, 1PHAL
C1	1AT, 1PELV(f), 1SC, 1PR, 1PHAL	E2	2PELV(f), 1SC, 1PR, 1DR, 1DMC/T, 3AST, 2CAL, 2PHAL	H4	1DF
C2	1PR, 1DF, 1CAL, 1PHAL			J2	1PELV(f), 1PH, 1DR(f), 1TARS, 1AST(f), 1CAL(f)
C3	4VERT, 1PELV(f) 1PH, 1DH, 1DF(f), 1AST, 2PHAL	E4	1VERT		
		F1	1PELV(f), 2SC, 1DH(f), 1DR, 1DMC/T, 2PT, 1PT(f), 1DT, 1CAL(f), 1PHAL, 1PHAL(f)	J4	1VERT, 1DU, 1AST, 1CAL
C4	1PR, 1DF			J5	1PELV(f), 1DU
C5	1AX, 1DH, 1DR			K2	3PELV(f), 1DH, 1PR(f), 1DF, 1PT(f), 1DT, 1AST
D1	1PT, 2PHAL				
D2	1SC, 1DH, 1R, 1PT, 1CAL, 1PHAL	F2	1PH, 1DR, 1DF, 1DT, 1PHAL		
D3	2SK(f), 2VERT	F3	1DH, 2DT, 2AST, 1AST(f), 1CAL,	K3	1VERT, 3SC,

Section XXXV continued

	1PHAL		1DH(f), 1DU(f),
G2	1AT, 1U, 1PF, 1DF,		1DMC/T, 1DT,
	1DT, 1TARS, 1AST,		1TARS, 1AST(f),
	1CAL,		1CAL(f)
G3	1DH, 1CAL(f),	K5	1PELV(f),
	1PHAL		1SC(f)
G5	1MAN(f), 1TARS		

Section XXXVI

Unit		Unit		Unit	
A2	1CAL(f)	C10	1VERT, 1SC	E3	1SC, 1F, 2PF,
A3	1PELV(f)	D1	5RIB, 1PH, 1DH(f),		1DT, 1CAL
A4	1AX, 1PHAL		1DT, 1PHAL(f)	E5	1AT, 1PELV(f),
B2	1AST	D3	1VERT, 3RIB, 1DU,		1DMC/T, 1DF
B8	1CAL		1PF	E6	2MAN(f)
B10	1PELV(f)	D4	1TARS, 2PHAL(f)	E9	1SC, 1DH, 1PR,
C3	1DU(f), 1AST	D5	1PELV(f)		1DR, 1AST,
C4	1PELV(f), 1SC,	D7	1SC, 1PF, 1T,		1CAL, 1PHAL
	1DH(f), 1PF		1AST, 1CAL, 1PHAL	F1	1DH, 1DT, 3CAL,
C7	1DR	D8	1DH, 1DR, 1PMC,		1PHAL
C8	2VERT, 1SC, 1PH,		1DMC/T, 1PHAL(f)	F2	1PELV(f), 1DH,
	1F, 1DT	D10	1SC		1CAL(f)
		E1	1SC, 1PHAL(f)	F3	1AX, 1PELV(f),
		E2	1TARS, 1AST, 1CAL		1DH, 1DMC/T,
					1PHAL
				F5	1PELV(f),
					1DU(f), 1DF,
					1DT, 1DMT
				F6	2VERT, 1PT,
					3PHAL
				F7	1VERT, 1DU(f),
					1AST, 1AST(f)

Unit		Unit		Unit	
F9	1VERT, 2PELV(f),	H4	1DU, 2PT, 1DT,	J7	1VERT,
	1SC, 1PR, 1F,		1PHAL		1PELV(f), 1SC,
	3DF, 1DF(f), 1PT,	H5	1PR, 1DU, 2DMC/T,		1DU, 1DT,
	4PHAL, 1PHAL(f)		1PHAL, 1PHAL(f)		2TARS, 1CAL,
F10	1U	H7	1VERT, 1PELV(f),		3PHAL(f)
G1	3VERT		2DH, 1PR, 2PHAL,	J8	1AX, 1VERT,
G4	1AT, 2PELV(f),		1PHAL(f)		1SC, 1PH,
	1DU(f), 1DMC/T,	H8	1SC, 1H, 1U,		1DU(f), 1DT,
	1PF, 1T, 1DT,		1DMC/T, 2PT, 1AST,		1AST, 1CAL(f),
	1AST, 1CAL,		2CAL		1PHAL
	2PHAL, 1PHAL(f)	H10	1SC(f), 1DF	J9	1VERT(f), 1SC,
G6	1DR, 1DMC/T,	J1	1VERT, 1DMC/T,		1DH, 1DMC/T,
	1PF, 1DF, 2AST,	J3	2PT,1AT(f), 1DR, 1U,		1DT, 3AST,
	1PHAL		1AST, 1CAL		2CAL, 1CAL(f),
G8	2SC, 1PR, 1DU,	J4	2PELV(f), 1SC, 1U,		1PHAL, 1PHAL(f)

	1DMC/T, 1PF, 1DT, 3AST, 3CAL, 2PHAL, 1PHAL(f)		1PT, 2DT, 1DMC/T, 1AST, 2CAL, 1PHAL, 1PHAL(f)	K1	1MAN, 1DMC/T, 2PF, 1PT(f)
G10	1VERT	J5	1MAX(f), 1VERT, 3PELV(f), 2RIB, 1DU	K2	1AT(f), 1PF, 1PT, 1AST, 2PHAL, 2PHAL(f)
H1	1VERT, 1PELV(f), 1DF, 1PT, 1PMT	J6	2PELV(f), 1PR, 2PF, 1DF(f), 1DT, 2TARS, 2AST, 1PMT	K3	1PELV(f), 4PHAL
H2	1PELV, 1DF, 1AST			K4	1VERT, 1PELV(f), 1SC, 1DH, 1PR, 1DT
H3	1CAL			K7	1MAN(f), 3VERT, 1DU, 1DMC/T, 1PT, 1CAL, 1CAL(f), 1PHAL
				K8	1RIB, 2DR, 1U(f), 1PU, 1PMC, 1PMC(f), 2PF, 1PT, 1AST, 2AST(f), 1CAL, 2CAL(f), 3PHAL, 1PHAL(f)
				K9	1SC, 1DR, 1DMC/T, 2PF, 1DT, 1TARS, 1PHAL, 1PHAL(f)

Section XXXVII

Unit		Unit		Unit	
A2	1F	B2	1PELV(f)	B4	1TARS
B1	1CAL	B3	1SC, 1DF		

Section XXXVIII

Unit		Unit		Unit	
A1	1PR	A7	2DT	B5	1VERT
A4	1DT	B2	1MAX(f)		

Section XXXIX

Unit	
B10	1CAL

Elk

Section XXIII

Unit		Unit		Unit	
A4	1PU, 1PHAL, 1PHAL(f)	C4	2AST	D5	1PF, 1PHAL(f)
B5	1TARS	C5	1PHAL	F5	1TARS

Section XXIV

Unit	
A1	1MC
A3	1U, 1TARS, 1PHAL(f)
A4	2PELV(f), 4PHAL, 1PHAL(f)
A5	1PELV(f), 1AST, 2PHAL, 1PHAL(f)
A8	1DH, 2AST, 1PHAL
B2	1PELV, 1AST
B3	1TARS, 1PHAL
B4	1DF(f), 1PT(f), 5PHAL
B5	1DT, 1PHAL(f)
B8	1DMT, 2DMT(f), 1TARS, 3PHAL

Unit	
C1	1AST
C2	2AST, 1PHAL, 1PAHL(f)
C3	2DMT, 1TARS
C4	1DF, 1CAL, 2PHAL
C5	1PT, 2PHAL

Section XXXIV

Unit	
K9	2CAL, 1PHAL

Section XXXV

Unit	
A1	1PT
B2	1PHAL
C1	1SC(f), 1AST
C2	1PHAL(f)
C3	1PELV(f)
C4	1PHAL(f)
C5	1PHAL(f)
D1	1PELV(f)
D2	1PHAL(f)
D3	1MAN, 1LUM 1PHAL

Unit	
E1	1TARS, 1DMT, 1PHAL
F1	1PELV(f)
F2	1PELV(f), 2DMT(f)
F3	2PELV(f), 1DR, 2PHAL
G3	1·AT(f), 1PHAL, 1PHAL(f)
H2	1SK+ANT
H3	2AST, 1CAL(f),
H4	1VERT, 1DR, 1PT(f), 1PHAL(f)
J2	1DF(f), 1PT, 2PHAL
J3	1DH

Unit	
J4	1TARS, 1AST, 1PHAL
J5	1AST
K2	1THOR, 1CERV
K3	2CAL, 1PHAL
K5	1PH, 1PHAL

Section XXXVI

Unit	
A1	1CAL(f)
A3	1AST
A5	1PF, 1PHAL(f)
B2	1SC, 2AST
B3	1DF
B5	1PH
C1	3ANT(f)

Unit	
C8	1THOR(f)
C10	1CERV, 1CAL, 1PHAL(f)
D1	1PELV(f), 1DH
D3	1PHAL
D4	1DF(f), 2PHAL, 1PHAL(f)

Unit	
E1	1PELV(f)
E2	1CAL, 2PHAL
E3	1PHAL(f)
E5	1PHAL
E9	1AT(f), 1PELV(f), 1SC, 1DR, 1DMC, 1PT

C2	1PHAL	D5	1PF, 1TARS	F1	1DF	
C3	1THOR	D6	1ANT(f)	F3	1PELV(f), 2PHAL	
C5	1ANT(f), 1RIB	D7	1DU, 1DMC, 1PHAL	F6	1ANT(f), 1MAN,	
		D8	2PHAL		1CERV(f),	
		D9	1PELV(f), 1CAL,		2THOR, 1PF,	
			1PHAL		1CAL, 2PHAL	
				F9	11ANT(f),	
					1MAN(f), 1THOR,	
					1LUM, 1CAL,	
					2PHAL, 1PHAL(f)	
				F10	1SC	

Unit		Unit		Unit		
G1	1AT, 1LUM	H8	1PELV(f), 1AST	K2	1PELV(f), 1DF,	
G4	1DH, 1PHAL	H10	2DMC(f), 1CAL,		1CAL	
G6	1PHAL		1PHAL	K3	1PT(f),	
G8	4ANT, 7ANT(f),	J1	1AT(f), 1PELV(f),		1MC/T(f), 2PHAL	
	1PAT, 1TARS,		1DMC	K4	4ANT, 2RIB,	
	1CAL, 1PHAL(f)	J3	1PT(f)		2DH, 1DT, 2PHAL	
G9	1THOR, 3LUM	J4	1PELV(f),	K7	2ANT(f), 1CERV,	
H1	1PHAL(f)		1MC/T(f), 1AST,		2PELV(f), 1DH,	
H2	1DU		2PHAL, 1PHAL(f)		2PAT, 2TARS	
H3	1AT(f), 1DR	J5	2CAL	K8	1PR, 1PHAL,	
H5	1ANT(f), 1AT(f),	J6	1SC, 1MC/T(f)		2PHAL(f)	
	1SC	J7	3ANT, 1THOR, 1SC,	K9	2ANT, 1PELV(f),	
H7	1AT(f), 1ANT,		2CAL, 1PHAL		1TARS	
	1PHAL	J8	1ANT(f), 1THOR,			
			1DU			
		K1	2THOR, 1VERT(f),			
			1RIB, 1AST(f),			
			2PHAL			

Section XXXVII

Unit		Unit		Unit	
J1	1U, 1PHAL	K1	1DF	K3	1DH, 1PR
J2	1SC, 1PR, 1DR, 1TARS	K2	1TARS		

Section XXXVIII

Unit		Unit		Unit	
J7	1AST	J8	1PHAL	K2	1RIB(f)

Section XL

Unit		Unit		Unit	
A10	1TARS	C10	1DT, 1AST, 1PHAL	E10	1DT
B10	1PHAL				

Aurochs

Section XXIII

Unit		*Unit*		*Unit*	
A4	1DMC(f), 4PHAL, 4PHAL(f)	C5	1DH(f)	F5	2PHAL, 1PHAL(f)
B4	1AST, 1CAL, 1PHAL	D5	1DMT, 1AST, 1CAL, 2PHAL	G5	1DT(f), 1TARS
C4	1AX, 1PELV(f), 1DH, 1MC, 1PMC, 2DMC/T, 2PF, 1PT, 1PT(f),2AST, 2PHAL	E5	1PHAL		

Section XXIV

Unit		*Unit*	
A2	1AST, 1PHAL(f)	B8	3PHAL, 2PHAL(f)
A3	1CAL, 2PHAL	C2	1CAL(f), 2PHAL, 1PHAL(f)
A4	1PELV(f), 1PR, 2DMT(f), 2PHAL, 2PHAL(f)	C3	1PH, 1AST, 1PHAL
A5	1PELV(f), 3CAL 3PHAL, 1PHAL(f)	C4	1PELV(f), 1DMC(f), 3PHAL, 4PHAL(f)
A8	1PELV(f), 2CAL(f) 2PHAL	C5	1DR(f), 1DMC(f), 1DF, 5PHAL, 3PHAL(f)
B1	2PHAL(f)	C8	1DU, 1AST, 1PHAL
B2	2PELV(f), 1PMC, 2PHAL, 2PHAL(f)		
B3	2PELV(f), 1DH, 1DR, 4PHAL, 1PHAL(f)		
B4	1AST		
B5	6PHAL		

Section XXXIV

Unit		*Unit*	
C5	1PMC	K8	1PHAL

Section XXXV

Unit		*Unit*		*Unit*	
A4	1PELV(f)	E3	1SAC, 1RIB(f), 1DMC(f)	J4	1CAL(f), 1PHAL, 1PHAL(f)
A5	1PHAL	F1	2SC, 1CAL, 7PHAL	J5	1DF, 2PHAL
B2	1PR, 1PHAL	F2	2PELV(f)	K2	1PELV, 1SC(f), 1PF, 2PHAL
B4	1AST	F3	3PELV(f), 1PHAL(f)	K3	1VERT, 2PELV(f), 1DR, 1DU, 2CAL, 3PHAL, 4PHAL(f)
C1	1CAL	G2	1AST		
C2	1CAL, 1PHAL	G3	1PHAL(f)		
C3	1CAL, 2PHAL	H2	1PELV(f), 2AST, 2PHAL		
C4	1PR, 1PHAL				
E1	1SC	H3	1RIB, 2PHAL		
E2	1PHAL				

| | I2 | | | 1PELV(f), 1PF,
1DF(f), 3PHAL,
2PHAL(f) |
| | | | J3 | 1PELV(f), 1PF,
1PHAL, 2PHAL(f) |

Section XXXVI

Unit		*Unit*		*Unit*	
A3	1DR, 1DU, 1PHAL, 1PHAL(f)	C4	1VERT, 1DU, 1PHAL(f)	D9	1U, 2PHAL
A5	1PHAL	C7	1PHAL, 2PHAL(f)	E1	1DT, 3PHAL
A7	1PHAL	C8	1VERT, 1PHAL	E3	2PHAL
B1	1SC(f)	C10	1PELV(f), 1CAL	E4	1DR(f), 2PHAL
B3	1SC(f)	D1	1DU, 2PHAL(f)	E5	1DU, 1CAL(f)
B5	1VERT	D3	1PELV(f), 1DT, 3PHAL	E9	1PHAL
B6	2PELV(f), 1PHAL			E10	1PHAL, 1PHAL(f)
B8	1PELV(f), 1PHAL, 1PHAL(f)	D5	1PH, 1PF, 1PHAL(f)	F1	1PELV(f), 1PHAL(f)
B10	1PR, 1DR	D6	1VERT, 1PF	F3	3PHAL
C2	1PHAL	D7	1PHAL(f)	F4	1DMC(f), 1PHAL
		D8	1PELV(f), 1DR, 1DU, 1DF		

Unit		*Unit*		*Unit*	
F5	2PHAL(f)	G6	1PELV(f), 1DU, 1PHAL(f)	J9	1PELV(f), 1SC, 1PHAL(f)
F6	1RIB, 1DMC/T(f), 3PHAL	G7	2PHAL	H1	1VERT
F7	1PELV(f), 1PAT, 1PHAL, 1PHAL(f)	G8	1CERV, 1PELV(f), 2PHAL, 1PHAL(f)	H2	1AT, 1AX
				H3	1PELV(f), 1DT, 1PHAL(f)
F9	1DU, 1DMC(f), 2PHAL, 2PHAL(f)	G10	1VERT	H4	1PELV(f), 1PHAL, 1PHAL(f)
F10	1AT(f), 1PH	J3	1PR, 1PHAL, 1PHAL(f)	H5	1VERT, 1SC, 2PHAL
G1	1RIB, 1CAL	J4	1VERT, 1PELV(f), 1PH, 1PU, 5PHAL		
G2	1AST	J5	1PELV(f), 3PHAL	H6	2PHAL(f)
G3	1MC	J6	1SC(f), 1DF(f), 1PHAL	H7	1PR, 1DU(f), 1PHAL(f)
G4	1SC, 1PHAL	J7	1VERT, 1DMT, 1PHAL(f)	H8	1PELV(f), 1AST(f)
G5	1PHAL	J8	1SC, 1SC(f), 1PHAL, 1PHAL(f)		

Unit	
K1	1PH, 1PHAL
K2	1PF
K3	1PR, 1PHAL
K4	1PELV(f)
K5	1U, 1PHAL, 3PHAL(f)
K6	3PHAL

Section XXXV continued

K7	1DR, 1AST(f), 1PHAL(f)
K8	1SC(f), 6PHAL(f)
K9	1VERT, 1PR(f), 1DT, 1TARS, 1AST

Section XXXVII

Unit		*Unit*	
K3	1PELV(f), 1PH, 1PF, 1CAL	K5	1PHAL

Section XXXVIII

Unit		*Unit*		*Unit*	
J1	1PHAL(f)	J9	1PHAL(f)	K6	1DMC(f), 1PHAL(f)
J4	1AST	K5	1PHAL(f)	K10	1VERT
J7	1PHAL(f)				

Section XXXIX

Unit	
J10	1PHAL

Section XL

Unit		*Unit*	
B10	1DT	F9	1PHAL

Sværdborg I, 1943-44. Area A

Red deer

Section LI

Unit
A4   1H

Section LII

Unit		*Unit*	
B10	1ANT(f)	H6	1SESAM
C7	1T	H7	2PHAL
D7	1AST	H9	1RIB(f)
E8	3MC, 1PHAL	J7	1PT
F8	4TARS, 2PHAL	K5	1AT(f)
G5	1U, 1PHAL		
G6	1AST		
G7	1DMC, 1DT		
G8	2DMC/T		
H5	2DMC/T, 1CAL		

Section LV

Unit
A1   1PHAL
A8   1T(f), 1CAL
B1   1RIB
B5   1VERT
B6   1PHAL
B7   1AT, 1CERV
C4   1T(f), 2MT, 1CAL
C6   1PHAL
E1   1PHAL
E3   1PHAL

Section LVI

Unit
G6   1AST
J1   1CAL
J2   1PHAL
K3   1MAN(f)
K4   1PHAL

Roe deer

Section LI

Unit		Unit	
A4	1AST	A5	1SK(f), 1PELV(f), 1DR, 1PHAL

Section LII

Unit		Unit		Unit	
C7	1T	F5	1VERT	H6	1PHAL
C9	1CAL(f)	F6	1SC, 1PHAL	H7	1PHAL
C10	1H	F8	1SK(f), 1ANT(f),	H8	2SK(f), 2VERT,
D6	1PR	F9	1PT		2PHAL
D7	1AST	F10	1DF, 1T(f), 1TARS	H9	1H, 1T(f), 1AST
D10	1SK, 2PH, 1PF,		1PHAL	J4	1DH, 1PHAL(f)
	1PHAL	G4	1SC	J5	1VERT, 1MC(f)
E6	1T	G6	1AST	J7	1VERT, 1RIB
E7	1PHAL	G7	1PR, 1CAL	J8	3SC, 1PH, 1DR,
E8	1MAN	G8	2DR, 2U, 1MC		1MC, 1PT
E10	1SK(f),	G9	1DMC, 1F(f),	J10	1PT, 2CAL,
	1PELV(f), 1DH,		1T(f)		1PHAL
	1MC, 1MT	G10	1MC, 1MT, 1CAL	K4	1DH, 1PHAL
F4	3ANT(f)				

Unit	
K5	2PELV(f), 1CAL
K6	1U(f)
K7	1R

Section LIV

Unit	
A7	1ANT

Section LV

Unit		Unit		Unit	
A1	1MAN(f)	B5	1PELV(f)	C9	1ANT
A2	1ANT	B6	1DH	D2	1DT, 1AST
A4	1H, 1DT, 1AST	B7	2MAN, 2F, 1AST	D3	1MC(f), 1T(f)
A5	1PELV(f), 1PHAL	B8	1MAN, 1CAL	D4	1DH
A6	3MT(f)	C1	1DH, 1PU	D7	1VERT, 1H, 1T,
A7	2ANT, 1VERT,	C4	1DF, 1DT, 1T(f)		1CAL, 1PHAL
	2PH, 1R, 1DF	C5	1ANT, 1MAN, 2F	D9	1DH, 1PHAL
A8	1MAN(f), 1MC,	C6	1CAL	E1	1MAN, 1DMC
	1MT,	C7	1DH, 1PHAL	E2	1TARS
A9	1MT(f)	C8	1ANT, 1MAX, 1PAT,	E3	1PHAL
B1	1H(f)		1T, 1CAL	E4	1PELV(f), 1DR,
B2	1MAN				1MT(f)

Unit		Unit		Unit	
E5	1VERT, 1T(f), 1AST	G8	1SK(f), 2MT(f)	K8	1ANT, 1AST
E6	1DMT, 1PHAL	H7	1CAL	K9	1PF
F1	1AST, 2PHAL				

Section LVI

Unit		Unit	
F6	1MAN	J7	1PELV(f), 1PT
G5	1PR	J8	1H(f)
G6	1AST	K3	1ANT(f)
H5	1DF, 1DT	K4	1T(f), 1PHAL
H6	1PH	K6	1ANT
H7	1VERT	K8	1PAT
J2	1TARS, 1MT	K9	2MAN, 1MC(f),
J3	1PMC		1F, 1MT(f), 1CAL
J4	1DH, 1T(f)		
J6	1PT		

Section LVIII

Unit		Unit		Unit	
A1	1AST, 1PHAL	A2	2H(f)	F1	1MT(f), 1CAL

Pig

Section LI

Unit	
A5	1PELV(f)

Section LII

Unit		Unit		Unit	
C7	1PHAL	G5	1PHAL	J9	1DMT
C9	1PHAL(f)	G8	2CAL(f), 2PHAL	K4	1MAN(f)
C10	1DR	G9	1MAN(f), 1MC(f),	K7	1PHAL
D7	1SC		1AST, 2PHAL	K8	1DT
E7	1PELV, 1PHAL	G10	1DH		
F5	1PHAL	H6	1DH, 1MT(f)		
F7	1PF	H7	1PAT, 1FIB(f)		
F8	1DMT	H8	1T, 2PHAL		
F9	1DH, 1PHAL(f)	J6	3PHAL		
F10	1SC	J7	3MC, 2PHAL		
		J8	1RIB, 1DR, 2MC, 1PF, 1DT		

Section LV

Unit		Unit		Unit	
A1	1SC	B4	1TARS, 1PHAL	D4	1DF

Section LV continued

A2	1MC/T(f), 1PAT, 1T(f)	B6	1MAN	D5	1RIB, 1U(f)
A3	1MAN(f), 1R(f), 1U, 1MT	B8	1MAN(f), 1T	E2	1CARP, 1MC
A4	1SC	C1	1DF	F6	1PELV(f)
A5	1SC, 1F	C2	1PHAL	H8	1CAL
A6	1F(f)	C3	2MC	J8	1MC
A7	1AST, 1CAL	C7	2PHAL	K6	1SESAM
A9	1MAN(f)	C8	1PT, 1PHAL		
B2	1MAN(f), 1MC(f)	C9	1DH		
B3	1MAN, 2T	D1	1PHAL		

Section LVI

Unit		Unit	
F6	1PHAL	K6	1PHAL
H1	1AST	K8	1DR
H2	1PELV(f)	K9	1DT
H8	1PF		
J1	1DR		
J2	1SC(f)		
J3	1U		
J6	1CAL		
K4	1DMC		
K5	1SC(f)		

Elk

Section LII

Unit	
D10	5ANT(f)
E6	1DT
F4	1RIB(f), 1MC/T(f)
F8	1CAL
F10	1DT, 1FIB
G4	1PT
G5	1CAL
G8	1SESAM

Section LV

Unit		Unit		Unit	
A3	1MAN(f), 1SAC(f)	D2	1MC, 1PHAL	D3	1PF

Section LVI

Unit		Unit		Unit	
G8	1DMC/T	H5	1CAL	J7	1PHAL

Section LVIII

Unit
A2   14ANT(f)

Aurochs

Section LII

Unit
H5   1PHAL

Section LV

Unit
A5   1DH

Section LVI

Unit		*Unit*	
I8	1SC(f)	K2	1VERT

Section LVIII

Unit
A1   1PMC(f)

Sværdborg I, 1943-44. Area B

Red deer

Section LXV

Unit		Unit	
A5	1CERV	D4	1T(f)
A7	1MAN(f), 2VERT	E4	1F(f)
A8	1PHAL(f)	E8	2TARS
A9	1VERT		
B4	1MAN(f)		
B6	1MAN(f)		
B10	2TARS		
C1	1PHAL		
C4	3ANT(f)		
C10	1DT		

Section LXVI

Unit		Unit		Unit	
G5	1MC/T(f), 1PHAL	J7	1DMC/T	J10	1DMC/T
G6	1DT, 1PHAL(f)	J9	1PHAL	K5	4ANT(f)
J6	1DMC/T				

Section LXVII

Unit	
B2	1PHAL

Section LXVIII

Unit		Unit		Unit	
F3	1SAC	H1	1ANT(f)	J2	1PELV(f)
F4	1CAL	H4	1MC(f), 2DMC/T,	J3	1CAL(f)
G4	1ANT(f)		1AST, 1CAL	J4	1DF

Roe deer

Section LXV

Unit		Unit	
A8	1PELV(f)	E6	1RIB(f), 1DH, 1DF
A9	1R(f)	F5	1T(f)
A10	1PU	F7	1DH, 1PMC
B2	3MC/T	G7	1PELV(f), 1MC(f)
B9	1R, 1DF		
C4	1PELV(f), 1SC(f)		
C5	1DF, 1PT		
C10	1MC		
D3	1T(f)		
D7	1DH		

Section LXVI

Unit		Unit	
G7	1PU	K8	1SC(f), 1MC(f)
H9	1PR, 1PF	K9	1SC, 1PR
H10	1SC(f)	K10	1CERV
J5	1H		
J6	1SC(f)		
J7	1SC(f)		
J10	1DMC, 1T(f)		
K4	1T(f)		
K5	2TARS		
K6	1DR, 1MC/T		

Section LXVIII

Unit		Unit		Unit	
F4	2H	H2	1SK(f)	J3	1PH, 1DMC, 2PHAL
G3	1DH, 1PMC	H4	1DMC/T	J4	1DR
H1	1SK+ANT, 1PELV(f), 1DR, 1PHAL				

Pig

Section LXV

Unit		Unit	
A3	1MAN(f), 1SC	C6	1SC(f)
A4	1SC(f), 1MT	C8	1SAC(f), 1MT, 1TARS, 1CAL, 1PHAL
A5	1CAL		
B1	1MAX(f)		
B6	1DR	C10	1AST
B8	1U(f)	D4	1MC(f), 1F(f)
B10	1DT	D6	1DMT
C1	1MAN(f)	D7	1MC(f)
C3	1CERV, 1MT	D10	1DF
C4	1MAN(f), 1T(f), 1AST	E5	1MT(f)
		F6	1MAN(f)
		F7	1MAN

Section LXVI

Unit		Unit	
G6	1PF	I10	1SK(f), 1PF
H4	1DR, 1DMT	K4	1SC, 1CAL
H6	1SC(f), 1PH, 2PHAL	K6	1MAN(f), 1U(f), 1PAT, 1DT, 1TARS
H7	1MAN(f), 1AST	K7	1MAN(f), 1PHAL
H8	1DR	K8	1MT
H10	1AST	K10	1MT(f), 1PHAL
J5	1FIB(f)		

Section LXVI continued

J6	1MAN(f), 1SC, 1DU, 1MC, 1PF, 1DFIB
J7	2MC
J8	1SC(f), 1PHAL

Section LXVIII

Unit		Unit		Unit	
F2	1DR	G3	1DH, 1PAT, 1AST	J2	1U(f)
G2	1FIB, 1PHAL	G4	1CAL	J3	1PHAL

Elk

Section LXV

Unit		Unit		Unit	
A2	1VERT	A8	1DMC/T(f)	B7	1SK(f), 1CAL
A4	1AT	B6	1DMT	B8	5ANT(f)
A6	4ANT(f), 1MAN(f), 2RIB(f)				

Section LXVI

Unit		Unit	
G7	1F(f)	K8	1DMC/T(f)
G8	1PF		
H6	1DT		
J5	1DT		
J6	1RIB		
J7	1PF		
J8	1CAL(f)		
J9	2TARS		
K6	1ANT(f), 1PHAL		
K7	1R		

Section LXVIII

Unit		Unit	
H1	1SC(f)	J4	1CARP

Aurochs

Section LXV

Unit		Unit		Unit	
A5	1DMC/T(f)	A6	1PHAL	A7	1PHAL

Section LXVI

Unit		*Unit*		*Unit*	
G4	1PHAL	J6	1PHAL, 1SESAM	K5	1PHAL
H6	1SESAM	J7	1RIB(f), 1SESAM, 1PHAL	K6	1PHAL

Section LXVIII

Unit	
F2	1LUM

Sværdborg I, 1943-44. Area C

Red deer

Section LIX

Unit		Unit		Unit	
A10	3DMC/T, 1PHAL	C9	1RIB(f), 1DMC/T	D10	1DMC/T
B10	1ANT(f), 1PHAL	C10	1PHAL		

Section LX

Unit		Unit		Unit	
E9	1PHAL	G9	1PHAL(f)	J9	1PHAL(f)
F7	1ANT(f)	G10	1SESAM	K7	1DMC/T(f)
G7	1ANT(f)				

Section LXII

Unit	
A1	1PHAL
A2	1VERT, 1RIB, 2PHAL
A3	1ANT(f)
A8	1ANT
A9	1AST
B1	2ANT(f), 1PHAL(f), 2SESAM
B2	1DMC/T(f), 1SESAM
C1	3DMC/T, 1PHAL, 1SESAM
D1	1VERT, 2RIB(f), 1PHAL, 1SESAM
E1	1PHAL

Section LXIII

Unit		Unit	
F2	1ANT(f), 1VERT	J6	1R, 3DMC/T
G5	1DMC/T	J9	1RIB(f), 1PHAL
G6	1DMC/T	J10	1PELV(f)
G9	1PHAL(f)	K3	1RIB(f)
H3	1DMC/T	K8	1PSAC
H8	1DMC/T(f)	K9	1DH, 1PT
H9	1MAN(f), 1PHAL		
H10	1TARS		
J1	1DMC/T(f)		
J5	2ANT(f)		

Roe deer

Section LIX

Unit		Unit	
A8	1DMC, 1T(f), 1PHAL	D8	1VERT, 1PMC, 1PHAL
A9	3MC/T(f), 1TARS, 1PHAL	D9	1ANT(f), 1MAN(f), 1PR, 1MC(f), 1PHAL
A10	2SK(f), 2VERT(f), 2PELV(f), 4DH, 6MC/T(f), 2DMC/T, 1PAT, 1TARS, 3PHAL	D10	1ANT, 1SK(f), 1VERT(f), 3H(f), 4R(f), 1PU, 3DMC/T, 1PT, 2AST, 3CAL, 1MT, 3PHAL
B9	1MC/T(f), 1AST, 1PHAL	E8	1CAL
B10	1ANT, 3VERT, 3H, 1PH, 1U, 3F, 1DF, 1PT, 1CAL, 3MT, 9PHAL	E10	1SC, 1DH, 1R(f), 1PR, 2DF, 1T, 1PT, 1AST, 1CAL
C6	1DR, 1DMC/T, 1PHAL	F10	2ANT(f), 1SK(f), 1VERT, 1PT, 1CAL, 2PHAL
C7	1CAL		
C8	1H(f)		
C9	1RIB(f), 1DR, 6MC/T(f), 1TARS, 1PHAL		
C10	3RIB(f), 2SC, 1R, 1DMC/T, 1DF, 1T(f), 1CAL		

Section LX

Unit		Unit		Unit	
B10	2ANT(f)	F10	1SK(f), 1VERT, 1AST, 1PHAL	K8	1ANT(f)
C10	1DR	G7	1DH, 1TARS, 1MT	K9	1SK(f), 1PR, 1PHAL
D8	1DR, 2MC/T(f)	G9	1MAN(f), 1PR, 1PHAL	K10	1ANT(f), 1MAN(f), 2RIB, 1PR, 2MC/T(f), 2PAT, 1TARS, 3PHAL
D9	1MC, 1DMC/T, 1PF, 1DF, 5PHAL	G10	1VERT, 1PHAL		
D10	1MAN(f), 1SC(f), 1MT(f), 1PHAL	H7	1DMC/T(f)		
E8	1ANT(f), 1SC(f), 1MT(f)	H9	3SC, 3MC/T(f), 1PF, 1PHAL		
E9	1ANT(f), 1H, 1DR, 1MC, 1PHAL	H10	2DMC/T		
E10	2SK+ANT, 1SC(f), 5MC/T(f)	J9	1MT, 1PHAL(f)		
F8	1ANT(f)	J10	1SK(f), 3MC/T(f), 1PAT		
F9	2DH(f), 1MC(f), 1MC/T	K7	2MT(f)		

Section LXII

Unit		Unit	
A1	1ANT(f), 1MAN(f), 2VERT, 1RIB, 1H, 1PR, 3DR, 8MC(f), 1DF, 2T(f), 1PT, 1DT, 3TARS, 4AST, 2CAL, 4MT(f), 9PHAL	B6	3ANT(f), 1PHAL
		C1	2MAN(f), 4RIB(f), 1SC(f), 4H(f), 1DR, 1PU, 1MC, 3MC/T(f), 2DMC/T, 1T(f), 3PHAL
A2	1SK, 1VERT, 2PELV(f), 4MC/T(f), 2PT, 1TARS, 1DMT, 4PHAL	C4	1PAT, 1CAL
		D1	1SK(f), 1MAN(f), 1RIB(f), 2MC(f), 1T(f), 1CAL, 1PHAL
A3	1DMC/T	D2	1CAL(f)
A4	1ANT(f)	G2	1MAN(f), 6MC/T(f), 1PF, 1PH, 1CAL 1PHAL
A5	1MT(f)		
A6	1SC(f), 1H(f)		
A9	1SC, 1PF, 1MT(f)		
B1	1ANT(f), 1SK+ANT, 2SK(f), 2MAN(f), 3PELV(f), 3SC(f), 7PH, 6DR, 3U(f), 4MC, 21MC/T(f), 1DF, 2DT, 2TARS, 3AST, 3CAL, 10PHAL		
B2	3R(f), 1U(f), 3MC, 4MC/T(f), 1PAT, 2DT, 2AST, 4PHAL		
B3	1MAN(f), 1SC(f), 1U(f), 1MT(f)		

Section LXIII

Unit		Unit		Unit	
C1	1PHAL	G4	1R(f), 1AST	H5	1ANT(f), 2SK+ANT, 1RIB, 3H, 1R, 5MC/T(f), 1AST, 1PHAL
D1	1SK+ANT, 1MC(f), 1T(f), 1PHAL	G5	4MAN(f), 1SC(f), 1H(f), 1R, 1U(f), 2MC, 4T, 1AST, 1CAL,		
E1	1ANT, 1MAN(f)			H6	1SK(f), 2PELV(f), 2DH, 1PT, 2MT
E6	1MT(f)	G6	1MAN(f), 1VERT, 1U(f), 6MC/T(f), 1T(f), 1PHAL		
E9	1DR			H7	1MAN(f), 3MC/T(f), 1AST
F5	1MAN(f), 1MC, 2MC/T(f), 1AST	G7	1PH, 1PAT		
F6	1ANT, 2MC/T(f), 1CAL	G8	1PH	H8	1MAN(f), 1DH, 1PU
F7	1U	G9	1MAX, 1RIB, 1DH, 1DMC, 1DT, 1CAL 1DMT		
G1	1MAN(f)			H10	3SK+ANT, 1SC(f), 1R, 1U, 1DF, 1AST,
G3	3ANT(f), 1DT, 1CAL	G10	1R(f)		
		H1	1PHAL(f)		

H3	1DF, 2PHAL		1PHAL
H4	2MAN(f), 2MC/T(f)	J1	1MC/T(f), 1F, 1PHAL
		J2	1MAN(f), 1MC, 2PHAL
		J4	1MT(f), 1CAL
		J5	1SK(f),1MAN(f), 1SC(f), 1MC/T(f), 1DT, 1AST, 2CAL, 1PHAL
		J6	3ANT(f) 3SK(f), 3SC(f), 2H, 1R, 1MC, 4MC/T(f), 1T(f), 1CAL, 1PHAL

Unit		Unit	
J7	3ANT, 2SK(f), 2SC, 2H, 1R, 3MC/T(f), 1T, 1PHAL	K8	1MAN, 2SC, 1DH(f), 2MC, 2MT, 1CAL
J9	1SK+ANT, 1MAN(f), 1RIB(f), 1PH, 1U(f), 8MC/T(f), 1DF, 2PAT, 1T(f), 1AST, 5PHAL	K9	1VERT, 1R, 1MC(f), 1DF, 1T, 1PHAL
J10	1ANT(f), 2SC, 2MT(f), 1CAL	K10	1DT, 1AST
K1	2ANT(f), 1SK+ANT, 4VERT, 1RIB(f), 3PR, 7MC/T(f), 1PAT, 3PHAL(f)		
K2	1ANT, 1TARS, 1CAL		
K3	1AST		
K4	1ANT(f)		
K5	1DF(f)		
K6	1MAN(f), 1VERT, 1R, 1MT(f)		
K7	1DH, 1DT		

Section LXX

Unit		Unit	
G1	1DF	H1	1SC(f), 1DMC

Pig

Section LIX

Unit		Unit	
A7	1RADIALE	C10	2PHAL

Section LIX continued

A8	1DMT, 3PHAL, 1ULNARE
A9	1PELV(f), 1MT
A10	4SK(f), 2RIB, 1CARP, 7MC/T, 1TARS, 10PHAL
B6	1SK(f)
B8	1VERT, 1FIB, 1MT
B9	1INTERM., 5PHAL
B10	2MAN(f), 1AT, 5VERT, 1U, 5MC/T, 1PAT, 1TARS, 7PHAL
C7	1PISIFORME
C9	1PAT, 1TARS, 1AST, 1DMC, 2PHAL

D8	1MAN(f), 1VERT, 1H, 1T, 1FIB(f), 5PHAL
D9	1MAN(f), 5MC/T, 1AST, 1CAL, 4PHAL
D10	1TARS, 1AST, 1CAL, 2MC, 4PHAL
E9	1VERT, 2MT(f), 2PHAL
E10	1U(f), 1MC(f), 1PAT, 2PHAL
F9	1CARP, 1PHAL
F10	1RIB, 2PHAL

Section LX

Unit	
C9	1RADIALE
C10	1PR
D7	1PAT
D8	1PU, 1TEMPORALE
D9	1DH, 1PR, 1PU, 1CAL, 1MT, 1PHAL
E8	1MC(f), 1PHAL
E9	1U(f), 1PHAL
E10	1MC/T(f), 1DT, 1PHAL(f)
F7	1CARP(f)
F8	1T

Unit	
F9	1AT, 4VERT(f), 1PELV(f), 1ST, 1R(f), 1MT, 8PHAL
F10	1MAN(f), 1THOR(f), 1MC, 1PAT, 1AST, 2PHAL, 2PHAL(f)
G10	2SK(f), 1MT(f)
H9	2PHAL(f)
H10	1CENTRALE
K7	1ST(f), 1DMC, 1PHAL
K8	1TARS
K9	1DR, 1MT, 1CENTR.
K10	1DFIB, 1MC/T, 1PAT, 5PHAL

Section LXII

Unit	
A1	1PU, 1F(f), 2MT, 1CENTR.
A2	2MC, 1DT
A3	1SC, 1CAL, 1PHAL
A5	1CAL
A6	1R
A10	1AST
B1	1ST(f), 1PAT, 1TARS, 1CAL, 2MT, 16PHAL
B2	1CARP, 1PFIB,

Unit	
C1	2SK(f), 1MAN, 2VERT, 1PELV(f), 4MC(f), 1F(f), 1T(f), 1AST, 1CAL, 6PHAL
D1	1SK(f), 3VERT, 1PHAL, 1PHAL(f)
E2	1CAL
E5	1SC(f)
G2	1PHAL(f)

```
          1AST, 4PHAL,
          1SESAM
B3        1RADIALE
B4        1MAX(f)
```

Section LXIII

Unit		Unit		Unit	
F4	1DH, 1PHAL	G10	1SC(f), 1CAL	J1	1PHAL
F5	1H(f), 2MC(f)	H2	1R(f), 1PHAL	J3	1CAL
F6	1MAN, 2H(f),	H3	1F(f), 1AST(f),	J4	1PHAL(f)
	1R(f), 1U(f),		1CAL(f)	J5	1VERT, 1SAC(f),
	2PHAL	H4	1PR		2SC(f), 1R,
F9	1DH	H5	1MAX(f), 1MC,		1DFIB, 1CAL
F10	1AST, 1CAL		1F(f), 2MT	J6	2MAN(f), 1PH,
G2	1SK(f)	H6	1MAN(f), 1SC,		1R(f), 1DU,
G3	1MAN(f)		1SC(f), 1H,		1MC, 1T(f),
G5	2PELV(f), 2SC(f),		2MC/T(f), 1F(f),		1AST, 1CAL,
	1R(f), 1U(f),		1T(f), 1CAL,		2PHAL
	1MC, 1AST,		2PHAL	J7	1SK(f), 1DU,
	1PHAL(f)	H7	1SC(f)		3MC/T(f)
G6	1SK(f), 1SC(f),	H8	1MAX(f), 1SC(f),	J9	1MAX, 1MAN,
	1CAL, 4PHAL		1DU, 1PHAL		2PH, 1CARP,
G8	1MT	H9	1SC(f)		2MC(f), 2TARS,
		H10	1THOR(f), 1SC(f),		6PHAL
			1PHAL	J10	1MAN, 1VERT,
					1U(f), 1T,1CAL
				K1	2MAN(f), 1CARP,
					5MC/T(f),
					1F(f), 5PHAL
				K5	1PHAL

```
Unit
K6        1AT(f), 3MC(f)
K7        1THOR(f), 1CARP,
          2PHAL
K8        2MC, 1DF
K9        1MAN(f), 1VERT,
          1PELV(f), 1SC(f),
          1AST
K10       1SC(f), 1H, 2MT(f)
```

Section LXX

Unit		Unit	
H1	1FIB(f)	J1	1VERT, 1PH

Elk

Section LIX

Unit	
D10	1PT, 1DT

Section LX

Unit		Unit		Unit	
C10	1PT(f)	E10	1PHAL	J10	1RIB(f)
D10	1F(f)	G10	1SESAM	K10	1SK(f)

Section LXII

Unit		Unit		Unit	
A1	1PHAL	B1	2DMC/T, 1PHAL,	B3	1SESAM
A7	1AST		1SESAM	C1	1VERT, 3RIB(f),
					1TARS, 1AST, 1CAL

Section LXIII

Unit		Unit		Unit	
C1	1LUM	H10	1T(f)	K5	1DMT
G3	1SESAM	J10	3ANT(f), 1MAN	K8	1ANT(f)
H9	1ANT(f)	K1	1PHAL(f)		

Section LXX

Unit	
H1	4ANT(f)

Aurochs

Section LIX

Unit		Unit		Unit	
A10	1RIB(f), 1PHAL,	C10	2PHAL	D10	1DR, 1MC, 1CARP
	1SESAM				

Section LX

Unit	
F10	2RIB(f), 1PHAL(f)

Section LXIII

Unit	
J5	1RIB(f)

Sværdborg II

Red deer

Unit		Unit	
A4	1PELV(f)	F3	1ANT(f), 1PHAL
A5	1DR	F4	12ANT(f), 1T(f)
A6	1T(f)	F5	5ANT(f)
B4	1PMT, 1PHAL	G1	1DMT
D2	1T(f)	G2	1H(f)
D5	10ANT(f), 1T(f)		
E3	2PHAL		
E5	3ANT(f)		
F1	1T(f)		
F2	1T(f)		

Roe deer

Unit		Unit	
-A4	1F(f)	E5	1PHAL
A2	1MAN(f)	F1	1PF
A3	1DF	F2	1ANT, 1CAL
A6	1PAT, 1PHAL	G1	1R(f)
B4	1SK(f)	G2	1SK(f), 1T(f)
B6	1CAL		
C2	2PELV(f)		
D2	1SC(f)		
E2	1DR, 1DH, 1AST, 1MT		
E3	1R, 1DU, 2CAL, 1CAL(f)		

Pig

Unit		Unit	
-A3	1MC	E5	1F(f)
-A4	1H	K3	1H(f)
A2	1PHAL		
A3	1DF		
A4	1PF, 1DF, 1TARS		
A5	1SC		
B4	1SC		
D2	1MC		
D3	1MC		
E3	1DT, 1PHAL		

Appendix B

Element frequencies, MNI and %MNI per species per site

Technical notes
Where element counts include fragments not dealt with analytically, the number of these fragments is given in parantheses. For example, a scapula count listed 14(6) means that 6 out of 14 are fragments not analytically dealt with, resulting in 8 usable for analysis, giving a MNI of 8 divided by 2 = 4.

The element frequencies for Star Carr, Stellmoor and Meiendorf are derived in only slightly modified form from Legge & Rowley-Conwy (1988) and Grønnow (1987) and have thus been omitted as redundant.

Zoological determinations

Mullerup Syd	Winge (1903) and in original files in the National Museum, Copenhagen.
Mullerup Nord	Winge, original files in the National Museum, Copenhagen.
Ulkestrup I & II	Richter (1982) and Richter, private files.
Sværdborg I, 1917-18	Winge (1919) and in original files in the National Museum, Copenhagen.
Sværdborg I, 1923	P. Rowley-Conwy, private files, and G. Jensen, files in Universitetets Zoologiske Museum, Copenhagen.
Sværdborg I, 1943-44	Aaris-Sørensen (1976) and Aaris-Sørensen, private files.
Sværdborg II	Rosenlund (1972) and in original files in the National Museum, Copenhagen.
Lundby I	P. Rowley-Conwy, private files, Degerbøl (1933) and in original files in the National Museum, Copenhagen.
Lundby II	Rosenlund (1979) and 1991 for the author.
Skottemarke	Møhl (1978).
Ageröd I:B	Lepiksaar (1978) and in original files in Lunds Universitets Historiska Museum.
Ageröd I:D	Lepikssaar (1978) and in original files in Lunds Universitets Historiska Museum.
Ageröd V	Lepiksaar (1983).
Segebro	Lepiksaar (1982).

B1. Mullerup Syd. Red deer.

Element	Count	MNI	%MNI
ANT(shed)	1	-	-
ANT(mass.)	3	-	-
SK+ANT	-	-	-
SK(frag.)	1	-	-
MAX	2	1.0	18
MAN	5	2.5	45
AT	-	-	-
AX	-	-	-
VERT	1	0.0	0
SAC	-	-	-
PELV	2	1.0	18
RIB	-	-	-
ST	-	-	-
SC	6	3.0	54
PH	-	-	-
DH	6	3.0	54
PR	3	1.5	27
DR	6	3.0	54
PU	-	-	-
DU	-	-	-
PMC	-	-	-
DMC	-	-	-
PF	2	1.0	18
DF	2	1.0	18
PT	3	1.5	27
DT	3	1.5	27
FIB	-	-	-
AST	3	1.5	27
CAL	2	1.0	18
PMT	11	5.5	100
DMT	11	5.5	100
PHAL	10	0.4	7

B2. Mullerup Syd. Roe deer.

Element	Count	MNI	%MNI
ANT(shed)	1	-	-
ANT(mass.)	9	-	-
SK+ANT	5	-	-
SK	11	-	-
MAX	2	1.0	10
MAN	15	7.5	71
AT	2	2.0	19
AX	1	1.0	10
VERT	2	0.1	1
SAC	-	-	-
PELV	11	5.5	52
RIB	1	0.0	0
ST	-	-	-
SC	21	10.5	100
PH	-	-	-
DH	13	6.5	62
PR	6	3.0	29
DR	6	3.0	29
PU	-	-	-
DU	-	-	-
PMC	2	1.0	10
DMC	2	1.0	10
PF	4	2.0	19
DF	4	2.0	19
PT	9	4.5	43
DT	9	4.5	43
FIB	-	-	-
AST	2	1.0	10
CAL	6	3.0	29
PMT	18	9.0	86
DMT	18	9.0	86
PHAL	-	-	-

B3. Mullerup Syd. Pig.

Element	Count	MNI	%MNI
ANT(shed)			
ANT(mass.)			
SK+ANT			
SK	5	-	-
MAX	20	10.0	59
MAN	21	10.5	62
AT	-	-	-
AX	1	1.0	6
VERT	7	0.2	1
SAC	-	-	-
PELV	20	10.0	59
RIB	-	-	-
ST	-	-	-
SC	34	17.0	100
PH	-	-	-
DH	-	-	-
PR	17	8.5	50
DR	-	-	-
PU	22	11.0	65
DU	-	-	-
PMC	-	-	-
DMC	-	-	-
PF	3	1.5	9
DF	3	1.5	9
PT	-	-	-
DT	21	10.5	62
FIB	1	0.5	3
AST	15	7.5	44
CAL	18	9.0	53
PMT	9	1.1	6
DMT	9	1.1	6
PHAL	5	0.2	1

B4. Mullerup Syd. Elk.

Element	Count	MNI	%MNI
ANT(shed)	(8)	-	-
ANT(mass.)	(8)	-	-
SK+ANT	1	-	-
SK	4	-	-
MAX	2	1.0	25
MAN	1	0.5	13
AT	-	-	-
AX	1	1.0	25
VERT	1	0.0	0
SAC	-	-	-
PELV	3	1.5	38
RIB	7	0.2	5
ST	-	-	-
SC	4	2.0	50
PH	-	-	-
DH	3	1.5	38
PR	3	1.5	38
DR	2	1.0	25
PU	1	0.5	13
DU	1	0.5	13
PMC	1	0.5	13
DMC	2	1.0	25
PF	6	3.0	75
DF	6	3.0	75
PT	-	-	-
DT	-	-	-
FIB	1	0.5	13
AST	8	4.0	100
CAL	5	2.5	63
PMT	7	3.5	88
DMT	7	3.5	88
PHAL	63	2.6	65

B5. Mullerup Syd. Aurochs.

Element	Count	MNI	%MNI
ANT(shed)	-	-	-
ANT(mass.)	-	-	-
SK+ANT	-	-	-
SK	3	-	-
MAX	-	-	-
MAN	-	-	-
AT	-	-	-
AX	-	-	-
VERT	3	0.2	8
SAC	-	-	-
PELV	6	3.0	100
RIB	2	0.1	3
ST	1	1.0	33
SC	5	2.5	83
PH	-	-	-
DH	-	-	-
PR	1	0.5	17
DR	2	1.0	33
PU	-	-	-
DU	-	-	-
PMC	1	0.5	17
DMC	4	2.0	67
PF	2	1.0	33
DF	-	-	-
PT	3	1.5	50
DT	2	1.0	33
FIB	-	-	-
AST	2	1.0	33
CAL	4	2.0	67
PMT	2	1.0	33
DMT	2	1.0	33
PHAL	34	1.4	47

B6. Mullerup Nord. Red deer.

Element	Count	MNI	%MNI
ANT(shed)	0	0.0	0
ANT(mass.)	0	0.0	0
SK+ANT	0	0.0	0
SK(frag.)	0	0.0	0
MAX	0	0.0	0
MAN	1	0.5	50
AT	0	0.0	0
AX	0	0.0	0
VERT	0	0.0	0
SAC	0	0.0	0
PELV	0	0.0	0
RIB	0	0.0	0
ST	0	0.0	0
SC	1	0.5	50
PH	0	0.0	0
DH	0	0.0	0
PR	0	0.0	0
DR	0	0.0	0
PU	2	1.0	100
DU	1	0.5	50
PMC	1	0.5	50
DMC	1	0.5	50
PF	0	0.0	0
DF	0	0.0	0
PT	0	0.0	0
DT	1	0.5	50
FIB	0	0.0	0
AST	1	0.5	50
CAL	0	0.0	0
PMT	1	0.5	0
DMT	1	0.5	50
PHAL	1	0.0	5

B7. Mullerup Nord. Roe deer.

Element	Count	MNI	%MNI
ANT(shed)	0	0.0	0
ANT(mass.)	0	0.0	0
SK+ANT	0	0.0	0
SK(frag.)	1	1.0	100
MAX	0	0.0	0
MAN	1	0.5	50
AT	0	0.0	0
AX	0	0.0	0
VERT	0	0.0	0
SAC	0	0.0	0
PELV	0	0.0	0
RIB	0	0.0	0
ST	0	0.0	0
SC	1	0.5	50
PH	0	0.0	0
DH	0	0.0	0
PR	2	1.0	100
DR	2	1.0	100
PU	1	0.5	50
DU	1	0.5	50
PMC	0	0.0	0
DMC	0	0.0	0
PF	2	1.0	100
DF	2	1.0	100
PT	0	0.0	0
DT	1	0.5	50
FIB	0	0.0	0
AST	1	0.5	50
CAL	1	0.5	50
PMT	1	0.5	50
DMT	1	0.5	50
PHAL	1	0.05	5

B8. Mullerup Nord. Pig.

Element	Count	MNI	%MNI
ANT(shed)			
ANT(mass.)			
SK+ANT			
SK(frag.)	2	1.0	100
MAX	-	-	-
MAN	2	1.0	100
AT	-	-	-
AX	-	-	-
VERT	1	-	-
SAC	-	-	-
PELV	2	1.0	100
RIB	1	0.0	0
ST	-	-	-
SC	1	0.5	50
PH	-	-	-
DH	-	-	-
PR	2	1.0	100
DR	1	0.5	50
PU	2	1.0	100
DU	2	1.0	100
PMC	-	-	-
DMC	-	-	-
PF	1	0.5	50
DF	1	0.5	50
PT	2	1.0	100
DT	2	1.0	100
FIB	-	-	-
AST	2	1.0	100
CAL	1	0.5	50
PMT	2	0.25	25
DMT	2	0.25	25
PHAL	3	0.06	6

B9. Mullerup Nord. Elk.

Element	Count	MNI	%MNI
ANT(shed)	-	-	-
ANT(mass.)	1	0.5	10
SK+ANT	-	-	-
SK(frag.)	2	1.0	20
MAX	-	-	-
MAN	2	1.0	20
AT	-	-	-
AX	-	-	-
VERT	-	-	-
SAC	-	-	-
PELV	-	-	-
RIB	-	-	-
ST	-	-	-
SC	3	1.5	30
PH	-	-	-
DH	-	-	-
PR	1	0.5	10
DR	2	1.0	20
PU	-	-	-
DU	-	-	-
PMC	10	5.0	100
DMC	10	5.0	100
PF	3	1.5	30
DF	3	1.5	30
PT	-	-	-
DT	-	-	-
FIB	-	-	-
AST	1	0.5	10
CAL	-	-	-
PMT	3	1.5	30
DMT	3	1.5	30
PHAL	7	0.3	6

B10. Mullerup Nord. Aurochs.

Element	Count	MNI	%MNI
ANT(shed)	-	-	-
ANT(mass.)	-	-	-
SK+ANT	-	-	-
SK(frag.)	1	1.0	40
MAX	-	-	-
MAN	-	-	-
AT	-	-	-
AX	-	-	-
VERT	1	0.2	8
SAC	-	-	-
PELV	1	0.5	20
RIB	1	0.03	1
ST	2	2.0	80
SC	4	2.0	80
PH	-	-	-
DH	-	-	-
PR	-	-	-
DR	-	-	-
PU	1	0.5	20
DU	1	0.5	20
PMC	5	2.5	100
DMC	5	2.5	100
PF	-	-	-
DF	-	-	-
PT	1	0.5	20
DT	1	0.5	20
FIB	-	-	-
AST	3	1.5	60
CAL	2	1.0	40
PMT	-	-	-
DMT	-	-	-
PHAL	5	0.2	8

B11. Ulkestrup I. Red deer.

Element	Count	MNI	%MNI
ANT(shed)			
ANT(mass.)	3(3)	-	-
SK+ANT			
SK(frag.)	1(1)	-	-
MAX	-	-	-
MAN	2(2)	-	-
AT	1	1.0	50
AX	2	2.0	100
VERT	38(30)	0.3	15
SAC	2	2.0	100
PELV	6(6)	-	-
RIB	16(15)	-	-
ST	-	-	-
SC	8(6)	1.0	50
PH	2	1.0	50
DH	4	2.0	100
PR	-	-	-
DR	-	-	-
PU	-	-	-
DU	-	-	-
PMC	-	-	-
DMC	-	-	-
PF	1(1)	-	-
DF	2	-	-
PT	-	-	-
DT	-	-	-
FIB	-	-	-
AST	2	1.0	50
CAL	1	0.5	25
PMT	-	-	-
DMT	1	0.5	25
PHAL	6	0.25	13

B12. Ulkestrup I. Roe deer.

Element	Count	MNI	%MNI
ANT(shed)	-	-	-
ANT(mass.)	1(1)	-	-
SK+ANT	-	-	-
SK(frag.)	2(2)	-	-
MAX	-	-	-
MAN	1(1)	-	-
AT	-	-	-
AX	-	-	-
VERT	2(2)	-	-
SAC	-	-	-
PELV	2(2)	-	-
RIB	2(2)	-	-
ST	1	1.0	50
SC	-	-	-
PH	-	-	-
DH	1	0.5	25
PR	-	-	-
DR	-	-	-
PU	-	-	-
DU	-	-	-
PMC	4	2.0	100
DMC	3	1.5	75
PF	-	-	-
DF	-	-	-
PT	-	-	-
DT	1	0.5	25
FIB	-	-	-
AST	1	0.5	25
CAL	-	-	-
PMT	1	0.5	25
DMT	-	-	-
PHAL	1	-	-

B13. Ulkestrup I. Pig.

Element	Count	MNI	%MNI
ANT(shed)			
ANT(mass.)			
SK+ANT			
SK(frag.)	4(4)	-	-
MAX	3(3)	-	-
MAN	4(2)	1.0	50
AT	2	2.0	100
AX	1	1.0	50
VERT	6(6)	-	-
SAC	1	1.0	50
PELV	3(3)	-	-
RIB	13(13)	-	-
ST	-	-	-
SC	4	2.0	100
PH	1	0.5	25
DH	3	1.5	75
PR	2	1.0	50
DR	1	0.5	25
PU	-	-	-
DU	-	-	-
PMC	-	-	-
DMC	2	0.2	10
PF	-	-	-
DF	3	1.5	75
PT	-	-	-
DT	2	1.0	50
FIB	-	-	-
AST	-	-	-
CAL	1	0.5	25
PMT	2	0.2	10
DMT	1	0.1	5
PHAL	25	0.5	25

B14. Ulkestrup I. Elk.

Element	Count	MNI	%MNI
ANT(shed)	-	-	-
ANT(mass.)	-	-	-
SK+ANT	-	-	-
SK(frag.)	1(1)	-	-
MAX	1(1)	-	-
MAN	1	0.5	100
AT	-	-	-
AX	-	-	-
VERT	-	-	-
SAC	-	-	-
PELV	2(2)	-	-
RIB	6(6)	-	-
ST	-	-	-
SC	-	-	-
PH	-	-	-
DH	-	-	-
PR	1	0.5	100
DR	1	0.5	100
PU	-	-	-
DU	-	-	-
PMC	1	0.5	100
DMC	1	0.5	100
PF	-	-	-
DF	-	-	-
PT	-	-	-
DT	-	-	-
FIB	-	-	-
AST	-	-	-
CAL	-	-	-
PMT	-	-	-
DMT	-	-	-
PHAL	4	0.1	20

B15. Ulkestrup I. Aurochs.

Element	Count	MNI	%MNI
ANT(shed)			
ANT(mass.)			
SK+ANT			
SK(frag.)	3(3)	-	-
MAX	2(2)	-	-
MAN	3(3)	-	-
AT	1	1.0	67
AX	1	1.0	67
VERT	14(14)	-	-
SAC	1	1.0	67
PELV	4(4)	-	-
RIB	13(13)	-	-
ST	-	-	-
SC	-	-	-
PH	1	0.5	33
DH	3	1.5	100
PR	-	-	-
DR	1	0.5	33
PU	-	-	-
DU	-	-	-
PMC	-	-	-
DMC	-	-	-
PF	-	-	-
DF	-	-	-
PT	-	-	-
DT	-	-	-
FIB	-	-	-
AST	1	0.5	33
CAL	-	-	-
PMT	-	-	-
DMT	-	-	-
PHAL	7(7)	-	-

B16. Ulkestrup II. Red deer.

Element	Count	MNI	%MNI
ANT(shed)	-	-	-
ANT(mass.)	3(3)	-	-
SK+ANT	1	-	-
SK(frag.)	7(7)	-	-
MAX	3(3)	-	-
MAN	7(7)	-	-
AT	3	3.0	66
AX	3	3.0	66
VERT	35(32)	0.1	0
SAC	-	-	-
PELV	2(2)	-	-
RIB	35(32)	0.1	0
ST	1	1.0	22
SC	4(3)	0.5	11
PH	-	-	-
DH	6	3.0	66
PR	3	1.5	33
DR	5	2.5	55
PU	1	0.5	11
DU	-	-	-
PMC	1	0.5	11
DMC	9	4.5	100
PF	1	0.5	11
DF	1	0.5	11
PT	4	2.0	22
DT	8	4.0	88
FIB	1	0.5	11
AST	3	1.5	33
CAL	1	0.5	11
PMT	-	-	-
DMT	8	4.0	88
PHAL	46	1.9	42

B17. Ulkestrup II. Roe deer.

Element	Count	MNI	%MNI
ANT(shed)	-	-	-
ANT(mass.)	1(1)	-	-
SK+ANT	-	-	-
SK(frag.)	4(4)	-	-
MAX	3(3)	-	-
MAN	6(6)	-	-
AT	1	1.0	33
AX	1	1.0	33
VERT	5(5)	-	-
SAC	1	1.0	33
PELV	7(7)	-	-
RIB	24(24)	-	-
ST	-	-	-
SC	3	1.5	50
PH	1	0.5	16
DH	3	1.5	50
PR	-	-	-
DR	3	1.5	50
PU	1	0.5	16
DU	2	1.0	33
PMC	2	1.0	33
DMC	3	1.5	50
PF	6	3.0	100
DF	6	3.0	100
PT	2	1.0	33
DT	3	1.5	50
FIB	-	-	-
AST	4	2.0	67
CAL	3	1.5	50
PMT	3	1.5	50
DMT	1	0.5	16
PHAL	14	0.6	20

B18. Ulkestrup II. Pig.

Element	Count	MNI	%MNI
ANT(shed)			
ANT(mass.)			
SK+ANT			
SK(frag.)	3(3)	-	-
MAX	2(2)	-	-
MAN	3(3)	-	-
AT	-	-	-
AX	-	-	-
VERT	4(4)	-	-
SAC	-	-	-
PELV	4(4)	-	-
RIB	5(5)	-	-
ST	-	-	-
SC	1	0.5	50
PH	-	-	-
DH	2	1.0	100
PR	-	-	-
DR	1	0.5	50
PU	-	-	-
DU	-	-	-
PMC	-	-	-
DMC	-	-	-
PF	-	-	-
DF	1	0.5	50
PT	1	0.5	50
DT	-	-	-
FIB	-	-	-
AST	1	0.5	50
CAL	2	1.0	100
PMT	1	0.5	50
DMT	-	-	-
PHAL	-	-	-

B19. Ulkestrup II. Elk.

Element	Count	MNI	%MNI
ANT(shed)	-	-	-
ANT(mass.)	-	-	-
SK+ANT	-	-	-
SK(frag.)	1(1)	-	-
MAX	-	-	-
MAN	-	-	-
AT	-	-	-
AX	-	-	-
VERT	-	-	-
SAC	-	-	-
PELV	-	-	-
RIB	-	-	-
ST	-	-	-
SC	-	-	-
PH	-	-	-
DH	-	-	-
PR	2	1.0	100
DR	1	0.5	50
PU	-	-	-
DU	-	-	-
PMC	-	-	-
DMC	-	-	-
PF	-	-	-
DF	-	-	-
PT	-	-	-
DT	-	-	-
FIB	-	-	-
AST	-	-	-
CAL	2	1.0	100
PMT	-	-	-
DMT	1	0.5	50
PHAL	-	-	-

B20. Ulkestrup II. Aurochs.

Element	Count	MNI	%MNI
ANT(shed)			
ANT(mass.)			
SK+ANT			
SK(frag.)	10(10)	-	-
MAX	6(5)	0.5	25
MAN	5(2)	1.5	75
AT	2	2.0	100
AX	-	-	-
VERT	11(11)	-	-
SAC	1	1.0	50
PELV	-	-	-
RIB	20(20)	-	-
ST	-	-	-
SC	5(2)	1.5	75
PH	-	-	-
DH	1	0.5	25
PR	1	0.5	25
DR	-	-	-
PU	4	2.0	100
DU	1	0.5	25
PMC	-	-	-
DMC	1	0.5	25
PF	-	-	-
DF	-	-	-
PT	1	0.5	25
DT	-	-	-
FIB	-	-	-
AST	1	0.5	25
CAL	-	-	-
PMT	1	0.5	25
DMT	1	0.5	25
PHAL	8	0.3	15

B21. Sværdborg I, 1917-18. Red deer.

Element	Count	MNI	%MNI
ANT(shed) *			
ANT(mass.)	33(33)	-	-
SK+ANT	3(1)	-	-
SK(frag.)	1(1)	-	-
MAX	-	-	-
MAN	9(4)	2.5	42
AT	-	-	-
AX	-	-	-
VERT	3	0.1	2
SAC	-	-	-
PELV	4(2)	1.0	17
RIB	-	-	-
ST	-	-	-
SC	9(5)	2.0	33
PH	-	-	-
DH	1	0.5	8
PR	1	0.5	8
DR	1	0.5	8
PU	1	0.5	8
DU	1	0.5	8
PMC	4	2.0	33
DMC	4	2.0	33
PF	2	1.0	17
DF	2	1.0	17
PT	1	0.5	8
DT	2	1.0	17
FIB	1	0.5	8
AST	9	4.5	75
CAL	7	3.5	58
PMT	10	5.0	83
DMT	12	6.0	100
PHAL	30	1.3	22

B22. Sværdborg I, 1917-18. Roe deer.

Element	Count	MNI	%MNI
ANT(shed)			
ANT(mass.)	8(8)	-	-
SK+ANT	17	-	-
SK(frag.)	2(2)	-	-
MAX	-	-	-
MAN	12(9)	1.5	23
AT	-	-	-
AX	-	-	-
VERT	6	0.25	4
SAC	-	-	-
PELV	6(6)	-	-
RIB	-	-	-
ST	-	-	-
SC	12(8)	2.0	31
PH	3	1.5	23
DH	4	2.0	31
PR	2	1.0	15
DR	1	0.5	8
PU	-	-	-
DU	-	-	-
PMC	-	-	-
DMC	-	-	-
PF	-	-	-
DF	-	-	-
PT	3	1.	23
DT	3	1.5	23
FIB	-	-	-
AST	9	4.5	69
CAL	13	6.5	100
PMT	3	1.5	23
DMT	3	1.5	23
PHAL	17	0.7	11

B23. Sværdborg I, 1917-18. Pig.

Element	Count	MNI	%MNI
ANT(shed)			
ANT(mass.)			
SK+ANT			
SK(frag.)	3(3)	-	-
MAX	2(2)	-	-
MAN	12(12)	-	-
AT	-	-	-
AX	-	-	-
VERT	6	0.2	2
SAC	-	-	-
PELV	16(13)	1.5	10
RIB	13(13)	-	-
ST	-	-	-
SC	34(20)	7.0	48
PH	3	1.5	10
DH	3	1.5	10
PR	-	-	-
DR	-	-	-
PU	-	-	-
DU	-	-	-
PMC	-	-	-
DMC	-	-	-
PF	1	0.5	3
DF	1	0.5	3
PT	1	0.5	3
DT	1	0.5	3
FIB	1(1)	-	-
AST	29	14.5	100
CAL	19	9.5	65
PMT	10	1.25	9
DMT	8	1.0	7
PHAL	27	0.56	4

B24. Sværdborg I, 1917-18. Elk.

Element	Count	MNI	%MNI
ANT(shed)			
ANT(mass.)	25(25)	-	-
SK+ANT	3	-	-
SK(frag.)	7(7)	-	-
MAX	5(5)	-	-
MAN	15(15)	-	-
AT	-	-	-
AX	-	-	-
VERT	6(3)	0.1	1
SAC	-	-	-
PELV	3(3)	-	-
RIB	-	-	-
ST	-	-	-
SC	6(3)	1.5	21
PH	1	0.5	7
DH	4	2.0	29
PR	1	0.5	7
DR	4	2.0	29
PU	1	0.5	7
DU	1	0.5	7
PMC	-	-	-
DMC	-	-	-
PF	1	0.5	7
DF	-	-	-
PT	1	0.5	7
DT	2	1.0	14
FIB	1	0.5	7
AST	14	7.0	100
CAL	11	5.5	79
PMT	-	-	-
DMT	7	3.5	50
PHAL	40(3)	1.5	2

B25. Sværdborg I, 1917-18. Aurochs.

Element	Count	MNI	%MNI
ANT(shed)	-	-	-
ANT(mass.)	-	-	-
SK+ANT	-	-	-
SK(frag.)	2(2)	-	-
MAX	-	-	-
MAN	7(3)	2.0	50
AT	-	-	-
AX	-	-	-
VERT	14(1)	0.7	18
SAC	-	-	-
PELV	7(7)	-	-
RIB	9(9)	-	-
ST	-	-	-
SC	6(6)	-	-
PH	-	-	-
DH	1	0.5	13
PR	2	1.0	25
DR	1	0.5	13
PU	-	-	-
DU	-	-	-
PMC	2	1.0	25
DMC	1	0.5	13
PF	1	0.5	13
DF	1	0.5	13
PT	-	-	-
DT	2	1.0	25
FIB	-	-	-
AST	5	2.5	63
CAL	8	4.0	100
PMT	-	-	-
DMT	-	-	-
PHAL	54(23)	1.3	32

B26. Sværdborg I, 1923. Red deer.

Element	Count	MNI	%MNI
ANT(shed)	-	-	-
ANT(mass.)	-	-	-
SK+ANT	-	-	-
SK(frag.)	-	-	-
MAX	1(1)	-	-
MAN	3(1)	1.0	9
AT	11(9)	2.0	19
AX	8(4)	4.0	38
VERT	42(6)	1.5	14
SAC	-	-	-
PELV	17(17)	-	-
RIB	8(2)	0.2	2
ST	-	-	-
SC	7(1)	3.0	29
PH	7(1)	3.0	29
DH	15(0)	7.5	71
PR	10(1)	4.5	43
DR	8(0)	4.0	38
PU	-	-	-
DU	8(0)	4.0	38
PMC	-	-	-
DMC	23(16)	3.5	33
PF	13	6.5	62
DF	7	3.5	33
PT	17(1)	8.0	76
DT	6	3.0	29
FIB	-	-	-
AST	24(3)	10.5	100
CAL	22(1)	10.5	100
PMT	1	0.5	4
DMT	16(12)	2.0	19
PHAL	66(4)	2.6	25

B27. Sværdborg I, 1923. Roe deer.

Element	Count	MNI	%MNI
ANT(shed)	-	-	-
ANT(mass.)	-	-	-
SK+ANT	-	-	-
SK(frag.)	-	-	-
MAX	1(1)	-	-
MAN	18(6)	6.0	14
AT	16(12)	4.0	10
AX	8(4)	4.0	10
VERT	13(2)	0.45	1
SAC	-	-	-
PELV	99(99)	-	-
RIB	-	-	-
ST	-	-	-
SC	90(7)	41.5	100
PH	15	7.5	18
DH	81(1)	40.0	96
PR	32(1)	15.5	37
DR	18(2)	8.0	19
PU	21	10.5	25
DU	28	14.0	34
PMC	13	6.5	16
DMC	14(6)	4.0	10
PF	25(3)	11.0	27
DF	40(2)	19.0	46
PT	23	11.5	28
DT	14	7.0	17
FIB	-	-	-
AST	28(2)	13.0	31
CAL	51(7)	22.0	53
PMT	8	4.0	10
DMT	17(13)	2.0	5
PHAL	61(4)	2.4	6

B28. Sværdborg I, 1923. Pig.

Element	Count	MNI	%MNI
ANT(shed)	-	-	-
ANT(mass.)	-	-	-
SK+ANT	-	-	-
SK(frag.)	2(2)	-	-
MAX	4(3)	0.5	2
MAN	11(8)	1.5	5
AT	7(3)	4.0	14
AX	6	6.0	21
VERT	44(5)	1.5	5
SAC	-	-	-
PELV	65(65)	-	-
RIB	13(1)	0.4	1
ST	-	-	-
SC	56(3)	26.5	95
PH	12	6.0	21
DH	36(4)	16.0	57
PR	23(1)	11.0	39
DR	20(2)	9.0	32
PU	12(0)	6.0	21
DU	33(6)	13.5	48
PMC	3(1)	0.25	1
DMC	2	0.25	1
PF	29(1)	14.0	50
DF	39(5)	17.0	61
PT	35(4)	15.5	55
DT	58(2)	28.0	100
FIB	-	-	-
AST	52(6)	23.0	82
CAL	67(17)	25.0	89
PMT	8	1.0	4
DMT	-	-	-
PHAL	108(42)	1.4	5

B29. Sværdborg I, 1923. Elk.

Element	Count	MNI	%MNI
ANT(shed)	-	-	-
ANT(mass.)	-	-	-
SK+ANT	-	-	-
SK(frag.)	-	-	-
MAX	-	-	-
MAN	3(1)	1.0	7
AT	9(7)	2.0	14
AX	-	-	-
VERT	26(7)	0.8	5
SAC	-	-	-
PELV	29(29)	-	-
RIB	-	-	-
ST	-	-	-
SC	12(2)	5.0	34
PH	4	2.0	14
DH	12(1)	5.5	38
PR	5(1)	2.0	14
DR	5	2.5	17
PU	4	2.0	14
DU	8(1)	3.5	24
PMC	1	0.5	3
DMC	7(3)	2.0	14
PF	5	2.5	17
DF	13(4)	4.5	31
PT	10(5)	2.5	17
DT	5	2.5	17
FIB	-	-	-
AST	30(1)	14.5	100
CAL	28(2)	13.0	90
PMT	-	-	-
DMT	8(3)	2.5	17
PHAL	126(41)	3.5	24

B30. Sværdborg I, 1923. Aurochs.

Element	Count	MNI	%MNI
ANT(shed)	-	-	-
ANT(mass.)	-	-	-
SK+ANT	-	-	-
SK(frag.)	-	-	-
MAX	-	-	-
MAN	-	-	-
AT	3(2)	1.0	13
AX	2	2.0	25
VERT	13	0.5	7
SAC	1	1.0	13
PELV	45(45)	-	-
RIB	4(1)	0.1	1
ST	-	-	-
SC	14(6)	4.0	50
PH	7	3.5	44
DH	6(1)	2.5	31
PR	11(2)	4.5	56
DR	10(3)	3.5	44
PU	4	2.0	25
DU	13(1)	6.0	75
PMC	5	2.5	31
DMC	9(7)	1.0	13
PF	10	5.0	63
DF	3(2)	0.5	6
PT	4(1)	1.5	19
DT	6(2)	2.0	25
FIB	-	-	-
AST	19(3)	8.0	100
CAL	22(6)	8.0	100
PMT	2(2)	-	-
DMT	5(3)	1.0	13
PHAL	221(87)	5.6	70

B31. Sværdborg I, 1943-44, Area A, NE. Red deer.

Element	Count	MNI	%MNI
ANT(shed)	-	-	-
ANT(mass.)	1?	-	-
SK+ANT	-	-	-
SK(frag.)	-	-	-
MAX	-	-	-
MAN	1	0.5	33
AT	1	1.0	66
AX	-	-	-
VERT	2	0.0	75
SAC	-	-	-
PELV	-	-	-
RIB	1	0.0	43
ST	-	-	-
SC	-	-	-
PH	-	-	-
DH	-	-	-
PR	-	-	-
DR	-	-	-
PU	-	-	-
DU	-	-	-
PMC	-	-	-
DMC	-	-	-
PF	-	-	-
DF	-	-	-
PT	-	-	-
DT	-	-	-
FIB	-	-	-
AST	1	0.5	33
CAL	3	1.5	100
PMT	2	1.0	66
DMT	2	1.0	66
PHAL	7	0.3	20

B32. Sværdborg I, 1943-44, Area A, NE. Roe deer.

Element	Count	MNI	%MNI
ANT(shed)	-	-	-
ANT(mass.)	4	-	-
SK+ANT	-	-	-
SK(frag.)	-	-	-
MAX	1	0.5	13
MAN	9(1)	4.0	100
AT	-	-	-
AX	-	-	-
VERT	3	0.1	2
SAC	-	-	-
PELV	3(3)	-	-
RIB	-	-	-
ST	-	-	-
SC	-	-	-
PH	5	2.5	63
DH	8	4.0	100
PR	2	1.0	25
DR	3	1.5	38
PU	1	0.5	13
DU	-	-	-
PMC	1	0.5	13
DMC	2	1.0	25
PF	4	2.0	50
DF	6	3.0	75
PT	3	1.5	38
DT	6	3.0	75
FIB	-	-	-
AST	5	2.5	63
CAL	6	3.0	75
PMT	1	0.5	13
DMT	2	1.0	25
PHAL	9	0.4	10

B33. Sværdborg I, 1943-44, Area A, NE. Pig.

Element	Count	MNI	%MNI
ANT(shed)	-	-	-
ANT(mass.)	-	-	-
SK+ANT	-	-	-
SK(frag.)	-	-	-
MAX	-	-	-
MAN	6(3)	1.5	75
AT	-	-	-
AX	-	-	-
VERT	-	-	-
SAC	-	-	-
PELV	1(1)	-	-
RIB	1	0.0	42
ST	-	-	-
SC	5(2)	1.5	75
PH	-	-	-
DH	1	0.5	25
PR	-	-	-
DR	3	1.5	75
PU	2	1.0	50
DU	2	1.0	50
PMC	3	0.38	19
DMC	4	0.5	25
PF	2	1.0	50
DF	3	1.5	75
PT	4	2.0	100
DT	4	2.0	100
FIB	-	-	-
AST	2	1.0	50
CAL	2	1.0	50
PMT	2	0.25	13
DMT	2	0.25	13
PHAL	8	0.2	8

B34. Sværdborg I, 1943-44, Area A, NE. Elk.

Element	Count	MNI	% MNI
ANT(shed)	-	-	-
ANT(mass.)	19(19)	-	-
SK+ANT	-	-	-
SK(frag.)	-	-	-
MAX	-	-	-
MAN	-	-	-
AT	-	-	-
AX	-	-	-
VERT	-	-	-
SAC	-	-	-
PELV	-	-	-
RIB	-	-	-
ST	-	-	-
SC	-	-	-
PH	-	-	-
DH	-	-	-
PR	-	-	-
DR	-	-	-
PU	-	-	-
DU	-	-	-
PMC	1	0.5	50
DMC	2	1.0	100
PF	1	0.5	50
DF	-	-	-
PT	-	-	-
DT	-	-	-
FIB	-	-	-
AST	-	-	-
CAL	1	0.5	50
PMT	-	-	-
DMT	1	0.5	50
PHAL	2	0.08	8

B35. Sværdborg I, 1943-44, Area A, NE. Aurochs.

Element	Count	MNI	%MNI
ANT(shed)	-	-	-
ANT(mass.)	-	-	-
SK+ANT	-	-	-
SK(frag.)	-	-	-
MAX	-	-	-
MAN	-	-	-
AT	-	-	-
AX	-	-	-
VERT	1	0.04	8
SAC	-	-	-
PELV	-	-	-
RIB	-	-	-
ST	-	-	-
SC	1(1)	-	-
PH	-	-	-
DH	1	0.5	100
PR	-	-	-
DR	-	-	-
PU	-	-	-
DU	-	-	-
PMC	1(1)	-	-
DMC	-	-	-
PF	-	-	-
DF	-	-	-
PT	-	-	-
DT	-	-	-
FIB	-	-	-
AST	-	-	-
CAL	-	-	-
PMT	-	-	-
DMT	-	-	-
PHAL	1	0.04	8

Save for 1 PHAL in Sværdborg I, 1943-44, Area A, S this totals
aurochs for Sværdborg I, 1943-44, Area A.

B36. Sværdborg I, 1943-44, Area A, S. Red deer.

Element	Count	MNI	%MNI
ANT(shed)	-	-	-
ANT(mass.)	-	-	-
SK+ANT	-	-	-
SK(frag.)	-	-	-
MAX	-	-	-
MAN	-	-	-
AT	1(1)	-	-
AX	-	-	-
VERT	-	-	-
SAC	-	-	-
PELV	-	-	-
RIB	1(1)	-	-
ST	-	-	-
SC	-	-	-
PH	1	0.5	13
DH	1	0.5	13
PR	-	-	-
DR	-	-	-
PU	1	0.5	13
DU	1	0.5	13
PMC	3	1.5	38
DMC	8	4.0	100
PF	-	-	-
DF	-	-	-
PT	2	1.0	25
DT	2	1.0	25
FIB	-	-	-
AST	2	1.0	25
CAL	1	0.5	13
PMT	-	-	-
DMT	4	2.0	50
PHAL	6	0.25	6

B37. Sværdborg I, 1943-44, Area A, S. Roe deer.

Element	Count	MNI	%MNI
ANT(shed)	-	-	-
ANT(mass.)	4(3)	-	-
SK+ANT	6	-	-
SK(frag.)	-	-	-
MAX	-	-	-
MAN	1	0.5	20
AT	-	-	-
AX	-	-	-
VERT	5	0.2	8
SAC	-	-	-
PELV	5(3)	1.0	40
RIB	1	0.04	2
ST	-	-	-
SC	4	2.0	80
PH	4	2.0	80
DH	5	2.5	100
PR	3	1.5	60
DR	5	2.5	100
PU	2	1.0	40
DU	2	1.0	40
PMC	4	2.0	80
DMC	5	2.5	100
PF	2	1.0	40
DF	1	0.5	20
PT	5	2.5	100
DT	2	1.0	40
FIB	-	-	-
AST	4	2.0	80
CAL	5	2.5	100
PMT	2	1.0	40
DMT	2	1.0	40
PHAL	12	0.5	20

B38. Sværdborg I, 1943-44, Area A, S. Pig.

Element	Count	MNI	%MNI
ANT(shed)	-	-	-
ANT(mass.)	-	-	-
SK+ANT	-	-	-
SK(frag.)	-	-	-
MAX	-	-	-
MAN	2(2)	-	-
AT	-	-	-
AX	-	-	-
VERT	-	-	-
SAC	-	-	-
PELV	2(1)	0.5	33
RIB	1	0.04	3
ST	-	-	-
SC	2	1.0	66
PH	-	-	-
DH	3	1.5	100
PR	-	-	-
DR	1	0.5	33
PU	-	-	-
DU	-	-	-
PMC	5	0.63	42
DMC	5	0.63	42
PF	2	1.0	66
DF	-	-	-
PT	1	0.5	33
DT	3	1.5	100
FIB	1(1)	-	-
AST	1	0.5	33
CAL	2	1.0	66
PMT	-	-	-
DMT	2	0.25	17
PHAL	17	0.35	23

B39. Sværdborg I, 1943-44, Area A, S. Elk.

Element	Count	MNI	%MNI
ANT(shed)	-	-	-
ANT(mass.)	-	-	-
SK+ANT	-	-	-
SK(frag.)	-	-	-
MAX	-	-	-
MAN	-	-	-
AT	-	-	-
AX	-	-	-
VERT	-	-	-
SAC	-	-	-
PELV	-	-	-
RIB	-	-	-
ST	-	-	-
SC	-	-	-
PH	-	-	-
DH	-	-	-
PR	-	-	-
DR	-	-	-
PU	-	-	-
DU	-	-	-
PMC	1(1)	-	-
DMC	1(1)	-	-
PF	-	-	-
DF	-	-	-
PT	2	1.0	100
DT	2	1.0	100
FIB	1	0.5	50
AST	-	-	-
CAL	2	1.0	100
PMT	-	-	-
DMT	-	-	-
PHAL	-	-	-

B40. Sværdborg I, 1943-44, Area B. Red deer.

Element	Count	MNI	%MNI
ANT(shed)	-	-	-
ANT(mass.)	9(9)	-	-
SK+ANT	-	-	-
SK(frag.)	-	-	-
MAX	-	-	-
MAN	3(3)	-	-
AT	-	-	-
AX	-	-	-
VERT	3	0.12	5
SAC	1	1.0	40
PELV	1(1)	-	-
RIB	-	-	-
ST	-	-	-
SC	-	-	-
PH	-	-	-
DH	-	-	-
PR	-	-	-
DR	-	-	-
PU	-	-	-
DU	-	-	-
PMC	-	-	-
DMC	5	2.5	100
PF	-	-	-
DF	1	0.5	20
PT	-	-	-
DT	2	1.0	40
FIB	-	-	-
AST	1	0.5	20
CAL	3	1.5	60
PMT	-	-	-
DMT	5	2.5	100
PHAL	6	0.25	10

B41. Sværdborg I, 1943-44, Area B. Roe deer.

Element	Count	MNI	%MNI
ANT(shed)	-	-	-
ANT(mass.)	-	-	-
SK+ANT	1	-	-
SK(frag.)	1	-	-
MAX	-	-	-
MAN	-	-	-
AT	-	-	-
AX	-	-	-
VERT	1	0.2	5
SAC	-	-	-
PELV	4(3)	0.5	13
RIB	1(1)	-	-
ST	-	-	-
SC	6(5)	0.5	13
PH	4	2.0	50
DH	7	3.5	87
PR	3	1.5	38
DR	4	2.0	50
PU	2	1.0	25
DU	-	-	-
PMC	7	3.5	87
DMC	8	4.0	100
PF	1	0.5	13
DF	3	1.5	38
PT	1	0.5	13
DT	-	-	-
FIB	-	-	-
AST	-	-	-
CAL	-	-	-
PMT	4	2.0	50
DMT	5	2.5	62
PHAL	3	0.12	3

B42. Sværdborg I, 1943-44, Area B. Pig.

Element	Count	MNI	%MNI
ANT(shed)	-	-	-
ANT(mass.)	-	-	-
SK+ANT	-	-	-
SK(frag.)	-	-	-
MAX	-	-	-
MAN	9(7)	1.0	40
AT	-	-	-
AX	-	-	-
VERT	1	0.04	2
SAC	1(1)	-	-
PELV	-	-	-
RIB	-	-	-
ST	-	-	-
SC	7(4)	1.5	60
PH	1	0.5	20
DH	1	0.5	20
PR	-	-	-
DR	4	2.0	80
PU	-	-	-
DU	1	0.5	20
PMC	3	0.38	15
DMC	3	0.38	15
PF	3	1.5	60
DF	1	0.5	20
PT	-	-	-
DT	2	1.0	40
FIB	3(1)	1.0	40
AST	4	2.0	80
CAL	5	2.5	100
PMT	4	0.5	20
DMT	6	0.75	30
PHAL	8	0.17	7

B43. Sværdborg I, 1943-44, Area B. Elk.

Element	Count	MNI	%MNI
ANT(shed)	-	-	-
ANT(mass.)	10(10)	-	-
SK+ANT	-	-	-
SK(frag.)	1	-	-
MAX	-	-	-
MAN	1(1)	-	-
AT	1	1.0	100
AX	-	-	-
VERT	1	0.04	4
SAC	-	-	-
PELV	-	-	-
RIB	3(2)	0.04	4
ST	-	-	-
SC	1(1)	-	-
PH	-	-	-
DH	-	-	-
PR	1	0.5	50
DR	1	0.5	50
PU	-	-	-
DU	-	-	-
PMC	-	-	-
DMC	2(2)	-	-
PF	2	1.0	100
DF	-	-	-
PT	-	-	-
DT	2	1.0	100
FIB	-	-	-
AST	-	-	-
CAL	2	1.0	100
PMT	-	-	-
DMT	3(2)	0.5	50
PHAL	1	0.04	4

B44. Sværdborg I, 1943-44, Area B. Aurochs.

Element	Count	MNI	%MNI
ANT(shed)	-	-	-
ANT(mass.)	-	-	-
SK+ANT	-	-	-
SK(frag.)	-	-	-
MAX	-	-	-
MAN	-	-	-
AT	-	-	-
AX	-	-	-
VERT	1	0.16	55
SAC	-	-	-
PELV	-	-	-
RIB	1(1)	-	-
ST	-	-	-
SC	-	-	-
PH	-	-	-
DH	-	-	-
PR	-	-	-
DR	-	-	-
PU	-	-	-
DU	-	-	-
PMC	-	-	-
DMC	1(1)	-	-
PF	-	-	-
DF	-	-	-
PT	-	-	-
DT	-	-	-
FIB	-	-	-
AST	-	-	-
CAL	-	-	-
PMT	-	-	-
DMT	1(1)	-	-
PHAL	7	0.3	100

B45. Sværdborg I, 1943-44, Area C, NE. Red deer.

Element	Count	MNI	%MNI
ANT(shed)	-	-	-
ANT(mass.)	4(3)	-	-
SK+ANT	-	-	-
SK(frag.)	-	-	-
MAX	-	-	-
MAN	1(1)	-	-
AT	-	-	-
AX	-	-	-
VERT	1	0.04	1
SAC	1	1.0	33
PELV	1(1)	-	-
RIB	1(1)	-	-
ST	-	-	-
SC	-	-	-
PH	-	-	-
DH	1	0.5	17
PR	1	0.5	17
DR	1	0.5	17
PU	-	-	-
DU	-	-	-
PMC	-	-	-
DMC	7(1)	3.0	100
PF	-	-	-
DF	-	-	-
PT	1	0.5	17
DT	-	-	-
FIB	-	-	-
AST	1	0.5	17
CAL	-	-	-
PMT	-	-	-
DMT	7(1)	3.0	100
PHAL	3	0.13	4

B46. Sværdborg I, 1943-44, Area C, NE. Roe deer.

Element	Count	MNI	%MNI
ANT(shed)	-	-	-
ANT(mass.)	16(13)	-	-
SK+ANT	6	-	-
SK(frag.)	7(7)	-	-
MAX	1	0.5	8
MAN	14(13)	0.5	8
AT	-	-	-
AX	-	-	-
VERT	3	0.13	2
SAC	-	-	-
PELV	2(2)	-	-
RIB	3(1)	0.08	1
ST	-	-	-
SC	15(8)	3.5	58
PH	7	3.5	58
DH	10(1)	4.5	75
PR	7	3.5	58
DR	8	4.0	67
PU	4	2.0	33
DU	3	1.5	25
PMC	6	3.0	50
DMC	8	4.0	67
PF	1	0.5	8
DF	6(1)	2.5	42
PT	7	3.5	58
DT	11	5.5	92
FIB	-	-	-
AST	8	4.0	67
CAL	12	6.0	100
PMT	4	2.0	33
DMT	5	2.5	42
PHAL	15	0.63	11

B47. Sværdborg I, 1943-44, Area C, NE. Pig.

Element	Count	MNI	%MNI
ANT(shed)	-	-	-
ANT(mass.)	-	-	-
SK+ANT	-	-	-
SK(frag.)	2(2)	-	-
MAX	4(3)	0.5	10
MAN	8(5)	1.5	30
AT	1	1.0	20
AX	-	-	-
VERT	6	0.24	5
SAC	1(1)	-	-
PELV	3(3)	-	-
RIB	-	-	-
ST	-	-	-
SC	15(14)	0.5	10
PH	6	3.0	60
DH	4	2.0	40
PR	3	1.5	30
DR	2	1.0	20
PU	-	-	-
DU	3	1.5	30
PMC	5	0.63	13
DMC	5	0.63	13
PF	-	-	-
DF	1	0.5	10
PT	1	0.5	10
DT	1	0.5	10
FIB	2	1.0	20
AST	6	3.0	60
CAL	10	5.0	100
PMT	3	0.38	8
DMT	3	0.38	8
PHAL	25	0.52	10

B48. Sværdborg I, 1943-44, Area C, NE. Elk.

Element	Count	MNI	%MNI
ANT(shed)	-	-	-
ANT(mass.)	9(9)	-	-
SK+ANT	-	-	-
SK(frag.)	-	-	-
MAX	-	-	-
MAN	1	0.5	100
AT	-	-	-
AX	-	-	-
VERT	-	-	-
SAC	-	-	-
PELV	-	-	-
RIB	-	-	-
ST	-	-	-
SC	-	-	-
PH	-	-	-
DH	-	-	-
PR	-	-	-
DR	-	-	-
PU	-	-	-
DU	-	-	-
PMC	-	-	-
DMC	-	-	-
PF	-	-	-
DF	-	-	-
PT	-	-	-
DT	-	-	-
FIB	-	-	-
AST	1	0.5	100
CAL	-	-	-
PMT	-	-	-
DMT	1	0.5	100
PHAL	-	-	-

B49. Sværdborg I, 1943-44, Area C, SE. Red deer.

Element	Count	MNI	%MNI
ANT(shed)	-	-	-
ANT(mass.)	2(2)	-	-
SK+ANT	-	-	-
SK(frag.)	-	-	-
MAX	-	-	-
MAN	-	-	-
AT	-	-	-
AX	-	-	-
VERT	-	-	-
SAC	-	-	-
PELV	-	-	-
RIB	-	-	-
ST	-	-	-
SC	-	-	-
PH	-	-	-
DH	-	-	-
PR	-	-	-
DR	-	-	-
PU	-	-	-
DU	-	-	-
PMC	-	-	-
DMC	-	-	-
PF	-	-	-
DF	-	-	-
PT	-	-	-
DT	-	-	-
FIB	-	-	-
AST	-	-	-
CAL	-	-	-
PMT	-	-	-
DMT	-	-	-
PHAL	2	-	-

B50. Sværdborg I, 1943-44, Area C, SE. Roe deer.

Element	Count	MNI	%MNI
ANT(shed)	-	-	-
ANT(mass.)	6(5)	-	-
SK+ANT3	-	-	
SK(frag.)	2	-	-
MAX	-	-	-
MAN	4(4)	-	-
AT	-	-	-
AX	-	-	-
VERT	2	0.08	4
SAC	-	-	-
PELV	-	-	-
RIB	-	-	-
ST	-	-	-
SC	2(2)	-	-
PH	1	0.5	25
DH	4(2)	1.0	50
PR	1	0.5	25
DR	2	1.0	50
PU	-	-	-
DU	-	-	-
PMC	3	1.5	75
DMC	4	2.0	100
PF	1	0.5	25
DF	1	0.5	25
PT	-	-	-
DT	-	-	-
FIB	-	-	-
AST	1	0.5	25
CAL	-	-	-
PMT	2	1.0	50
DMT	3	1.5	75
PHAL	12	0.5	25

B51. Sværdborg I, 1943-44, Area C, SE. Pig.

Element	Count	MNI	%MNI
ANT(shed)	-	-	-
ANT(mass.)	-	-	-
SK+ANT	-	-	-
SK(frag.)	2(2)	-	-
MAX	-	-	-
MAN	1(1)	-	-
AT	1	1.0	100
AX	-	-	-
VERT	5	0.2	20
SAC	-	-	-
PELV	1(1)	-	-
RIB	-	-	-
ST	1	1.0	100
SC	-	-	-
PH	-	-	-
DH	1	0.5	50
PR	2	1.0	100
DR	-	-	-
PU	2	1.0	100
DU	1	0.5	50
PMC	1	0.13	13
DMC	1	0.13	13
PF	-	-	-
DF	-	-	-
PT	1	0.5	50
DT	2	1.0	100
FIB	-	-	-
AST	1	0.5	50
CAL	1	0.5	50
PMT	2	0.25	25
DMT	2	0.25	25
PHAL	16	0.33	33

B52. Sværdborg I, 1943-44, Area C, SW. Red deer.

Element	Count	MNI	%MNI
ANT(shed)	-	-	-
ANT(mass.)	4(4)	-	-
SK+ANT	-	-	-
SK(frag.)	-	-	-
MAX	-	-	-
MAN	-	-	-
AT	-	-	-
AX	-	-	-
VERT	2	0.1	3
SAC	-	-	-
PELV	-	-	-
RIB	6(4)	0.08	2
ST	-	-	-
SC	-	-	-
PH	-	-	-
DH	-	-	-
PR	-	-	-
DR	-	-	-
PU	-	-	-
DU	-	-	-
PMC	-	-	-
DMC	11(3)	4.0	100
PF	-	-	-
DF	-	-	-
PT	-	-	-
DT	-	-	-
FIB	-	-	-
AST	-	-	-
CAL	-	-	-
PMT	-	-	-
DMT	11(3)	4.0	100
PHAL	11	0.5	12

B53. Sværdborg I, 1943-44, Area C, SW. Roe deer.

Element	Count	MNI	%MNI
ANT(shed)	-	-	-
ANT(mass.)	12(7)	-	-
SK+ANT	2	-	-
SK(frag.)	10	-	-
MAX	-	-	-
MAN	10(9)	0.5	4
AT	-	-	-
AX	-	-	-
VERT	15(1)	0.6	5
SAC	-	-	-
PELV	7(7)	-	-
RIB	13(10)	0.1	0
ST	-	-	-
SC	10(4)	3.0	25
PH	13	6.5	54
DH	9	4.5	37
PR	9	4.5	37
DR	13	6.5	54
PU	3	1.5	13
DU	1	0.5	4
PMC	11	5.5	46
DMC	24	12.0	100
PF	6	3.0	25
DF	10	5.0	42
PT	8	4.0	33
DT	4	2.0	17
FIB	-	-	-
AST	12	6.0	50
CAL	18	9.0	75
PMT	5	2.5	20
DMT	19(1)	9.0	75
PHAL	64	2.7	23

B54. Sværdborg I, 1943-44, Area C, SW. Pig.

Element	Count	MNI	%MNI
ANT(shed)	-	-	-
ANT(mass.)	-	-	-
SK+ANT	-	-	-
SK(frag.)	7	-	-
MAX	-	-	-
MAN	7(6)	0.5	15
AT	1	1.0	30
AX	-	-	-
VERT	13	0.5	15
SAC	-	-	-
PELV	2(2)	-	-
RIB	3	0.1	3
ST	2(2)	-	-
SC	1	0.5	15
PH	1	0.5	15
DH	1	0.5	15
PR	-	-	-
DR	1	0.5	15
PU	2	1.0	30
DU	1	0.5	15
PMC	22	2.75	85
DMC	24	3.0	92
PF	-	-	-
DF	-	-	-
PT	1	0.5	15
DT	2	1.0	30
FIB	4(1)	1.5	46
AST	5	2.5	77
CAL	6	3.0	92
PMT	25	3.12	96
DMT	26	3.25	100
PHAL	93	1.94	60

B55. Sværdborg I, 1943-44, Area C, SW. Elk.

Element	Count	MNI	%MNI
ANT(shed)	-	-	-
ANT(mass.)	-	-	-
SK+ANT	-	-	-
SK(frag.)	1	-	-
MAX	-	-	-
MAN	-	-	-
AT	-	-	-
AX	-	-	-
VERT	1	0.04	8
SAC	-	-	-
PELV	-	-	-
RIB	4(4)	-	-
ST	-	-	-
SC	-	-	-
PH	-	-	-
DH	-	-	-
PR	-	-	-
DR	-	-	-
PU	-	-	-
DU	-	-	-
PMC	-	-	-
DMC	2(2)	-	-
PF	-	-	-
DF	-	-	-
PT	1	0.5	100
DT	1	0.5	100
FIB	-	-	-
AST	1	0.5	100
CAL	1	0.5	100
PMT	-	-	-
DMT	2(2)	-	-
PHAL	2(1)	0.04	8

B56. Sværdborg I, 1943-44, Area C. Aurochs.

Element	Count	MNI	%MNI
ANT(shed)	-	-	-
ANT(mass.)	-	-	-
SK+ANT	-	-	-
SK(frag.)	-	-	-
MAX	-	-	-
MAN	-	-	-
AT	-	-	-
AX	-	-	-
VERT	1	0.04	8
SAC	-	-	-
PELV	-		-
RIB	7(7)	-	-
ST	-	-	-
SC	-	-	-
PH	-	-	-
DH	-	-	-
PR	-	-	-
DR	1	0.5	100
PU	-	-	-
DU	-	-	-
PMC	-	-	-
DMC	1	0.5	100
PF	-	-	-
DF	-	-	-
PT	-	-	-
DT	-	-	-
FIB	-	-	-
AST	-	-	-
CAL	-	-	-
PMT	-	-	-
DMT	-	-	-
PHAL	5	0.2	40

B57. Sværdborg II. Red deer.

Element	Count	MNI	%MNI
ANT(shed)	1	-	-
ANT(mass.)	31	-	-
SK+ANT	-	-	-
SK(frag.)	-	-	-
MAX	-	-	-
MAN	-	-	-
AT	-	-	-
AX	-	-	-
VERT	-	-	-
SAC	-	-	-
PELV	1	0.5	14
RIB	-	-	-
ST	-	-	-
SC	-	-	-
PH	1	0.5	14
DH	1	0.5	14
PR	1	0.5	14
DR	1	0.5	14
PU	-	-	-
DU	-	-	-
PMC	-	-	-
DMC	-	-	-
PF	-	-	-
DF	-	-	-
PT	7	3.5	100
DT	7	3.5	100
FIB	-	-	-
AST	-	-	-
CAL	-	-	-
PMT	2	1.0	28
DMT	2	1.0	28
PHAL	5	0.3	7

B58. Sværdborg II. Roe deer.

Element	Count	MNI	%MNI
ANT(shed)	-	-	-
ANT(mass.)	2	-	-
SK+ANT	-	-	-
SK(frag.)	2	-	-
MAX	-	-	-
MAN	1	0.5	20
AT	-	-	-
AX	-	-	-
VERT	-	-	-
SAC	-	-	-
PELV	2	1.0	40
RIB	-	-	-
ST	-	-	-
SC	1	0.5	20
PH	-	-	-
DH	1	0.5	20
PR	2	1.0	40
DR	3	1.5	60
PU	-	-	-
DU	1	0.5	20
PMC	-	-	-
DMC	-	-	-
PF	2	1.0	40
DF	2	1.0	40
PT	1	0.5	20
DT	1	0.5	20
FIB	-	-	-
AST	1	0.5	20
CAL	5	2.5	100
PMT	1	0.5	20
DMT	1	0.5	20
PHAL	-	-	-

B59. Sværdborg II. Pig.

Element	Count	MNI	%MNI
ANT(shed)			
ANT(mass.)			
SK+ANT			
SK(frag.)	-	-	-
MAX	-	-	-
MAN	-	-	-
AT	-	-	-
AX	-	-	-
VERT	-	-	-
SAC	-	-	-
PELV	-	-	-
RIB	1	0.03	1
ST	-	-	-
SC	2	1.0	50
PH	3	1.5	75
DH	3	1.5	75
PR	-	-	-
DR	-	-	-
PU	-	-	-
DU	-	-	-
PMC	3	0.38	19
DMC	3	0.38	19
PF	3	1.5	75
DF	4	2.0	100
PT	-	-	-
DT	1	0.5	25
FIB	-	-	-
AST	-	-	-
CAL	-	-	-
PMT	-	-	-
DMT	-	-	-
PHAL	2	0.04	2

B60. Lundby I. Red deer.

Element	Count	MNI	%MNI
ANT(shed)	-	-	-
ANT(mass.)	-	-	-
SK+ANT	-	-	-
SK(frag.)	-	-	-
MAX	-	-	-
MAN	-	-	-
AT	2(2)	-	-
AX	2	2.0	50
VERT	4	0.2	5
SAC	-	-	-
PELV	4(4)	-	-
RIB	-	-	-
ST	-	-	-
SC	7	3.5	88
PH	-	-	-
DH	4	2.0	50
PR	8	4.0	100
DR	6	3.0	75
PU	1	0.5	13
DU	3(1)	1.0	25
PMC	-	-	-
DMC	6(3)	1.5	38
PF	4	2.0	50
DF	1	0.5	13
PT	2(1)	0.5	13
DT	1	0.5	13
FIB	-	-	-
AST	5	2.5	63
CAL	6(6)	-	-
PMT	3	1.5	38
DMT	5(2)	1.5	38
PHAL	29(20)	0.4	10

B61. Lundby I. Roe deer.

Element	Count	MNI	%MNI
ANT(shed)	-	-	-
ANT(mass.)	-	-	-
SK+ANT	-	-	-
SK(frag.)	-	-	-
MAX	3(1)	1.0	7
MAN	3(1)	1.0	7
AT	3(3)	-	-
AX	3	3.0	22
VERT	3(2)	0.0	0
SAC	-	-	-
PELV	14(14)	-	-
RIB	-	-	-
ST	-	-	-
SC	26(1)	12.5	93
PH	7	3.5	26
DH	27	13.5	100
PR	8(1)	3.5	26
DR	7	3.5	26
PU	6	3.0	22
DU	6	3.0	22
PMC	3	1.5	11
DMC	6(1)	2.5	19
PF	13	6.5	48
DF	18(1)	8.5	63
PT	3	1.5	11
DT	10	5.0	37
FIB	-	-	-
AST	9	4.5	33
CAL	12(2)	5.0	37
PMT	5(1)	2.0	15
DMT	9(3)	3.0	22
PHAL	15(3)	0.5	4

B62. Lundby I. Pig.

Element	Count	MNI	%MNI
ANT(shed)			
ANT(mass.)			
SK+ANT			
SK(frag.)	-	-	-
MAX	1	0.5	2
MAN	-	-	-
AT	4(3)	1.0	4
AX	2	2.0	9
VERT	-	-	-
SAC	-	-	-
PELV	48(48)	-	-
RIB	-	-	-
ST	-	-	-
SC	54(12)	21.0	89
PH	7	3.5	15
DH	32(1)	15.5	66
PR	20	10.0	43
DR	21	10.5	45
PU	12	6.0	25
DU	33	16.5	70
PMC	8	1.0	4
DMC	-	-	-
PF	20	10.0	43
DF	29(3)	13.0	55
PT	27(3)	12.0	51
DT	47	23.5	100
FIB	1	0.5	2
AST	48(2)	23.0	98
CAL	48(9)	18.5	79
PMT	11	1.5	6
DMT	-	-	-
PHAL	47(21)	0.5	2

B63. Lundby I. Elk.

Element	Count	MNI	%MNI
ANT(shed)	-	-	-
ANT(mass.)	-	-	-
SK+ANT	-	-	-
SK(frag.)	-	-	-
MAX	-	-	-
MAN	1	0.5	5
AT	6(3)	3.0	30
AX	3(2)	1.0	10
VERT	3(2)	0.0	0
SAC	-	-	-
PELV	20(20)	-	-
RIB	1	0.0	0
ST	-	-	-
SC	24(4)	10.0	100
PH	6	3.0	30
DH	14	7.0	70
PR	6(1)	2.5	25
DR	17(1)	8.0	80
PU	6	3.0	30
DU	11(3)	4.0	40
PMC	-	-	-
DMC	3(2)	0.5	5
PF	4	2.0	20
DF	12(2)	5.0	50
PT	11	5.5	55
DT	10	5.0	50
FIB	-	-	-
AST	19	9.5	95
CAL	13(2)	5.5	55
PMT	-	-	-
DMT	8(6)	1.0	10
PHAL	62(52)	0.4	4

B64. Lundby I. Aurochs.

Element	Count	MNI	%MNI
ANT(shed)	-	-	-
ANT(mass.)	-	-	-
SK+ANT	-	-	-
SK(frag.)	-	-	-
MAX	-	-	-
MAN	-	-	-
AT	4(3)	1.0	20
AX	5	5.0	100
VERT	4(1)	0.1	2
SAC	-	-	-
PELV	22(22)	-	-
RIB	-	-	-
ST	-	-	-
SC	6	3.0	60
PH	1	0.5	10
DH	9(2)	3.5	70
PR	7(2)	2.5	50
DR	3(1)	1.0	20
PU	2(1)	0.5	10
DU	4	2.0	40
PMC	5(1)	2.0	40
DMC	5(1)	2.0	40
PF	4	2.0	40
DF	13(3)	5.0	100
PT	3(1)	1.0	20
DT	4	2.0	40
FIB	-	-	-
AST	8	4.0	80
CAL	12(3)	4.5	90
PMT	2	1.0	20
DMT	3(1)	1.0	20
PHAL	120(82)	1.5	30

B65. Lundby II. Red deer.

Element	Count	MNI	%MNI
ANT(shed)	-	-	-
ANT(mass.)	8	-	-
SK+ANT	-	-	-
SK(frag.)	3	-	-
MAX	-	-	-
MAN	-	-	-
AT	1	1.0	29
AX	-	-	-
VERT	4	0.2	6
SAC	-	-	-
PELV	3	1.5	43
RIB	4	0.2	6
ST	-	-	-
SC	5	2.5	71
PH	-	-	-
DH	7	3.5	100
PR	-	-	-
DR	1	0.5	14
PU	-	-	-
DU	-	-	-
PMC	-	-	-
DMC	-	-	-
PF	5	2.5	71
DF	2	1.0	29
PT	-	-	-
DT	2	1.0	29
FIB	-	-	-
AST	-	-	-
CAL	4	2.0	57
PMT	1	0.5	14
DMT	-	-	-
PHAL	12	0.5	14

B66. Lundby II. Roe deer.

Element	Count	MNI	%MNI
ANT(shed)	-	-	-
ANT(mass.)	5	-	-
SK+ANT	-	-	-
SK(frag.)	7	-	-
MAX	2(2)	-	-
MAN	6	3.0	67
AT	1	1.0	22
AX	-	-	-
VERT	2	0.1	0
SAC	-	-	-
PELV	2	1.0	22
RIB	3	0.1	0
ST	-	-	-
SC	9	4.5	100
PH	-	-	-
DH	6	3.0	67
PR	-	-	-
DR	-	-	-
PU	-	-	-
DU	-	-	-
PMC	3	1.5	33
DMC	1	0.5	11
PF	3	1.5	33
DF	4	2.0	44
PT	2	1.0	22
DT	5	2.5	55
FIB	-	-	-
AST	1	0.5	11
CAL	2	1.0	22
PMT	2	1.0	22
DMT	1	0.5	11
PHAL	6	0.25	5

B67. Lundby II. Pig.

Element	Count	MNI	%MNI
ANT(shed)			
ANT(mass.)			
SK+ANT			
SK(frag.)	27	-	-
MAX	8(8)	-	-
MAN	17	8.5	94
AT	5	5.0	56
AX	-	-	-
VERT	26	1.0	11
SAC	-	-	-
PELV	14	7.0	78
RIB	7	0.25	3
ST	-	-	-
SC	18	9.0	100
PH	8	4.0	44
DH	13	6.5	72
PR	7	3.5	39
DR	10	5.0	56
PU	3	1.5	17
DU	3	1.5	17
PMC	15	1.9	21
DMC	15	1.9	21
PF	8	4.0	44
DF	9	4.5	50
PT	10	5.0	56
DT	14	7.0	78
FIB	1	0.5	6
AST	10	5.0	56
CAL	6	3.0	33
PMT	15	1.9	21
DMT	15	1.9	21
PHAL	23	0.5	6

B68. Lundby II. Elk.

Element	Count	MNI	%MNI
ANT(shed)	l	-	-
ANT(mass.)	16	-	-
SK+ANT	-	-	-
SK(frag.)	4	-	-
MAX	1(1)	-	-
MAN	1	0.5	13
AT	1	1.0	25
AX	1	1.0	25
VERT	25	1.0	25
SAC	-	-	-
PELV	7	3.5	88
RIB	6	0.2	5
ST	-	-	-
SC	8	4.0	100
PH	3	1.5	38
DH	5	2.5	63
PR	4	2.0	50
DR	3	1.5	38
PU	-	-	-
DU	-	-	-
PMC	-	-	-
DMC	4	2.0	50
PF	4	2.0	50
DF	6	3.0	75
PT	3	1.5	38
DT	4	2.0	50
FIB	-	-	-
AST	3	1.5	38
CAL	2	1.0	25
PMT	2	1.0	25
DMT	4	2.0	50
PHAL	19	0.8	20

B69. Lundby II. Aurochs.

Element	Count	MNI	%MNI
ANT(shed)	-	-	-
ANT(mass.)	-	-	-
SK+ANT	-	-	-
SK(frag.)	2	-	-
MAX	-	-	-
MAN	-	-	-
AT	-	-	-
AX	1	1.0	29
VERT	27	1.0	29
SAC	-	-	-
PELV	7	3.5	100
RIB	6	0.2	6
ST	-	-	-
SC	5	2.5	71
PH	-	-	-
DH	1	0.5	14
PR	-	-	-
DR	-	-	-
PU	2	1.0	29
DU	-	-	-
PMC	-	-	-
DMC	1	0.5	14
PF	1	0.5	14
DF	-	-	-
PT	-	-	-
DT	1	0.5	14
FIB	1	0.5	14
AST	1	0.5	14
CAL	3	1.5	43
PMT	2	1.0	29
DMT	-	-	-
PHAL	14	0.6	17

B70. Skottemarke. Elk.

Element	Count	MNI	%MNI
ANT(shed)	-	-	-
ANT(mass.)	-	-	-
SK+ANT	-	-	-
SK(frag.)	1	-	-
MAX	2	1	20
MAN	4	2	40
AT	-	-	-
AX	-	-	-
VERT	79	3.3	66
SAC	2	2.0	40
PELV	6	3.0	60
RIB	66	2.5	50
ST	1	1.0	20
SC	6	3.0	60
PH	5	2.5	50
DH	4	2.0	40
PR	4	2.0	40
DR	6	3.0	60
PU	5	2.5	50
DU	6	3.0	60
PMC	-	-	-
DMC	-	-	-
PF	7	3.5	70
DF	9	4.5	90
PT	10	5.0	100
DT	5	2.5	50
FIB	-	-	-
AST	1	0.5	10
CAL	1	0.5	10
PMT	-	-	-
DMT	-	-	-
PHAL	5	0.2	4

B71. Ageröd I:B. Red deer.

Element	Count	MNI	%MNI
ANT(shed)	11(11)	-	-
ANT(mass.)	-	-	-
SK+ANT	-	-	-
SK(frag.)	1	-	-
MAX	-	-	-
MAN	-	-	-
AT	-	-	-
AX	1	1.0	100
VERT	-	-	-
SAC	-	-	-
PELV	-	-	-
RIB	-	-	-
ST	-	-	-
SC	2(2)	-	-
PH	-	-	-
DH	2	1.0	100
PR	-	-	-
DR	-	-	-
PU	-	-	-
DU	-	-	-
PMC	-	-	-
DMC	-	-	-
PF	1	0.5	50
DF	-	-	-
PT	-	-	-
DT	2	1.0	100
FIB	-	-	-
AST	1	0.5	50
CAL	1	0.5	50
PMT	-	-	-
DMT	-	-	-
PHAL	4(3)	-	-

B72. Ageröd I:B. Roe deer.

Element	Count	MNI	%MNI
ANT(shed)	5(5)	-	-
ANT(mass.)	-	-	-
SK+ANT	-	-	-
SK(frag.)	-	-	-
MAX	-	-	-
MAN	1(1)	-	-
AT	-	-	-
AX	-	-	-
VERT	-	-	-
SAC	-	-	-
PELV	-	-	-
RIB	1(1)	-	-
ST	-	-	-
SC	-	-	-
PH	-	-	-
DH	-	-	-
PR	-	-	-
DR	-	-	-
PU	1	0.5	50
DU	1	0.5	50
PMC	-	-	-
DMC	-	-	-
PF	1	0.5	50
DF	-	-	-
PT	2	1.0	100
DT	2	1.0	100
FIB	-	-	-
AST	1	0.5	50
CAL	2(2)	-	-
PMT	1	0.5	50
DMT	1	0.5	50
PHAL	1	0.0	0

B73. Ageröd I:B. Pig.

Element	Count	MNI	%MNI
ANT(shed)			
ANT(mass.)			
SK+ANT			
SK(frag.)	1	-	-
MAX	-	-	-
MAN	-	-	-
AT	-	-	-
AX	-	-	-
VERT	-	-	-
SAC	-	-	-
PELV	-	-	-
RIB	1(1)	-	-
ST	-	-	-
SC	1	0.5	33
PH	-	-	-
DH	2	1.0	66
PR	-	-	-
DR	-	-	-
PU	-	-	-
DU	-	-	-
PMC	-	-	-
DMC	-	-	-
PF	-	-	-
DF	-	-	-
PT	-	-	-
DT	1	0.5	33
FIB	-	-	-
AST	2	1.0	66
CAL	3	1.5	100
PMT	1	0.1	8
DMT	2	0.2	16
PHAL	3(2)	0.0	0

B74. Ageröd I:D. Red deer.

Element	Count	MNI	%MNI
ANT(shed)	-	-	-
ANT(mass.)	-	-	-
SK+ANT	-	-	-
SK(frag.)	6	-	-
MAX	-	-	-
MAN	-	-	-
AT	1(1)	-	-
AX	1(1)	-	-
VERT	8(5)	0.1	6
SAC	-	-	-
PELV	-	-	-
RIB	8(8)	-	-
ST	-	-	-
SC	-	-	-
PH	1	0.5	33
DH	1	0.5	33
PR	1	0.5	33
DR	-	-	-
PU	-	-	-
DU	-	-	-
PMC	-	-	-
DMC	-	-	-
PF	1	0.5	33
DF	1	0.5	33
PT	1	0.5	33
DT	1	0.5	33
FIB	-	-	-
AST	3	1.5	100
CAL	2(1)	0.5	33
PMT	1	0.5	33
DMT	1	0.5	33
PHAL	13(1)	0.5	33

B75. Ageröd I:D. Pig.

Element	Count	MNI	%MNI
ANT(shed)			
ANT(mass.)			
SK+ANT			
SK(frag.)	-	-	-
MAX	2(2)	-	-
MAN	5(5)	-	-
AT	1(1)	-	-
AX	-	-	-
VERT	-	-	-
SAC	-	-	-
PELV	-	-	-
RIB	-	-	-
ST	-	-	-
SC	2(2)	-	-
PH	-	-	-
DH	-	-	-
PR	-	-	-
DR	1	0.5	50
PU	-	-	-
DU	-	-	-
PMC	-	-	-
DMC	-	-	-
PF	-	-	-
DF	-	-	-
PT	-	-	-
DT	-	-	-
FIB	-	-	-
AST	1(1)	-	-
CAL	4(2)	1.0	100
PMT	1	0.12	12
DMT	1	0.12	12
PHAL	-	-	-

B76. Ageröd V. Red deer.

Element	Count	MNI	%MNI
ANT(shed)	2+	-	-
ANT(mass.)	-	-	-
SK+ANT	-	-	-
SK(frag.)	1+	-	-
MAX	-	-	-
MAN	2	1.0	15
AT	2	2.0	31
AX	2	2.0	31
VERT	18	0.7	12
SAC	1	1.0	15
PELV	-	-	-
RIB	21	0.8	12
ST	2	2.0	31
SC	1	0.5	8
PH	5	2.5	38
DH	5	2.5	38
PR	9	4.5	69
DR	9	4.5	69
PU	5	2.5	38
DU	5	2.5	38
PMC	13	6.5	100
DMC	13	6.5	100
PF	4	2.0	31
DF	4	2.0	31
PT	9	4.5	69
DT	9	4.5	69
FIB	2	1.0	15
AST	5	2.5	38
CAL	4	2.0	31
PMT	13	6.5	100
DMT	13	6.5	100
PHAL	26	1.0	15

B77. Ageröd V. Roe deer.

Element	Count	MNI	%MNI
ANT(shed)	-	-	-
ANT(mass.)	-	-	-
SK+ANT	-	-	-
SK(frag.)	1+	-	-
MAX	-	-	-
MAN	4	2.0	100
AT	1	1.0	50
AX	1	1.0	50
VERT	5	0.2	10
SAC	-	-	-
PELV	-	-	-
RIB	5	0.2	10
ST	-	-	-
SC	3	1.5	75
PH	2	1.0	50
DH	2	1.0	50
PR	1	0.5	25
DR	1	0.5	25
PU	2	1.0	50
DU	2	1.0	50
PMC	3	1.5	75
DMC	3	1.5	75
PF	3	1.5	75
DF	3	1.5	75
PT	2	1.0	50
DT	2	1.0	50
FIB	1	0.5	25
AST	-	-	-
CAL	-	-	-
PMT	3	1.5	75
DMT	3	1.5	75
PHAL	10	0.4	20

B78. Ageröd V. Pig.

Element	Count	MNI	%MNI
ANT(shed)			
ANT(mass.)			
SK+ANT			
SK(frag.)	1+	-	-
MAX	-	-	-
MAN	1	0.5	25
AT	-	-	-
AX	1	1.0	50
VERT	4	0.2	10
SAC	-	-	-
PELV	-	-	-
RIB	14	0.5	25
ST	-	-	-
SC	2	1.0	50
PH	4	2.0	100
DH	4	2.0	100
PR	1	0.5	25
DR	1	0.5	25
PU	1	0.5	25
DU	1	0.5	25
PMC	2	0.2	10
DMC	2	0.2	10
PF	2	1.0	50
DF	2	1.0	50
PT	4	2.0	100
DT	4	2.0	100
FIB	-	-	-
AST	2	1.0	50
CAL	1	0.5	25
PMT	1	0.1	5
DMT	1	0.1	5
PHAL	2	0.0	0

B79. Ageröd V. Elk.

Element	Count	MNI	%MNI
ANT(shed)	-	-	-
ANT(mass.)	-	-	-
SK+ANT	-	-	-
SK(frag.)	4	-	-
MAX	-	-	-
MAN	2	1.0	66
AT	1	1.0	66
AX	1	1.0	66
VERT	2	0.0	0
SAC	-	-	-
PELV	-	-	-
RIB	1	0.0	0
ST	-	-	-
SC	-	-	-
PH	3	1.5	100
DH	3	1.5	100
PR	3	1.5	100
DR	3	1.5	100
PU	2	1.0	66
DU	2	1.0	66
PMC	-	-	-
DMC	-	-	-
PF	1	0.5	33
DF	1	0.5	33
PT	1	0.5	33
DT	1	0.5	33
FIB	-	-	-
AST	2	1.0	66
CAL	2	1.0	66
PMT	1	0.5	33
DMT	1	0.5	33
PHAL	4	0.2	13

B80. Segebro. Red deer.

Element	Count	MNI	%MNI
ANT(shed)	10(10)	-	-
ANT(mass.)	-	-	-
SK+ANT	-	-	-
SK(frag.)	30(30)	-	-
MAX	-	-	-
MAN	40	20.0	100
AT	9	9.0	45
AX	4	4.0	20
VERT	55	2.3	12
SAC	4	4.0	20
PELV	20	10.0	50
RIB	28	1.1	6
ST	3	3.0	15
SC	7	3.5	18
PH	20	10.0	50
DH	20	10.0	50
PR	29	14.5	73
DR	29	14.5	73
PU	10	5.0	25
DU	10	5.0	25
PMC	39	18.5	93
DMC	39	18.5	93
PF	26	13.0	65
DF	26	13.0	65
PT	39	18.5	93
DT	39	18.5	93
FIB	-	-	-
AST	23	11.5	58
CAL	20	10.0	50
PMT	35	17.5	88
DMT	35	17.5	88
PHAL	111	4.6	23

B81. Segebro. Roe deer.

Element	Count	MNI	%MNI
ANT(shed)	-	-	-
ANT(mass.)	12(7)	-	-
SK+ANT	-	-	-
SK(frag.)	13	-	-
MAX	-	-	-
MAN	11	5.5	30
AT	6	6.0	33
AX	8	8.0	44
VERT	19	0.8	4
SAC	-	-	-
PELV	13	6.5	36
RIB	13	0.5	3
ST	-	-	-
SC	18	9.0	50
PH	31	15.5	86
DH	31	15.5	86
PR	15	7.5	42
DR	15	7.5	42
PU	8	4.0	22
DU	8	4.0	22
PMC	27	13.5	75
DMC	27	13.5	75
PF	36	18.0	100
DF	36	18.0	100
PT	23	11.5	64
DT	23	11.5	64
FIB	-	-	-
AST	13	6.5	36
CAL	11	5.5	30
PMT	35	17.5	97
DMT	35	17.5	97
PHAL	40	1.7	9

B82. Segebro. Pig.

Element	Count	MNI	%MNI
ANT(shed)			
ANT(mass.)			
SK+ANT			
SK(frag.)	18	-	-
MAX	-	-	-
MAN	27	13.5	93
AT	6	6.0	41
AX	-	-	-
VERT	12	0.5	3
SAC	1	1.0	7
PELV	8	4.0	28
RIB	12	0.4	3
ST	1	1.0	7
SC	14	7.0	48
PH	29	14.5	100
DH	29	14.5	100
PR	15	7.5	51
DR	15	7.5	51
PU	11	5.5	38
DU	11	5.5	38
PMC	16	2.0	14
DMC	16	2.0	14
PF	14	7.0	48
DF	14	7.0	48
PT	15	7.5	51
DT	15	7.5	51
FIB	7	3.5	24
AST	21	10.5	72
CAL	6	3.0	21
PMT	16	2.0	14
DMT	16	2.0	14
PHAL	62	1.3	9

B83. Segebro. Elk.

Element	Count	MNI	%MNI
ANT(shed)	-	-	-
ANT(mass.)	3	-	-
SK+ANT	-	-	-
SK(frag.)	8	-	-
MAX	-	-	-
MAN	6	3.0	100
AT	-	-	-
AX	-	-	-
VERT	2	0.2	7
SAC	-	-	-
PELV	-	-	-
RIB	-	-	-
ST	-	-	-
SC	-	-	-
PH	1	0.5	17
DH	1	0.5	17
PR	-	-	-
DR	-	-	-
PU	2	1.0	33
DU	2	1.0	33
PMC	-	-	-
DMC	-	-	-
PF	-	-	-
DF	-	-	-
PT	-	-	-
DT	-	-	-
FIB	-	-	-
AST	-	-	-
CAL	-	-	-
PMT	4	2.0	66
DMT	4	2.0	66
PHAL	2	-	-

Appendix C

Tools and debitage

This appendix contains the raw database of flint, bone, and antler tools plus debitage. Only sites used in the spatial analysis (Section 6) are included, and only to the extent that these data have not previously been published in readily accessible form.

Abbreviations

AIA	Axe inset of antler
AXA	Antler axe
BAX	Bone axe
BBP	Barbed bone point
BOR	Borer
BRB	Bilaterally retouched blade
BSC	End of blade scraper
BUR	Burin
CAN	Chisel of antler
CAX	Core axe
DBP	Double plain bone point
FAX	Flake axe
FFL	Flint flaker
FHK	Fish hook
FSC	Flake scraper
MIC	Microlith
SBA	Socketed bone axe
SBP	Smooth (plain) bone point
TMI	Triangular Microlith
TUK	Tusk knife
URB	Unilaterally retouched blade

Mullerup Syd

Tools

Section I

Unit		Unit		Unit	
A1	1BSC	C5	2BBP	E4	1SBP
A7	1TUK	C7	1BBP	E5	1FSC, 1SBP
A10	1URB	D1	1CAX, 1DBP	E7	1CAX, 1SBP
B1	1SBP	D3	1BSC	E9	1SBP
B6	1SBP	D5	1SBP	E10	1SBP
B7	1CAN	D8	2SBP	F3	1BSC, 1URB, 2SBP
B9	1FSC	D9	1SBP		
B10	1AIA	E1	4BBP, 2SBP, 1BOR	F4	1URB, 1SBP
C2	1BSC	E2	1BSC	F5	1URB, 1SBP
C3	1BSC	E3	1BUR, 1SBP	F6	1SBP
				F7	1BUR

Unit		Unit		Unit	
F8	1URB	H3	1FSC, 3URB, 1SBP	K1	1FSC, 3URB, 1BBP, 1SBP
G1	1BUR, 1URB, 1SBP, 1FFL	H4	1FSC, 1CAX, 1URB,		
		H5	3FSC, 1BBP	K2	1BSC, 1URB,
G2	1FSC, 1BSC, 1SBP, 1TUK	H6	1URB, 1MIC	K3	1FSC, 1BUR
		H8	1FSC	K4	1FSC, 1BSC, 1URB
G3	2FSC, 1BUR, 1URB,	I1	1FSC, 1CAX, 1URB, 1AXA		
G4	1FSC, 1URB			K5	6BBP, 1SBP, 1SBA
G5	1FSC, 1AXA, 1BBP	I2	2BUR, 1CAX, 3URB, 2AXA		
G6	1CAX,			K6	1FSC, 1URB, 1SBP
G10	1BSC	I3	1FSC, 1CAN		
H1	1BSC, 1BUR, 1URB,	I4	2FSC, 1BUR, 1URB, 1AXA, 1SBP	K7	5BBP
H2	1CAX, 1URB, 1TUK, 1SBP			K9	1TUK
		I7	1BBP	K10	1URB

Section II

Unit		Unit	
I8	1BBP, 1TUK	I10	1BBP, 1SBP
I9	2FSC, 1DBP, 1FHK, 1AXA, 1CAN	K8	1BBP

Section III

Unit		Unit		Unit	
A3	1SBP	C4	1BUR, 2URB	G5	1URB
A5	1URB	C5	1URB, 1CAN	H3	1BBP
A6	1BBP	C6	1FSC, 1FAX	H5	1SBP
A7	1FSC, 1SBP	D2	1FHK		
A9	1FSC	D3	1BUR		
B2	2BUR, 1TUK	D4	1BUR, 2URB		
B3	1URB, 1BBP, 1SBP	D5	1URB, 1BBP		
B4	1FSC, 1URB, 1BBP	D6	1BSC		

Section III continued

B5	1URB, 1MIC		F4	1BSC
C2	1TUK		F6	1TUK

Section IV

Unit			*Unit*	
I2	1AXA		K6	1AXA

Section VII

Unit			*Unit*	
A5	1SBP		F5	1SBP, 1BOR
A6	1SBP		G8	1BUR, 1URB
B2	1FSC		H5	1TUK
B5	1BBP		I4	1URB
C3	1URB		I6	1SBP
D3	1SBA			
D4	1BSC			
D9	1URB			
E2	1URB, 2AIA			
E5	1BBP			

Debitage

Section I

Unit		*Unit*		*Unit*		*Unit*		*Unit*		*Unit*		*Unit*	
A1	141	B1	42	C1	40	D1	126	E1	304	F1	107	G1	114
A2	86	B2	49	C2	65	D2	169	E2	354	F2	226	G2	363
A3	46	B3	90	C3	49	D3	86	E3	115	F3	107	G3	244
A4	63	B4	64	C4	24	D4	160	E4	145	F4	92	G4	266
A5	23	B5	72	C5	36	D5	132	E5	166	F5	86	G5	133
A6	67	B6	60	C6	28	D6	73	E6	43	F6	68	G6	80
A7	94	B7	114	C7	72	D7	47	E7	25	F7	110	G7	115
A8	31	B8	62	C8	34	D8	37	E8	21	F8	41	G8	21
A9	56	B9	33	C9	51	D9	31	E9	49	F9	72	G9	38
A10	19	B10	35	C10	24	D10	38	E10	25	F10	13	G10	18

Unit		*Unit*		*Unit*	
H1	145	I1	151	K1	148
H2	138	I2	275	K2	284
H3	172	I3	176	K3	204
H4	179	I4	191	K4	221
H5	87	I5	48	K5	102
H6	51	I6	50	K6	73
H7	68	I7	55	K7	78
H8	46	I8	36	K8	49
H9	34	I9	33	K9	52
H10	27	I10	17	K10	25

Section II

Unit	
H6	27
H7	31
H8	23
H9	37
H10	22
I6	74
I7	103
I8	352
I9	179
I10	99

Section III

Unit		Unit		Unit		Unit		Unit		Unit	
A1	24	B1	26	C1	?	D4	35	F2	10	H5	18
A2	86	B2	61	C2	51	D5	61	F3	24	I3	18
A3	66	B3	82	C3	42	D6	34	F4	27	I4	11
A4	101	B4	67	C4	63	E1	13	F5	37	I5	19
A5	83	B5	58	C5	53	E2	9	F6	6	K3	11
A6	59	B6	73	C6	56	E3	21	G3	16	K4	11
A7	42	B7	35	C7	50	E4	37	G4	13	K5	8
A8	40	B8	27	D1	?	E5	28	G5	28		
A9	45	B9	21	D2	37	E6	35	H3	14		
A10	11	B10	19	D3	58	F1	5	H4	16		

Section IV

Unit		Unit		Unit	
D1	19	G2	18	K4	9
D2	15	G3	18	K5	10
D3	12	H1	23	K6	8
E1	10	H2	35	K7	7
E2	8	H3	18	K8	4
E3	17	I1	55	K9	4
F1	12	I2	31	K10	0
F2	15	I3	20		
F3	13	K2	15		
G1	12	K3	25		

Section VII

Unit		Unit		Unit		Unit		Unit		Unit		Unit	
A2	7	B4	23	C6	11	D8	4	F2	12	G4	17	H6	4
A3	11	B5	16	C7	12	D9	6	F3	10	G5	11	H7	5
A4	18	B6	9	C8	12	E2	30	F4	8	G6	7	H8	8
A5	13	B7	15	C9	8	E3	27	F5	11	G7	9	H9	7
A6	14	B8	10	D2	21	E4	12	F6	8	G8	7	I2	23
A7	5	B9	9	D3	20	E5	27	F7	8	G9	5	I3	3
A8	7	C2	21	D4	12	E6	11	F8	10	H2	19	I4	18

A9	0	C3	16	D5	12	E7	15	F9	6	H3	16	I5	17
B2	25	C4	14	D6	6	E8	10	G2	23	H4	19	I6	9
B3	15	C5	16	D7	6	E9	5	G3	14	H5	5	I7	13

Unit

I8	10
I9	7
K2	22
K3	15
K4	19
K5	15
K6	14
K7	12
K8	30
K9	14

Ulkestrup I

Debitage (excl. burned flint)

Unit		Unit		Unit		Unit		Unit	
E00,S09	3	V02,S14	22	V04,S11	297	V05,S14	5	V07,S07	89
E01,S09	5	V03,S09	42	V04,S12	305	V06,S07	63	V07,S08	259
E02,S09	1	V03,S10	3	V04,S13	196	V06,S08	147	V07,S09	165
E03,S09	2	V03,S11	82	V04,S14	10	V06,S09	184	V07,S10	444
E04,S09	1	V03,S12	117	V05,S08	72	V06,S10	305	V07,S11	387
V00,S09	3	V03,S13	17	V05,S09	107	V06,S11	229	V07,S12	244
V01,S09	4	V03,S14	12	V05,S10	187	V06,S12	78	V07,S13	100
V02,S09	29	V04,S08	24	V05,S11	745	V06,S13	23	V07,S14	6
V02,S12	31	V04,S09	96	V05,S12	671	V06,S14	18	V07,S15	24
V02,S13	22	V04,S10	77	V05,S13	386	V07,S03	4	V08,S06	38

Unit		Unit		Unit	
V08,S07	101	V09,S09	176	V11,S09	11
V08,S08	328	V09,S10	430	V11,S10	7
V08,S09	236	V09,S11	358	V11,S11	3
V08,S10	380	V09,S12	138	V12,S09	4
V08,S11	405	V10,S08	1		
V08,S12	228	V10,S09	18		
V08,S13	47	V10,S10	263		
V09,S06	8	V10,S11	163		
V09,S07	69	V11,S06	18		
V09,S08	769	V11,S08	25		

Burned flint

Unit		Unit		Unit		Unit		Unit	
V02,S09	6	V04,S09	20	V05,S12	134	V06,S14	1	V07,S15	3
V02,S12	10	V04,S10	24	V05,S13	30	V07,S03	1	V08,S06	2
V02,S13	5	V04,S11	95	V05,S14	1	V07,S07	10	V08,S07	3
V02,S14	16	V04,S12	53	V06,S07	9	V07,S08	18	V08,S08	19
V03,S09	4	V04,S13	23	V06,S08	30	V07,S09	23	V08,S09	20
V03,S11	15	V04,S14	1	V06,S09	37	V07,S10	115	V08,S10	71
V03,S12	34	V05,S08	17	V06,S10	57	V07,S11	37	V08,S11	41
V03,S13	4	V05,S09	22	V06,S11	18	V07,S12	84	V08,S12	10
V03,S14	3	V05,S10	35	V06,S12	2	V07,S13	10	V08,S13	3
V04,S08	2	V05,S11	201	V06,S13	3	V07,S14	1	V09,S07	6

Unit		Unit	
V09,S08	11	V11,S11	1
V09,S09	7		
V09,S10	14		
V09,S11	18		
V09,S12	6		
V10,S10	19		
V10,S11	7		
V11,S06	5		
V11,S08	3		
V11,S09	3		

Ulkestrup II

Debitage

Unit		Unit		Unit		Unit		Unit	
V15,S33	1	V19,S33	42	V21,S31	89	V22,S30	65	V22,S40	3
V16,S32	8	V19,S34	67	V21,S32	128	V22,S31	168	V22,S41	1
V16,S33	18	V19,S35	48	V21,S33	169	V22,S32	669	V22,S42	1
V17,S32	11	V20,S32	40	V21,S34	145	V22,S33	203	V23,S26	3
V17,S33	18	V20,S33	103	V21,S35	125	V22,S34	283	V23,S27	54
V18,S32	15	V20,S34	105	V22,S25	2	V22,S35	160	V23,S28	228
V18,S33	29	V20,S35	84	V22,S26	5	V22,S36	35	V23,S29	871
V18,S34	37	V21,S28	19	V22,S27	16	V22,S37	31	V23,S30	1731
V18,S35	8	V21,S29	20	V22,S28	120	V22,S38	20	V23,S31	581
V19,S32	17	V21,S30	16	V22,S29	105	V22,S39	13	V23,S32	509

Unit		Unit		Unit		Unit	
V23,S33	540	V24,S32	519	V25,S32	118	V26,S32	167
V23,S34	296	V24,S33	340	V25,S33	98	V26,S33	163
V23,S35	345	V24,S34	231	V25,S34	252	V26,S34	153
V23,S36	171	V24,S35	111	V25,S35	300	V26,S35	97
V24,S26	12	V24,S36	246	V25,S36	182	V27,S27	43
V24,S27	42	V25,S27	42	V26,S27	200	V27,S28	278
V24,S28	334	V25,S28	535	V26,S28	1509	V27,S29	250
V24,S29	1701	V25,S29	1246	V26,S29	624	V27,S30	271
V24,S30	1752	V25,S30	570	V26,S30	292	V27,S31	118
V24,S31	411	V25,S31	498	V26,S31	96	V28,S28	23

Unit	
V28,S29	51
V28,S30	98
V28,S31	99
V29,S30	16

Burned flint

Unit		Unit		Unit		Unit		Unit	
V16,S32	1	V19,S35	18	V21,S33	92	V22,S33	97	V23,S29	79
V16,S33	1	V20,S32	11	V21,S34	32	V22,S34	82	V23,S30	66
V17,S33	7	V20,S34	29	V21,S35	32	V22,S35	23	V23,S31	70
V18,S32	2	V20,S35	17	V22,S26	1	V22,S36	6	V23,S32	84
V18,S33	2	V21,S27	1	V22,S27	5	V22,S37	2	V23,S33	143
V18,S34	5	V21,S28	2	V22,S28	25	V22,S38	1	V23,S34	73
V18,S35	1	V21,S29	2	V22,S29	30	V22,S39	1	V23,S35	63
V19,S32	2	V21,S30	5	V22,S30	13	V22,S40	1	V23,S36	18
V19,S33	14	V21,S31	15	V22,S31	32	V23,S27	8	V24,S27	5
V19,S34	21	V21,S32	11	V22,S32	132	V23,S28	45	V24,S28	46

Unit		Unit		Unit		Unit	
V24,S29	337	V25,S29	247	V26,S29	85	V27,S30	36
V24,S30	209	V25,S30	200	V26,S30	77	V27,S31	7

V24,S31	63	V25,S31	84	V26,S31	11	V27,S32	5
V24,S32	109	V25,S32	41	V26,S32	33	V27,S33	5
V24,S33	108	V25,S33	44	V26,S33	58	V28,S28	2
V24,S34	68	V25,S34	154	V26,S34	44	V28,S29	5
V24,S35	27	V25,S35	139	V26,S35	11	V28,S30	5
V24,S36	41	V25,S36	128	V27,S27	7	V28,S31	12
V25,S27	8	V26,S27	17	V27,S28	74	V29,S30	2
V25,S28	97	V26,S28	330	V27,S29	23		

Sværdborg I, 1917-18

Debitage

Section I

Unit		Unit		Unit		Unit		Unit	
A1	139	B1	68	C1	124	D1	179	E1	1051
A2	196	B2	122	C2	90	D2	86	E2	294
A3	140	B3	171	C3	107	D3	138	E3	171
A4	125	B4	132	C4	111	D4	93	E4	190
A5	160	B5	104	C5	152	D5	100	E5	227
A6	70	B6	88	C6	116	D6	106	E6	190
A7	103	B7	60	C7	78	D7	124	E7	290
A8	18	B8	19	C8	55	D8	48	E8	20
A9	23	B9	31	C9	31	D9	73	E9	23
A10	107	B10	51	C10	55	D10	88	E10	124

Unit		Unit		Unit		Unit		Unit	
F1	1084	G1	651	H1	480	J1	686	K1	383
F2	493	G2	563	H2	914	J2	1167	K2	1068
F3	371	G3	331	H3	548	J3	1089	K3	1828
F4	356	G4	577	H4	764	J4	1301	K4	1430
F5	361	G5	729	H5	898	J5	685	K5	1211
F6	23	G6	696	H6	798	J6	222	K6	1245
F7	214	G7	211	H7	365	J7	293	K7	772
F8	102	G8	47	H8	278	J8	208	K8	408
F9	90	G9	53	H9	100	J9	137	K9	310
F10	64	G10	46	H10	108	J10	19	K10	281

Section X

Unit		Unit	
C7	161	E9	203
C8	163	E10	331
C9	286	F7	500
C10	124	F8	604
D7	182	F9	183
D8	222	F10	718
D9	333	G1	551
D10	607	G2	715
E7	314	G3	423
E8	253	G10	405

Section XI

Unit		Unit		Unit		Unit		Unit	
A1	310	C1	456	E1	252	G1	234	J1	128
A2*	1603	C2	331	E2	115	G2	112	J2	125
A3	504	C3	524	E3	488	G3	139	J3	165
A4	630	C4	283	E4	456	G4	136	J4	122
A5	77	C5	121	E5	116	G5	92	J5	97

B1	413	D1	437	F1	175	H1	122	K1	83
B2*		D2	561	F2	287	H2	130	K2	86
B3	566	D3	510	F3	162	H3	107	K3	56
B4	658	D4	577	F4	193	H4	48	K4	115
B5	196	D5	140	F5	70	H5	39	K5	89

*) Joint count for A2+B2

Section XVII

Unit		Unit		Unit	
A7	407	C9	892	F7	420
A8	748	C10	1412	F8	819
A9	1020	D7	1019	F9	387
A10	1016	D8	624	F10	308
B7	695	D9	444		
B8	645	D10	400		
B9	902	E7	692		
B10	793	E8	155		
C7	832	E9	210		
C8	386	E10	214		

Section XVIII

Unit		Unit		Unit		Unit	
A1	129	C3	92	F1	207	H3	197
A2	206	C4	147	F2	280	H4	345
A3	85	D1	215	F3	101	J1	225
A4	123	D2	165	F4	115	J2	708
B1	137	D3	67	G1	262	J3	257
B2	181	D4	124	G2	180	J4	380
B3	153	E1	189	G3	137	K1	273
B4	135	E2	103	G4	230	K2	1265
C1	83	E3	72	H1	276	K3	265
C2	201	E4	181	H2	317	K4	561

Section XIX

Unit		Unit		Unit		Unit	
A1	85	C3	89	F1	174	H3	136
A2	64	C4	89	F2	114	H4	194
A3	41	D1	130	F3	147	J1	325
A4	79	D2	81	F4	137	J2	158
B1	91	D3	71	G1	143	J3	150
B2	80	D4	49	G2	163	J4	186
B3	93	E1	112	G3	182	K1	123
B4	68	E2	134	G4	310	K2	212
C1	95	E3	144	H1	334	K3	116
C2	94	E4	121	H2	200	K4	128

Section XX

Unit		Unit		Unit		Unit	
B1	18	D3	24	G1	42	J3	38
B2	9	D4	36	G2	44	J4	79
B3	24	E1	24	G3	43	K1	56
B4	7	E2	31	G4	60	K2	80
C1	24	E3	19	H1	54	K3	47
C2	17	E4	36	H2	35	K4	51
C3	23	F1	30	H3	36		
C4	23	F2	24	H4	75		
D1	20	F3	31	J1	54		
D2	13	F4	34	J2	63		

Section XXXII

Unit		Unit		Unit	
K7	237	K9	543	K10	1003
K8	641				

Sværdborg I, 1923

Tools

Section XXIII

Unit		Unit	
A4	7MIC, 2SBP	H5	7FSC, 12MIC,
A5	10MIC,		1SBP
B4	2FSC, 10MIC, 2SBP	J5	2FSC, 3MIC
	2BBP	K5	7FSC, 2BSC, 8MIC
B5	3FSC, 6MIC		
C4	10MIC, 1BBP, 1SBP		
C5	4FSC, 12MIC, 2BBP		
D5	9FSC, 1BSC, 16MIC,		
	1BBP, 1SBP		
E5	9FSC, 1BSC, 32MIC,		
	2BBP, 1SBP		
F5	18FSC, 16MIC		
G5	5FSC, 15MIC		

Section XXIV

Unit		Unit	
A1	1MIC, 1BBP, 1SBP	B8	9MIC
A2	1FSC, 1MIC	C1	1BBP, 1SBP
A3	1MIC, 1SBP	C2	1FSC, 1MIC, 2SBP
A4	1FSC, 3MIC, 1SBP	C3	1MIC, 2BBP, 2SBP,
A5	6MIC		1AXA
A8	3MIC	C4	1MIC, 1BBP, 2SBP
B1	1MIC	C5	4MIC, 2BBP, 1SBP
B3	1MIC, 1BBP, 1SBP	C8	1FSC, 10MIC
B4	3FSC, 2MIC		
B5	2MIC		

Section XXXIII

Unit		Unit	
B10	2FSC	D10	1MIC

Section XXXIV

Unit		Unit		Unit	
A5	2FSC, 11MIC	H8	6MIC	K7	2FSC, 7MIC
B5	6FSC, 21MIC	H9	6MIC	K8	1CAX
C5	2FSC, 38MIC	H10	1FSC, 6MIC	K9	1FSC, 3MIC
D5	1FSC, 13MIC	J5	1FSC	K10	1FSC, 3MIC
E5	10MIC	J6	2FSC, 6MIC		
F5	1FSC, 19MIC, 1AXA	J8	1BSC, 3MIC		
G5	1FSC, 9MIC, 1CAX	J9	2MIC, 1CAX		
H5	1FSC, 5MIC	J10	3MIC		

Section XXXIV continued

H6	6FSC, 5MIC	K5	4FSC, 3MIC
H7	2MIC	K6	1BSC, 1MIC

Section XXXV

Unit		Unit		Unit	
A1	1MIC	D2	1FSC, 1BBP, 1SBP	F4	1FSC, 2MIC, 1BBP
A2	2BBP, 2SBP	D3	1FSC, 1CAX		
A5	1MIC	D4	3MIC, 1SBP	F5	2MIC
B2	2SBP, 1SBT, 1AXA	E1	1MIC	G1	2MIC, 3SBP, 1BBP
B4	1BBP, 1SBP	E2	1BSC, 1MIC, 1SBP, 1BAX		
B5	1FSC, 1MIC			G2	1AXA
C2	1MIC, 2SBP	E4	2FSC, 2MIC,	G3	2FSC
C3	1MIC, 2BBP	E5	2MIC, 1SBP	G4	1MIC
C4	2MIC, 1SBP, 1AXA	F1	1FSC	G5	2MIC
D1	1FSC, 1MIC, 1SBP	F2	1MIC, 1BBP	H1	6MIC, 1SBP, 2BBP, 1AXA
		F3	3MIC		
				H2	2FSC, 8SBP, 2BBP
				H3	3MIC, 2AXA

Unit		Unit		Unit	
H4	1BBP, 1CAX	J3	1FSC, 2MIC, 1BBP	K2	2MIC
H5	1FSC, 1BSC,	J4	2MIC	K3	1MIC, 1BBP, 1AXA
J2	3FSC, 4MIC, 1BBP, 1AXA	J5	1BAX	K5	1BAX

Section XXXVI

Unit		Unit		Unit	
A5	1BBP	C8	1AXA	E7	1BBP
A6	1FSC	C9	1FSC, 1AXA	E8	1MIC, 1BBP
A7	1SBP	C10	1FSC, 1BBP, 1SBP	E9	1FSC, 3MIC, 1SBP, 1AXA
A8	1SBP	D2	1FSC		
A9	1FSC	D3	1AXA	E10	4FSC
A10	1SBP	D5	1AXA	F1	1AXA
B8	1BSC, 1AXA	D7	2FSC, 1MIC, 1BBP, 1SBP	F2	1AXA
B10	1FSC			F6	1MIC, 1BBP, 1SBP
C6	1FSC	D8	2FSC, 2BBP		
C7	1MIC	D10	2SBP	F8	1BBP, 1SBP, 1AXA
		E6	1FSC	F9	5FSC, 2MIC, 2BBP, 1AXA
				F10	3MIC

Unit		Unit		Unit	
G1	1FSC, 1AXA	J3	1BBP	K5	1FSC, 1BBP
G6	SBP	J5	1FSC	K6	1FSC, 1MIC, 2SBP
G8	1FSC, 1MIC, 2BBP	J6	3FSC, 1MIC, 2SBP		
G9	1FSC, 1SBP	J7	1FSC, 2MIC, 2SBP,	K7	1BBP

G10	1MIC, 1BBP		1AXA		K8	2FSC, 4MIC,
H3	1BBP	J8	3MIC			3BBP
H4	2AXA	J9	2FSC, 2MIC			
H7	2FSC, 2MIC, 2SBP,	K1	1SBP			
	1AXA	K2	1SBP, 1AXA			
H8	3FSC, 7MIC, 4SBP,	K3	1SBP			
	2AXA	K4	1BBP, 1SBP			
H9	3MIC					

Section XXXVII

Unit		*Unit*		*Unit*	
J2	1BBP, 1SBP	K1	1BBP, 1SBP	K5	1BSC, 1AXA
J3	1SBP	K4	1MIC		

Section XXXVIII

Unit		*Unit*		*Unit*	
J9	1BBP	K5	1AXA	K9	1BBP
J10	1FSC				

Section XL

Unit		*Unit*		*Unit*	
A10	1SBP	E10	1FSC	H9	1BBP
B10	1FSC	F10	1AXA	J9	1AXA
D10	1FSC	G9	1FSC	J10	1MIC

Cores

Section XIII

Unit	
E10	2

Section XXIII

Unit		*Unit*	
A4	12	H5	51
A5	38	J5	25
B4	5	K5	16
B5	33		
C4	7		
C5	39		
D5	33		
E5	29		
F5	32		
G5	26		

Section XXIV

Unit		Unit	
A1	3	B8	7
A2	6	C1	3
A3	2	C2	12
A4	4	C4	2
A8	5	C5	3
B1	8	C8	7
B2	4		
B3	2		
B4	4		
B5	4		

Section XXXIII

Unit		Unit		Unit	
A10	2	D10	1	J10	1
B10	1	E10	1	K10	1
C10	1				

Section XXXIV

Unit		Unit		Unit	
A5	10	H9	10	K7	2
B5	14	H10	4	K8	7
C5	17	J5	5	K9	4
D5	6	J6	11	K10	1
E5	8	J7	5		
F5	4	J8	2		
H5	5	J9	4		
H6	7	J10	4		
H7	5	K5	4		
H8	6	K6	1		

Section XXXV

Unit		Unit		Unit		Unit	
A3	1	D3	2	F4	5	J2	6
A5	1	D4	2	F5	6	J3	11
B8	8	D5	3	G1	1	J4	7
C1	7	E1	1	G3	3	J5	6
C2	2	E2	4	G5	2	K2	4
C3	1	E3	1	H1	5	K3	6
C4	2	E5	2	H2	7	K4	3
C5	5	F1	1	H3	6	K5	10
D1	2	F2	4	H4	4		
D2	4	F3	6	H5	1		

Section XXXVI

Unit		Unit		Unit		Unit		Unit		Unit	
A3	1	B6	1	C8	3	E1	2	F6	5	G7	5
A4	2	B7	2	C9	2	E4	3	F7	7	G8	9
A5	2	B8	1	D2	5	E6	7	F8	5	G9	4
A6	2	B9	2	D3	1	E7	6	F9	13	G10	2
A8	2	B10	4	D4	4	E8	8	F10	3	H2	1
A9	1	C2	1	D6	4	E9	7	G1	2	H4	2
A10	3	C3	3	D7	1	E10	6	G3	4	H5	4
B1	1	C4	2	D8	5	F1	1	G4	2	H6	3
B3	2	C6	3	D9	2	F3	3	G5	4	H7	7
B4	2	C7	2	D10	1	F4	1	G6	9	H8	8

Unit		Unit	
H9	3	K3	2
H10	3	K5	6
J2	1	K6	10
J3	4	K7	10
J5	5	K8	11
J6	7	K9	4
J7	16		
J8	16		
J9	3		
K2	2		

Section XXXVII

Unit		Unit		Unit	
J2	1	J5	2	K4	2
J3	2	K2	2	K5	2
J4	2				

Section XXXVIII

Unit		Unit	
J1	1	K10	1
J3	1		
J6	1		
J7	1		
J9	1		
J10	3		
K1	1		
K2	2		
K7	2		
K8	1		

Section XXXIX

Unit	
J10	1

Section XL

Unit
B10   2
D10   1
E10   1
H9   1
J9   3
K9   2

Debitage

Section XIII

Unit		*Unit*		*Unit*	
C10	22	D10	54	E10	56

Section XXIII

Unit		*Unit*	
A4	1222	H5	2416
A5	724	J5	2271
B4	1164	K5	3044
B5	1271		
C4	1162		
C5	1490		
D5	2219		
E5	2446		
F5	3773		
G5	2147		

Section XXIV

Unit		*Unit*	
A1	103	B5	353
A2	219	B8	1237
A3	242	C1	124
A4	343	C2	337
A5	305	C3	251
A8	514	C4	191
B1	211	C5	241
B2	129	C8	1143
B3	161		
B4	233		

Section XXXIII

Unit
A10 212
B10   ?
C10 144
D10 118

E10 21
F10 14
G10 10
H10 31
J10 48
K10 49

Section XXXIV

Unit		Unit		Unit	
A5	3612	H8	296	K6	161
B5	1784	H9	358	K7	211
C5	2624	H10	418	K8	141
D5	1278	J5	154	K9	276
E5	1219	J6	154	K10	177
F5	708	J7	314		
G5	586	J8	149		
H5	329	J9	246		
H6	474	J10	128		
H7	320	K5	156		

Section XXXV

Unit		Unit		Unit		Unit		Unit	
A1	41	C1	116	E1	52	G1	114	J1	17
A2	52	C2	65	E2	243	G2	240	J2	426
A3	31	C3	192	E3	76	G3	356	J3	546
A4	?	C4	166	E4	104	G4	110	J4	262
A5	60	C5	61	E5	115	G5	154	J5	275
B1	64	D1	175	F1	51	H1	248	K1	5
B2	?	D2	164	F2	156	H2	331	K2	112
B3	32	D3	131	F3	228	H3	367	K3	14
B4	?	D4	118	F4	212	H4	192	K4	220
B5	99	D5	74	F5	206	H5	148	K5	689

Section XXXVI

Unit		Unit		Unit		Unit		Unit	
A1	67	B1	68	C1	109	D1	135	E1	143
A2	160	B2	49	C2	123	D2	198	E2	182
A3	50	B3	132	C3	77	D3	37	E3	27
A4	36	B4	24	C4	114	D4	224	E4	78
A5	21	B5	10	C5	8	D5	19	E5	23
A6	31	B6	40	C6	41	D6	26	E6	144
A7	55	B7	56	C7	87	D7	132	E7	157
A8	100	B8	86	C8	57	D8	186	E8	291
A9	72	B9	48	C9	74	D9	49	E9	287
A10	11	B10	46	C10	98	D10	117	E10	154

Unit		Unit		Unit		Unit		Unit	
F1	73	G1	197	H1	94	J1	121	K1	143
F2	88	G2	67	H2	86	J2	141	K2	210

Section XXXVI continued

F3	135	G3	86	H3	6	J3	108	K3	182
F4	26	G4	69	H4	18	J4	99	K4	91
F5	41	G5	59	H5	167	J5	60	K5	50
F6	65	G6	152	H6	86	J6	74	K6	133
F7	117	G7	113	H7	227	J7	346	K7	271
F8	40	G8	208	H8	362	J8	348	K8	202
F9	291	G9	144	H9	288	J9	167	K9	173
F10	164	G10	60	H10	233	J10	?	K10	?

Section XXXVII

Unit		*Unit*	
J1	23	K1	7
J2	15	K2	8
J3	31	K3	25
J4	38	K4	19
J5	17	K5	1

Section XXXVIII

Unit		*Unit*	
J1	74	K1	54
J2	48	K2	27
J3	0	K3	0
J4	12	K4	0
J5	5	K5	4
J6	12	K6	156
J7	3	K7	15
J8	74	K8	11
J9	18	K9	20
J10	23	K10	10

Section XXXIX

Unit		*Unit*	
J10	64	K10	39

Section XL

Unit		*Unit*	
A10	60	H9	39
B10	88	H10	53
C10	51	J9	52
D10	76	J10	18
E9	12	K9	17
E10	136	K10	61
F9	32		
F10	63		
G9	12		
G10	81		

Sværdborg I, 1943-44. Area A.

Tools

Section LI

Unit
A4   1BSC

Section LII

Unit		*Unit*		*Unit*	
A10	1TMI	E6	8TMI	F9	2TMI
B10	1TMI	E7	7TMI	F10	1FSC, 2TMI
C8	2TMI	E8	2TMI	G4	2TMI
C9	4TMI	E9	2TMI	G5	3TMI
C10	1TMI	E10	3TMI	G6	7TMI
D7	3TMI	F4	1TMI	G7	3TMI
D8	1FSC, 1TMI	F5	2TMI	G8	1TMI
D9	5TMI	F6	3TMI	G9	4TMI
D10	BSC, 2TMI	F7	1BSC, 6TMI	G10	2BSC, 1TMI
E5	1TMI	F8	5TMI	H4	5TMI

Unit		*Unit*	
H5	3TMI	J9	1TMI
H6	1TMI	K4	1BUR, 2TMI
H7	1TMI	K5	1BUR
H8	1BUR, 9TMI	K6	1BUR, 1TMI
H10	1BUR, 2TMI	K7	1BUR, 1TMI
J4	3TMI	K8	1BUR, 3TMI
J5	1TMI	K9	1TMI
J6	1TMI	K10	3TMI
J7	1TMI		
J8	3TMI		

Section LVI

Unit		*Unit*		*Unit*	
A3	1TMI	B4	4TMI	C5	10TMI
A4	5TMI	B5	9TMI	C6	16TMI
A5	4TMI	B6	6TMI	C7	7TMI
A6	1BUR, 9TMI	B7	8TMI	C8	3TMI
A7	5TMI	B8	6TMI	C9	3TMI
A8	5TMI	B9	5TMI	C10	2TMI
A9	7TMI	B10	1TMI	D2	3TMI
A10	4TMI	C2	2TMI	D3	4TMI
B2	3TMI	C3	1BUR, 8TMI	D4	5TMI
B3	3TMI	C4	15TMI	D5	1TMI

Unit		*Unit*		*Unit*	
D7	1BUR, 1TMI	E4	2TMI	E7	2TMI
D8	1TMI	E6	1TMI	E9	1BUR
D9	1TMI				

Section LV

Unit		Unit		Unit	
A1	1TMI	B5	1TMI	C5	1BSC, 2TMI
A2	2TMI	B6	2TMI	C6	1TMI
A3	1TMI	B7	2TMI	C7	2TMI
A4	1BUR, 1FSC, 2TMI	B8	1TMI	C9	1TMI
A5	1FSC, 2TMI	B9	1TMI	C10	1TMI
A7	1TMI	B10	1BUR	D1	1BSC, 1FSC,
A8	1TMI	C1	4TMI		3TMI
B1	7TMI	C2	1BSC, 1FSC	D2	2TMI
B3	1TMI	C3	1TMI	D3	2TMI
B4	1BUR, 3TMI	C4	2TMI	D4	1TMI

Unit		Unit		Unit	
D5	1TMI	F1	2TMI	G3	1FSC, 1TMI
D6	6TMI	F2	1TMI	G4	3TMI
D9	9TMI	F5	4TMI	G5	1BUR, 6TMI
E1	2TMI	F6	1BUR, 4TMI	G6	9TMI
E2	1BSC, 1TMI	F7	7TMI	G7	6TMI
E5	1FSC, 4TMI	F8	7TMI	G8	1TMI
E7	6TMI	F9	20TMI	G9	1BUR, 8TMI
E8	4TMI	F10	1TMI	G10	2TMI
E9	1TMI	G1	3TMI	H1	1TMI
E10	4TMI	G2	1TMI	H2	1TMI

Unit		Unit		Unit	
H4	1TMI	J4	1TMI	K6	1BUR, 8TMI
H5	4TMI	J5	3TMI	K8	1BSC, 1FSC,
H6	1BSC, 7TMI	J7	1BUR, 3TMI		11TMI
H7	3TMI	J8	3TMI	K9	1BSC, 8TMI
H8	3TMI	J9	1BSC, 4TMI		
H9	5TMI	J10	8TMI		
H10	1BSC, 7TMI	K1	7TMI		
J1	4TMI	K2	4TMI		
J2	4TMI	K3	2TMI		
J3	1TMI	K4	5TMI		

Section LVI

Unit		Unit	
F6	1TMI	J6	1TMI
F7	1TMI	J9	4TMI
G5	1BUR	K1	1TMI
G7	1TMI	K3	1TMI
H5	1BSC	K5	2BUR, 4TMI
H6	2TMI	K7	1TMI
H7	3TMI	K8	1BUR
J3	1TMI	K9	2TMI
J4	1BUR, 1FSC		
J5	2TMI		

Section LVII

Unit		Unit	
A1	2TMI	A2	2TMI

Section LVIII

Unit		Unit		Unit	
B1	1TMI	F3	2TMI	H5	1TMI
C1	1BUR	F4	1TMI	J1	4TMI
C3	1TMI	G1	3TMI	J2	3TMI
D1	3TMI	G2	2TMI	J3	3TMI
D2	1TMI	G3	2TMI	J4	1BSC, 1TMI
D3	1TMI	G4	1TMI	K1	1TMI
E1	1TMI	H1	12TMI	K2	2BUR, 1TMI
E2	1TMI	H2	2TMI		
F1	1BSC, 2TMI	H3	1BUR, 1TMI		
F2	4TMI	H4	1TM		

Cores

Section LI

Unit		Unit	
A4	1	B4	3

Section LII

Unit		Unit		Unit	
B9	1	G8	2	K4	3
B10	1	G10	1	K5	1
C8	1	H6	2	K6	1
D10	1	H7	2	K7	2
E10	1	J4	2	K8	1
F6	1	J5	1		
F8	1	J6	1		
F9	2	J7	1		
G4	2	J9	2		
G5	1	J10	1		

Section LIV

Unit		Unit	
A6	1	C10	1
A8	1	D4	2
A9	1	D6	1
A10	1	D9	1
B4	2	E8	2
B5	1		
B10	1		
C3	2		
C4	1		

Section LIV continued

C5   1

Section LV

Unit		Unit		Unit		Unit		Unit	
A2	1	B7	3	D3	1	E9	2	H6	2
A3	1	B8	1	D4	1	F1	1	J1	1
A5	2	B10	1	D5	5	F4	1	J3	1
A6	1	C2	1	D6	1	F6	4	J7	1
A7	1	C3	1	D8	1	F7	2	J8	1
B1	1	C4	3	E2	1	F8	2	K4	1
B2	1	C5	2	E5	1	F9	2	K5	2
B3	1	C7	2	E6	2	G5	3	K8	1
B5	2	C9	1	E7	2	G6	1		
B6	1	D2	3	E8	3	H5	1		

Section LVI

Unit		Unit	
E8	1	K4	1
F7	1	K5	2
G8	1	K7	1
G9	2	K8	1
H7	2	K9	1
H8	1		
H9	2		
J6	3		
J9	2		
K1	1		

Section LVII

Unit	
A1	1

Section LVIII

Unit		Unit	
A2	2	F2	1
A3	2	F3	2
B3	1	G2	2
C1	1	H1	5
C3	1	H5	1
E1	1	J1	2
E3	1	J2	2
E4	1	J3	1
F1	1	K2	3

Debitage

Section LI

Unit		Unit	
A4	59	B8	21
A5	18	B9	34
A6	8	B10	53
A8	28		
A9	265		
A10	47		
B4	150		
B5	22		
B6	11		
B7	19		

Section LII

Unit		Unit		Unit		Unit		Unit		Unit	
A10	13	D9	268	F6	73	G9	200	J5	60	K8	265
B9	12	D10	125	F7	71	G10	228	J6	101	K9	208
B10	27	E5	14	F8	283	H4	111	J7	151	K10	115
C7	11	E6	36	F9	134	H5	99	J8	432		
C8	48	E7	54	F10	133	H6	145	J9	187		
C9	48	E8	110	G4	57	H7	184	J10	140		
C10	37	E9	182	G5	83	H8	267	K4	44		
D6	26	E10	95	G6	124	H9	294	K5	105		
D7	74	F4	26	G7	164	H10	276	K6	102		
D8	38	F5	43	G8	497	J4	77	K7	106		

Section LIV

Unit		Unit		Unit		Unit		Unit	
A1	37	B1	28	C2	406	D3	292	E7	83
A2	81	B2	121	C3	411	D4	371	E8	74
A3	93	B3	151	C4	508	D5	206	E9	48
A4	164	B4	150	C5	325	D6	171		
A5	199	B5	171	C6	458	D7	153		
A6	371	B6	160	C7	243	D8	130		
A7	441	B7	288	C8	297	D9	92		
A8	345	B8	340	C9	503	E4	210		
A9	523	B9	583	C10	154	E5	232		
A10	185	B10	211	D2	174	E6	110		

Section LV

Unit		Unit		Unit		Unit		Unit		Unit	
A1	30	B1	82	C1	91	D1	107	E1	139	F1	116
A2	58	B2	64	C2	53	D2	111	E2	80	F2	127
A3	68	B3	90	C3	137	D3	171	E3	127	F3	51
A4	54	B4	102	C4	137	D4	141	E4	78	F4	132
A5	165	B5	94	C5	118	D5	422	E5	307	F5	390
A6	57	B6	120	C6	254	D6	13	E6	407	F6	241

Section LV continued

A7	162	B7	257	C7	178	D7	486	E7	611	F7	574
A8	115	B8	146	C8	56	D8	176	E8	348	F8	251
A9	55	B9	86	C9	149	D9	346	E9	276	F9	468
A10	27	B10	185	C10	143	D10	100	E10	86	F10	197

Unit		*Unit*		*Unit*		*Unit*	
G1	77	H1	127	J1	231	K1	334
G2	71	H2	178	J2	187	K2	166
G3	108	H3	187	J3	169	K3	254
G4	178	H4	135	J4	56	K4	234
G5	597	H5	239	J5	126	K5	366
G6	443	H6	266	J6	261	K6	396
G7	513	H7	298	J7	289	K7	467
G8	187	H8	307	J8	356	K8	578
G9	306	H9	193	J9	499	K9	507
G10	281	H10	274	J10	348	K10	287

Section LVI

Unit		*Unit*		*Unit*		*Unit*	
E6	11	G7	22	J1	24	K2	31
E7	13	G8	32	J2	28	K3	36
E8	21	G9	31	J3	32	K4	40
E9	13	H1	27	J4	32	K5	74
F6	16	H2	22	J5	26	K6	33
F7	26	H5	33	J6	31	K7	87
F8	20	H6	21	J7	58	K8	82
F9	22	H7	32	J8	77	K9	92
G5	9	H8	56	J9	74		
G6	20	H9	35	K1	47		

Section LVII

Unit		*Unit*	
A1	222	A2	205

Section LVIII

Unit		*Unit*		*Unit*		*Unit*	
A1	75	D2	139	F4	200	J1	452
A2	136	D3	136	G1	371	J2	194
A3	228	D4	68	G2	223	J3	366
B1	210	E1	219	G3	174	J4	116
B2	273	E2	117	G4	121	K1	145
B3	135	E3	189	H1	478	K2	272
C1	62	E4	156	H2	233	K3	185
C2	66	F1	291	H3	224	K4	116
C3	97	F2	340	H4	227		
D1	90	F3	394	H5	70		

Sværdborg I, 1943-44. Area B

Tools

Section LXV

Unit		Unit		Unit	
A8	1TMI	C3	1TMI	E10	1TMI
A9	5TMI	C5	1TMI	F9	1BSC
A10	2TMI	C6	1TMI	F10	1TMI
B1	1TMI	C8	4TMI	G7	1BUR
B6	1BUR, 2TMI	C10	1BSC	G10	1TMI
B7	3TMI	D1	1BUR, 1TMI		
B8	1TMI	D6	1TMI		
B9	2TMI	D9	1TMI		
B10	1FSC	D10	1TMI		
C2	1TMI	E6	1TMI		

Section LXVI

Unit		Unit	
G5	1TMI	K6	1TMI
G9	1TMI	K7	1BSC, 1BUR, 1TMI
H4	1BUR	K9	1BUR, 4TMI
H7	3TMI	K10	6TMI
H10	1BUR		
J4	1TMI		
J8	1FSC		
J9	2TMI		
J10	1TMI		
K4	1TMI		

Section LXVII

Unit		Unit	
A2	3TMI	D3	1FSC
A3	1BUR, 2TMI	D4	1BUR, 2TMI
A4	4TMI	E2	1TMI
B1	1BUR, 1FSC, 4TMI		
B3	2BUR, 2TMI		
B4	1BUR, 2TMI		
C1	1BSC, 1TMI		
C3	1TMI		
C4	6TMI		
D2	4TMI		

Section LXVIII

Unit		Unit	
E4	1TMI	K2	4TMI
G1	1TMI		
G3	1BUR, 1TMI		
G4	1BUR, 4TMI		
H2	2TMI		

Section LXVIII continued

H4	1BUR, 3TMI
J1	1BUR, 1TMI
J3	7TMI
J4	2TMI
K1	2TMI

Debitage

Section LXV

Unit		Unit		Unit		Unit		Unit		Unit	
A1	6	B1	9	C1	15	D1	15	E4	18	F7	69
A2	17	B2	7	C2	23	D2	72	E5	73	F8	72
A3	18	B3	34	C3	41	D3	21	E6	129	F9	45
A4	54	B4	45	C4	49	D4	36	E7	159	F10	116
A5	50	B5	44	C5	53	D5	34	E8	79	G7	57
A6	158	B6	98	C6	96	D6	97	E9	63	G8	37
A7	239	B7	116	C7	116	D7	154	E10	119	G10	38
A8	276	B8	93	C8	273	D8	111	F4	31		
A9	619	B9	449	C9	206	D9	88	F5	86		
A10	268	B10	319	C10	267	D10	230	F6	120		

Section LXVI

Unit		Unit		Unit	
G4	24	H7	123	J10	195
G5	27	H8	307	K4	37
G6	24	H9	249	K5	62
G7	34	H10	596	K6	141
G8	57	J4	43	K7	365
G9	73	J5	34	K8	488
G10	107	J6	106	K9	535
H4	29	J7	318	K10	834
H5	32	J8	649		
H6	56	J9	466		

Section LXVII

Unit		Unit	
A1	111	C3	658
A2	226	C4	476
A3	251	D1	74
A4	277	D2	524
B1	431	D3	346
B2	330	D4	368
B3	544	E1	117
B4	436	E2	233
C1	184	E3	178
C2	768	E4	248

Section LXVIII

Unit		Unit	
E4	34	H3	582
F2	50	H4	859
F3	31	J1	226
F4	91	J2	507
G1	244	J3	528
G2	344	J4	951
G3	177	K1	227
G4	306	K2	167
H1	383	K3	181
H2	416		

Sværdborg I:1943-44. Area C.

Tools

Section LIX

Unit	
A5	2TMI
A6	1FSC, 14TMI
A7	2BUR, 61TMI
A8	9TMI
A9	10TMI
A10	BSC, 1BUR, 37TMI
B5	1BSC, 6TMI
B6	27TMI
B7	1BUR, 24TMI
B8	1BUR, 1FSC, 19TMI

Unit	
B9	3TMI
B10	1BUR, 34TMI
C5	10TMI
C6	BSC, 1BUR, 1FSC, 26TMI
C7	1BSC, 2BUR, 33TMI
C8	14TMI
C9	1BUR, 6TMI
C10	28TMI
D5	1BUR, 7TMI
D6	16TMI

Unit	
D7	27TMI
D8	13TMI
D9	8TMI
D10	2BUR, 19TMI
E5	3TMI
E6	13TMI
E7	1BSC, 16TMI
E8	14TMI
E9	14TMI
E10	1FSC, 26TMI

Unit	
F5	3TMI
F6	9TMI
F7	1BUR
F8	10TMI
F9	5TMI
F10	11TMI
G5	1FSC
G6	1TMI
G7	8TMI
G8	6TMI

Unit	
G9	8TMI
G10	8TMI
H7	2TMI
H8	2TMI
H9	1BSC, 2TMI
H10	13TMI
J6	2TMI
J7	3TMI
J8	1TMI
J9	1BUR, 6TMI

Unit	
J10	4TMI
K7	1TMI
K9	1TMI
K10	1BUR, 4TMI

Section LX

Unit	
B9	1TMI
B10	5TMI
C7	1BSC, 2TMI
C8	3TMI
C9	1TMI
C10	4TMI
D6	1BUR, 3TMI
D7	1TMI
D8	1BUR, 8TMI
D9	1BUR, 3TMI

Unit	
D10	4TMI
E6	2TMI
E7	1BSC, 13TMI
E8	10TMI
E9	4TMI
E10	2TMI
F5	5TMI
F6	4TMI
F7	8TMI
F8	8TMI

Unit	
F9	6TMI
F10	11TMI
G5	1FSC, 2TMI
G6	1BUR, 1FSC, 10TMI
G7	7TMI
G8	1BUR, 15TMI
G9	3TMI
G10	1BUR, 9TMI
H5	2TMI
H6	4TMI

Unit	
H7	2BSC, 1BUR, 13TMI
H8	13TMI
H9	3TMI
H10	7TMI
J5	1TMI
J6	10TMI

Unit	
K6	3BUR, 7TMI
K7	7BUR, 38TMI
K8	3BUR, 20TMI
K9	1TMI
K10	3BUR, 1FSC, 33TMI

Section LX continued

J7	3BUR, 17TMI
J8	15TMI
J9	15TMI
J10	3BUR, 16TMI

Section LXII

Unit		*Unit*		*Unit*	
A1	6BUR, 37TMI	B1	5BUR, 48TMI	C2	1BUR, 11TMI
A2	2BUR, 1FSC, 13TMI	B2	2BUR, 1FSC, 9TMI	C3	1BSC, 5TMI
A3	4TMI	B3	3TMI	C4	6TMI
A4	1BUR, 5TMI	B4	1BUR, 2TMI	C5	1BUR, 3TMI
A5	1BSC, 1BUR, 2TMI	B5	1TMI	C6	1TMI
A6	1TMI	B6	8TMI	C7	2TMI
A7	2TMI	B7	2TMI	D1	1BSC, 18TMI
A9	1BUR	B9	1BUR	D2	9TMI
A10	1BUR	C1	2BUR, 28TMI	D4	2TMI

Unit		*Unit*		*Unit*	
D5	7TMI	F4	1TMI	K2	3TMI
D6	3TMI	F5	1TMI		
E1	17TMI	F6	4TMI		
E2	3TMI	G1	5TMI		
E4	2TMI	G2	1BUR, 1TMI		
E5	1TMI	H1	2TMI		
E6	3TMI	H2	2TMI		
E7	5TMI	J1	2TMI		
F1	1TMI	J2	1TMI		
F2	8TMI	K1	1TMI		

Section LXIII

Unit		*Unit*		*Unit*	
B1	2TMI	G5	9TMI	H6	5TMI
D1	2BUR	G6	1BUR, 4TMI	H7	3TMI
E1	3TMI	G7	2TMI	H8	1BUR
E2	1TMI	G8	3TMI	H10	3TMI
F1	6TMI	G9	1TMI	J1	2BUR, 7TMI
F2	1TMI	H1	6TMI	J2	1BUR, 5TMI
F4	3TMI	H2	8TMI	J3	1BUR
G1	2TMI	H3	3TMI	J4	1TMI
G3	1BUR, 4TMI	H4	1TMI	J5	1BUR, 4TMI
G4	1BSC, 1TMI	H5	4TMI	J6	2BUR, 7TMI

Unit		*Unit*	
J7	2TMI	K9	2TMI
J9	1BUR	K10	1TMI
J10	2TMI		
K1	6BUR, 15TMI		
K2	1BUR, 17TMI		

K3	4TMI
K4	5TMI
K6	2TMI
K7	8TMI
K8	2BUR

Debitage

Section LIX

Unit		Unit		Unit		Unit		Unit		Unit	
A4	196	B8	1300	D6	875	E10	1489	G8	942	J7	424
A5	286	B9	687	D7	2018	F5	466	G9	963	J8	412
A6	1594	B10	2103	D8	850	F6	684	G10	932	J9	887
A7	3593	C5	621	D9	1001	F7	969	H5	238	J10	546
A8	1400	C6	2311	D10	2341	F8	1748	H6	414	K6	300
A9	839	C7	2475	E5	620	F9	1022	H7	441	K7	354
A10	1489	C8	685	E6	840	F10	914	H8	594	K8	212
B5	775	C9	582	E7	1963	G5	436	H9	564	K9	1082
B6	2561	C10	3206	E8	1487	G6	531	H10	1287	K10	350
B7	4244	D5	470	E9	1837	G7	1028	J6	341		

Section LX

Unit		Unit		Unit		Unit		Unit	
A9	134	D8	591	F6	807	G10	652	J8	1014
A10	148	D9	558	F7	802	H5	244	J9	658
B9	184	D10	613	F8	750	H6	663	J10	623
B10	430	E5	112	F9	542	H7	965	K5	204
C7	194	E6	259	F10	546	H8	869	K6	788
C8	435	E7	1127	G5	423	H9	572	K7	2612
C9	811	E8	910	G6	820	H10	494	K8	1454
C10	475	E9	503	G7	1185	J5	168	K9	442
D6	220	E10	515	G8	830	J6	426	K10	1472
D7	310	F5	356	G9	538	J7	1270		

Section LXII

Unit		Unit		Unit		Unit		Unit		Unit	
A1	2948	B1	6201	C2	1246	D6	137	F4	102	K1	308
A2	1234	B2	976	C3	371	D7	137	F5	189	K2	283
A3	360	B3	430	C4	280	E1	1428	F6	151		
A4	275	B4	331	C5	364	E2	604	F7	100		
A5	552	B5	448	C6	138	E4	151	G1	508		
A6	336	B6	292	C7	55	E5	168	G2	229		
A7	162	B7	120	D1	1873	E6	228	H1	421		
A8	79	B8	71	D2	902	E7	229	H2	242		
A9	106	B9	49	D4	312	F1	619	J1	600		
A1	68	C1	4501	D5	414	F2	703	J2	317		

Section LXIII

Unit		Unit		Unit		Unit		Unit		Unit	
A1	107	E2	167	F5	238	G6	309	H6	473	J6	868
A10	45	E3	198	F6	170	G7	123	H7	232	J7	460
B1	482	E5	146	F7	71	G8	108	H8	196	J8	226
B10	25	E6	97	F9	65	G9	195	H9	154	J9	230
C1	315	E9	33	F10	66	G10	181	H10	191	J10	188
C10	32	E10	45	G1	238	H1	391	J1	662	K1	1250
D1	273	F1	338	G2	141	H2	348	J2	583	K2	749
D2	239	F2	228	G3	337	H3	281	J3	170	K3	357
D10	21	F3	298	G4	334	H4	325	J4	232	K4	291
E1	224	F4	226	G5	723	H5	655	J5	747	K5	361

Unit	
K6	297
K7	345
K8	179
K9	264
K10	140

Section LXIX

Unit	
A1	48

Section LXX

Unit	
G1	42
H1	13
J1	49
K1	72

Bibliography

Aaris-Sørensen, K. 1976. A Zoological Investigation of the Bone Material from Sværdborg I-1943. In B.B. Henriksen 1976: *Sværdborg I. Excavations 1943-44. A Settlement of the Maglemose Culture.* Arkæologiske Studier III. Copenhagen.

Aaris-Sørensen, K. 1980. Depauperation of the mammalian fauna of the island of Zealand during the Atlantic period. *Videnskabelige Meddelelser fra Dansk Naturhistorisk Forening i København* 142, pp. 131-8.

Aaris-Sørensen, K. 1984. Om en uroksetyr fra Prejlerup — og dens sammenstød med Maglemosekulturen. *Nationalmuseets Arbejdsmark*, pp. 165-73.

Aaris-Sørensen, K. 1988. *Danmarks Forhistoriske Dyreverden. Fra Istid til Vikingetid.* Gyldendal. Copenhagen.

Aaris-Sørensen, K. & E.B. Petersen 1986. The Prejlerup aurochs — an archaeo-zoological discovery from Boreal Denmark. *Striae* 24, pp. 111-17.

Albrethsen, S.E. & E.B. Petersen 1976. Excavations of a mesolithic cemetary at Vedbæk, Denmark. *Acta Archaeologica* 47, pp. 1-28.

Althin, C.-A. 1954. *The Chronology of the Stone Age Settlement of Scania, Sweden I. The Mesolithic Settlement.* Acta Archaeologica Lundensia. Series in 4°, No. 1. Lund.

Ammerman, A.J. & L.L. Cavalli-Sforza 1971. Measuring the rate of spread of early farming in Europe. *Man* 6, pp. 674-88.

Andersen, K. 1951. Hytter fra Maglemosetid. *Nationalmuseets Arbejdsmark* 1951, pp. 69-76.

Andersen, K. 1961. Verup bopladsen. *Årbøger for Nordisk Oldkyndighed og Historie* 1960, pp. 118-51.

Andersen, K., S. Jørgensen & J. Richter 1982. *Maglemose hytterne ved Ulkestrup Lyng.* Nordiske Fortidsminder. Serie B in quarto, Bind 5. Copenhagen.

Andersen, S.H. 1973. Overgangen fra ældre til yngre stenalder i Sydskandinavien set fra en mesolitisk synsvinkel. In P. Simonsen & G.S. Munch (eds.): Bonde-Veidemann. Bofast-ikke bofast i Nordisk Forhistorie. *Tromsø Museums Skrifter* 14, pp. 26-44.

Andersen, S.H. 1976. Et østjysk fjordsystems bebyggelse i stenalderen. in H. Thrane (ed.): Bebyggelsesarkæologi. Beretning fra et symposium d. 7-8 Nov. 1975. *Skrifter fra Institut for Historie og Samfundsvidenskab, Odense Universitet* 17, pp. 18-61.

Andersen, S.H. 1979. An 8000-year old Arrow from Vendsyssel, Northern Jutland. *Acta Archaeologica* 1979, pp. 203-8.

Andersen, S.H. 1981. *Stenalderen I. Jægerstenalderen.* Sesam. Copenhagen.

Andersen, S.H. 1983. The introduction of trapezes in the South Scandinavian Mesolithic. A brief survey. *Archaeologia Interregionalis*, pp. 257-62.

Andersen, S.H. 1991. Norsminde. A Køkkenmødding with Late Mesolithic and Early Neolithic Occupation. *Journal of Danish Archaeology* 8 (for 1989), pp. 13-40.

Bay-Petersen, J.L. 1978. Animal exploitation in Mesolithic Denmark. In P. Mellars (ed.): *The Early Postglacial Settlement of Northern Europe*, pp. 115-45. Duckworth London.

Becker, C.J. 1945. En 8000-årig Stenalderboplads i Holmegaards Mose. *Nationalmuseets Arbejdsmark* 1945.

Becker, C.J. 1947. Mosefundne Lerkar fra Yngre Stenalder. Studier over Tragt-bægerkulturen i Danmark. *Årbøger for Nordisk Oldkyndighed og Historie*, pp. 1-318.

Becker, C.J. 1951. Maglemosekultur på Bornholm. *Årbøger for Nordisk Oldkyndighed og Historie* 1951, pp. 96-177.

Becker, C.J. 1953. Die Maglemosekultur in Dänemark. In Vogt (ed.): *Actes de la IIIeme Session Zürich* 1950, pp. 180-83. Zürich.

Becker, C.J. 1958. 4000-årig minedrift i Thy. *Nationalmuseets Arbejdsmark*, pp. 73-82.

Becker, C.J. 1981. Feuerstein-Bergwerke Dänemarks. In *Veröffentlichungen aus dem Deutschen Bergbau-Museum Bochum* 22, pp. 456-70.

Berglund, B.E. 1966. *Late- Quarternary vegetation in Eastern Blekinge, Southeastern Sweden. A pollenanalytical study. II. Post-Glacial time.* Opera Botanica 12, 2.

Bettinger, R.L. 1991. *Hunter-Gatherers. Archaeological and Evolutionary Theory.* Plenum Press. New York.

Binford, L.R. 1968. Post-Pleistocene Adaptations. In S.R. Binford & L.R. Binford (eds.): *New Perspectives in Archaeology*, pp. 313-42. Aldine. Chicago.

Binford, L.R. 1978. *Nunamiut Ethnoarchaeology.* Academic Press. New York.

Binford, L.R. 1973. Interassemblage variability — the Mousterian and the 'functional' argument. In C. Renfrew (ed.): *The Explanation of Culture Change: models in prehistory*, pp. 227-54. Duckworth. London.

Binford, L.R. 1978a. Dimensional analysis of behaviour and site structure: learning from an eskimo hunting stand. *American Antiquity* 43, pp. 330-61.

Binford, L.R. 1978b. *Nunamiut Ethnoarchaeology.* Academic Press. New York.

Binford, L.R. 1979. Organization and formation processes: looking at curated technologies. *Journal of Anthropological Research* 35, pp. 255-73.

Binford, L.R. 1980. Willow smoke and dogs tails: hunter-gatherer settlement systems and archaeological site formation. *American Antiquity* 45, pp. 4-20.

Binford, L.R. 1981. *Bones. Ancient Men and Modern Myths.* Academic Press, New York.

Binford, L.R. 1983. *In Pursuit of the Past.* Thames & Hudson. London.

Binford, L.R. & N. Stone 1986. Zhoukoudian: A Closer Look. *Current Antrhopology*, Vol. 27, No. 5, pp. 453-75.

Blankholm, H.P. 1976. Site catchment analyse — metodik og anvendelsesmuligheder. *Kontaktstencil* 12, pp. 58-67. Turko.

Blankholm, H.P. 1980. *En analyse af Maglemosekulturens bebyggelse.* Unpublished konferensthesis, Århus Universitet.

Blankholm, H.P. 1981. Aspects of the Maglemose Settlement in Denmark. In B. Gramsch (ed.): *Mesolitikum in Europa, 2te Internationales Symposium, Potsdam 3 bis 8 April 1978, Bericht*, pp. 410-14. Veröffentlichungen des Museums für Ur- und Frühgeschichte, Potsdam 14/15.

Blankholm, H.P. 1985. Maglemosekulturens hyttegrundrids. En undersøgelse af bebyggelse og adfærdsmønstre i tidlig mesolitisk tid. *Årbøger for Nordisk Oldkyndighed og Historie* 1984, pp. 61-77.

Blankholm, H.P. 1987a. Maglemosian Hut floors: an Analysis of the Dwelling Unit, Social Unit and Intra-site Behavioural Patterns in Early Mesolithic Southern Scandinavia. In P. Rowley-Conwy, M. Zvelebil & H.P. Blankholm (ed.): *Mesolithic Northwest Europe: Recent Trends*, pp. 109-20. Department of Archaeology & Prehistory. Sheffield.

Blankholm, H.P. 1987b. Late Mesolithic Hunter-Gatherers and the Transition to Farming in Southern Scandinavia. In P. Rowley-Conwy, M. Zvelebil & H.P. Blankholm (ed.): *Mesolithic Northwest Europe: Recent Trends*, pp. 155-62. Department of Archaeology & Prehistory. Sheffield.

Blankholm, H.P. 1990. Stylistic Analysis of Maglemosian Microlithic Armatures in Southern Scandinavia: an Essay. In P.M. Vermeersch & Ph. van Peer (ed.): *Contributions to the Mesolithic in Europe*, pp. 239-57. Leuven.

Blankholm, H.P. 1991. *Intrasite spatial analysis in theory and practice*. Aarhus University Press.

Bratlund, B. 1991. A study of hunting lesions containing flint fragments on reindeer bones at Stellmoor, Schleswig-Holstein, Germany. *CBA Research Reports 77*, pp. 193-07.

Broholm, H.C. 1924. Nye Fund fra den ældste Stenalder. Holmegaard-og Sværdborgfundene. *Årbøger for Nordisk Oldkyndighed og Historie 1924*, pp. 1-144.

Brøndsted, J. 1938. *Danmarks Oldtid. Bind I. Stenalderen*. Gyldendal. Copenhagen.

Brøndsted, J. 1957. *Danmarks Oldtid. Bind I. Stenalderen*. 2nd. ed. Gyldendal. Copenhagen.

Burch, E.S. 1972. The Caribou/Wild Reindeer as a Human Resource. *American Antiquity 37*, pp. 339-68.

Bølviken, E., E. Helskog, K. Helskog, I.M. Holm-Olsen, L. Solheim & R. Bertelsen 1982. Correspondence analysis: an alternative to principal components. *World Archaeology 14(1)*, pp. 41-59.

Cahen, D., L.H. Keeley, & F. van Noten 1979. Stone tools, toolkits, and human behaviour in prehistory. *Current Anthropology 20(4)*, pp. 661-83.

Chaplin, R.E. 1971. *The study of animal bones from archaeological sites*. Seminar Press. London.

Clark, J.G.D. 1936. *The Mesolithic Settlement of Northern Europe*. CUP. Cambridge.

Clark, J.G.D. 1952. *Prehistoric Europe. The Economic Basis*. Methuen. London.

Clark, J.G.D. 1954. *Excavations at Star Carr, an Early Mesolithic Site at Seamer, near Scarborough, Yorkshire*. CUP. Cambridge.

Clark, J.G.D. 1971. *Excavations at Star Carr*, CUP. Cambridge.

Clark, J.G.D. 1972. Star Carr: a Case Study in Bioarchaeology. *Addison-Wesley Module in Anthropology 10*.

Clark, J.G.D. 1975. *The Earlier Stone Age Settlement of Scandinavia*. CUP. Cambridge.

Clark, J.G.D. 1978. Neothermal orientations. In P. Mellars (ed.): *The Early Postglacial Settlement of Northern Europe*, pp. 1-10, Duckworth. London.

Clark, J.G.D. 1980. *Mesolithic Prelude*. Edinburgh University Press. Edinburgh.

Clark, J.G.D. & M.W. Thompson 1953. The Groove and Splinter Technique of working antler in Upper Palaeolithic and Mesolithic Europe. *Proceedings of the Prehistoric Society 19*, pp. 148-60.

Constandse-Westermann, T.S., R.R. Newell & C. Meiklejohn 1984. Human biological background of population dynamics in the Western European Mesolithic. *Human Palaeontology*, B 87(2), pp. 139-223.

Constandse-Westermann, T.S. & R.R. Newell 1987. Social and Biological Aspects of the Western European Mesolithic Population Structure: a Comparison with the Demography of North American Indians. In C. Bonsall (ed.): *The Mesolithic in Europe*. John Donald Ltd. Glasgow, pp. 106-15.

Constandse-Westermann, T.S. & R.R. Newell 1990. A Diachronic and Chorological

Analysis of Lateralization Manifestations in the Western European Mesolithic Skeletal Sample: A novel Approach to the Assessment of Social Complexity. In P.M. Vermeersch & P. v. Peers (eds.): *Contributions to the Mesolithic in Europe*. Studia Praehistorica Belgica 5. Leuven, pp. 95-120.

David, N. 1973. On Upper Palaeolithic society, ecology and technological change. In C. Renfrew (ed.): *The Explanation of Culture Change*. Duckworth. London, pp. 277-303.

Degerbøl, M. 1964. Some remarks on Late- and Post-glacial vertebrate fauna and its ecological relations in Northern Europe. *Journal of Animal Ecology* 33, pp. 71-85.

Dumont, J.V. 1987. Mesolithic Microwear Research in Northwest Europe. In P. Rowley-Conwy, M. Zvelebil & H.P. Blankholm (eds.): *Mesolithic Northwest Europe: Recent Trends*, pp. 82-92.

Edwards, K.J. 1990. Fire and the Scottish Mesolithic: Evidence from Microscopic Charcoal. In P.M. Vermeersch & P. v. Peer (eds.): *Contributions to the Mesolithic in Europe*, pp. 71-80.

Fischer, A. 1978. På sporet af overgangen mellem palæoliticum og mesoliticum i Syd-skandinavien. *Hikuin* 4, pp. 27-50.

Fischer, A. 1981. Handel med skolæstøkser og landbrugets indførelse i Danmark. *Årbøger for Nordisk Oldkyndighed og Historie*, pp. 5-16.

Friis-Johansen, K. 1919. En Boplads fra den ældste Stenalder i Sværdborg Mose. *Årbøger for Nordisk Oldkyndighed og Historie*, pp. 106-235.

Gamble, C. 1986. The mesolithic sandwich: ecological approaches and the archae-ological record of the early postglacial. In M. Zvelebil (ed.): *Hunters in Transition*. CUP. Cambridge, pp. 33-42.

Gamble, C. & Boismier (eds.) 1991. *Ethnoarchaeological Approaches to Mobile Campsites*. International Monographs in Prehistory. Ethnoarchaeological Series 1. Ann Arbor.

Grayson, D.K. 1984. *Quantitative Zooarchaeology*. Academic Press.

Grøn, O. 1987. Seasonal variation in Maglemosian group size and structure: a new model. *Current Anthropology* 28, pp. 303-27.

Grønnow, B. 1987. Meiendorf and Stellmoor Revisited. An Analysis of Late Palaeolithic Reindeer Exploitation. *Acta Archaeologica*, Vol.56, 1985, pp. 131-66.

Hallam, E., B. Barnes & A.J. Stuart 1973. A late glacial elk with associated barbed points from High Furlong, Lancashire. *Proceedings of the Prehistoric Society* 39, pp. 100-27.

Hartz, N. & H. Winge 1906. Om Uroxen fra Vig. *Årbøger for Nordisk Oldkyndighed og Historie*, pp. 225ff.

Hatting, T. 1969. Er bæverens tænder benyttet som redskaber i stenalderens Danmark? *Årbøger for Nordisk Oldkyndighed og Historie*, pp. 116-25.

Henriksen, B.B. 1976. *Sværdborg I. Excavations 1943-44. A Settlement of the Maglemose Culture*. Arkæologiske Studier III. Copenhagen.

Henriksen, B.B. 1979. *Lundby-Holmen*. Nordiske Fortidsminder, Serie B — in quarto, Bd. 6. Copenhagen.

Hodder, I. 1982a. *The Present Past*. Batsford. London.

Hodder, I. 1982b. *Symbols in Action*. CUP. Cambridge.

Hodder, I. 1988. *Reading the Past. Current Approaches to Interpretation in Archaeology*. CUP, Cambridge.

Humaniora 1-6, 1972/74-1983/84. The Danish Research Council for the Humanities, Copenhagen.

Humaniora 1-5, 1987-91, The Danish Research Council for the Humanities, Copenhagen.

Indreko, R. 1948. *Die Mittlere Steinzeit in Estland*. Kungl. Vitterhets Historie och Antikvitets Akademiens Handlingar, Del 66. Stockholm.

Iversen, J. 1960. Problems of the Early Postglacial Forest Development in Denmark. *Danmarks Geologiske Undersøgelse*, IV, 4, 3.

Iversen, J. 1967. Naturens udvikling siden sidste istid. In *Danmarks Natur I*, pp. 343-445. Politikens Forlag. Copenhagen.

Jacobi, R.M. 1973. Aspects of the 'Mesolithic Age' in Britain. In S.K. Kozlowski (ed.): *The Mesolithic in Europe*, Warsaw University Press, pp. 237-66.

Jarman, M. 1972. A territorial model for archaeology: a behavioural and geographical approach. In D.L. Clarke (ed.): *Models in Archaeology*, pp. 705-33, Methuen, London.

Jennbert, K. 1984. *Den Produktiva Gåvan. Tradition och innovation i Sydskandinavien för omkring 5300 år sedan*. Acta Archaeologica Lundensia, Series in 4°. No.16.

Jensen, G. 1991. Ubrugelige økser? Forsøg med Kongemose- og Ertebøllekulturens økser af hjortetak. *Eksperimental Arkæologi 1991*, pp. 10-21.

Jensen, H.J. 1982. A preliminary analysis of blade scrapers from Ringkloster, a Danish Late Mesolithic site. *Studia Prehistorica Belgica* 2, pp. 323-7.

Jensen, H.J. 1983. A Microwear Analysis of Unretouched Blades from Ageröd V. In L. Larsson, *Ageröd V. An Atlantic Bog Site in Central Scania*, pp. 144-52.

Jensen, H.J. 1994. *Flint Tools and Plant Working. Hidden Traces of Stone Age Technology*. Aarhus University Press.

Jensen, J. 1982. *The Prehistory of Denmark*. Methuen. London.

Jessen, K. 1935a. Archaeological Dating in the History of North Jutland's Vegetation. *Acta Archaeologia* 5, pp. 185-214.

Jessen, K. 1935b. *The Composition of the Forest in Northern Europe in Epipalaeolithic Time*. Det Kongl. Danske Videnskabernes Selskab. Biologiske Meddelelser 12.

Jochim, M.A. 1976. *Hunter-Gatherer Settlement and Subsistence*. Academic Press. New York.

Jochim, M.A. 1981. *Strategies for Survival*. Academic Press. New York.

Jørgensen, S. 1954. A Pollen Analytical Dating of Maglemose Finds from the Bog Aamosen, Zealand. In *Studies in Vegetational History in Honour of Knud Jessen 29th November 1954*, Danmarks Geologiske Undersøgelse, II, 80, pp. 159-87.

Jørgensen, S. 1963. *Early Postglacial in Aamosen. Geological and Pollen-Analytical Investigations of Maglemosian Settlements in the West-Zealand Bog Aamosen I-II*. Danmarks Geologiske Undersøgelse, II, 87.

Keeley, L. 1978. Preliminary microwear analysis of the Meer assemblage. In F. v. Noten: *Les Chasseurs de Meer*. Dissertations Archaeologicae Gandenses 18, pp. 78-86. Bruges.

Klein, R.G. & K.Cruz-Uribe 1984. *The Analysis of Animal Bones from Archaeological Sites*. Chigago University Press. Chicago.

Koch, L. 1916. Nye Bidrag til Mullerupkulturens Alder. *Meddelelser fra Dansk Geologisk Forening* 5, 6.

Kollau, W. 1943. Zur Osteologie des Rentiers (Nach den Funden von Stellmoor in Holstein). In A. Rust 1943, *Die alt- und mittelsteinzeitlichen Funde von Stellmoor*, pp. 60-105.

Krause, W. 1937. Die eiszeitlichen Knochenfunde von Meiendorf. In A. Rust 1937, *Das alsteinzeitliche Rentierjägerlager Meiendorf*, pp. 48-61.

Kubitzki, K. 1961. Zur Synchronisierung der nordwesteuropäischen Pollendiagramme mit Beiträgen zur Waldgeschichte Nordwestdeutschlands. *Flora* 150, 1, pp. 43-52.

Kuhn, T. 1962. *The Structure of Scientific Revolutions*. University of Chicago Press. Chicago.

Larsson, L. 1978. *Ageröd I:B — Ageröd I:D. A Study of Early Atlantic Settlement in Scania*. Acta Archaeologica Lundensia. Series in 4 , No. 12. Lund.

Larsson, L. 1982. *Segebro. En tidigatlantisk boplats vid Sege Ås mynning*. Malmöfynd 4. Malmö Museum.

Larsson, L. 1983. *Ageröd V. An Atlantic Bog Site in Central Scania*. Acta Archaeologica Lundensia. Series in 8° , No. 12. Lund.

Larsson, L. 1984. The Skateholm Projekt. A late mesolithic settlement and cemetery complex at a southern Swedish bay. *Meddelanden från Lunds Universitets Historiska Museum* 1983-84, pp. 5-46.

Larsson, L. 1987. Late Mesolithic Settlements and Cemeteries at Skateholm, Southern Sweden. In C. Bonsall (ed.): *The Mesolithic in Europe*, Glasgow. John Donald, pp. 367-78.

Legge, A. & P. Rowley-Conwy 1988. *Star Carr Revisited. A Re-Analysis of the Large Mammals*. Centre for Extra-Mural Studies, Birkbeck College, London.

Leroi-Gourhan, A. & M. Brézillion 1966. L'habitation magdalénienne No.1 de Pincevent prés Montereau (Seine et Marne). *Gallia Préhistoire* 9, pp. 263-385.

Lepiksaar, J. 1978. Bone remains from the Mesolithic settlements Ageröd I:B and I:D. In L. Larsson: *Ageröd I:B — Ageröd I:D. A Study of Early Atlantic Settlement in Scania*. Acta Archaeologica Lundensia Series in 4°, No. 12, pp. 235-44. Lund.

Lepiksaar, J. 1982. Djurrester från den tidigatlantiska boplatsen vid Segebro nära Malmö i Skåne (Sydsverige). In L. Larsson: *Segebro. En Tidigatlantisk Boplats vid Sege Ås Mynning*. Malmöfynd 4, pp. 105-28.

Lepiksaar, J. 1983. Animal Remains from the Mesolithic Bog Site at Ageröd V in Central Scania. In L. Larsson: *Ageröd V. An Atlantic Bog Site in Central Scania*. Acta Archaeologica Lundensia. Series in 8°, No. 12, s. 159-68.

Louwe-Kooijmans, L.P. 1970-71. *Mesolithic Bone and Antler Implements from the North Sea and the Netherlands*. Berichten van de rijksdienst voor het oudheidkundig bodemonderzoek, Vol. 20-21, pp. 27-73.

Madsen, T. 1982. Settlement systems of early agricultural societies in East Jutland, Denmark: a regional study of change. *Journal of Anthropological Archaeology* 1(3), pp. 197-236.

Madsen, T & J.E. Petersen 1983. Tidlig-neolitiske anlæg ved Mosegården. Regionale og kronologiske forskelle i tidligneolitikum. *Kuml* 1982-83, pp. 61-110.

Mahler, D.L., C. Paludan-Müller & S. Stumann Hansen 1983. *Om arkæologi. Forskning, formidling, forvaltning — for hvem?* Reitzel. Copenhagen.

Mathiassen, Th. 1937. Gudenaa-Kulturen. En mesolitisk Indlandsbebyggelse i Jylland. *Årbøger for Nordisk Oldkyndighed og Historie*, pp. 1-186.

Mathiassen, Th. 1943. *Stenalderbopladser i Aamosen*. Nordiske Fortidsminder III, 3.

Mathiassen, Th. 1948. *Danske Oldsager I. Ældre Stenalder*. Copenhagen.

Mathiassen, Th., J. Degerbøl & J. Troels-Smith, 1942. *Dyrholmen. En Stenalderboplads paa*

Djursland. Det Kongl. Danske Videnskabernes Selskab. Arkaeologisk-Kunsthistoriske Skrifter, I, 1.

McGovern, T.H. 1980. Cows, Harp Seals, and Churchbells: Adaptation and Extinction in Norse Greenland. *Human Ecology* 8, 3, pp. 245-75.

McGovern, T.H. 1985. The Arctic Frontier of Norse Greenland. In S. Green & S. Pearlman (eds.): *The Archaeology of Frontiers & Boundaries*. Academic Press. New York, pp. 275-323.

McGovern, T.H. 1985. Contributions to the Paleoeconomy of Norse Greenland. *Acta Archaeologica* 54, 1983, pp. 73-122.

Meiklejohn, C. 1978. Ecological aspects of population size and growth in Late-Glacial and Early Postglacial Northwestern Europe. In P.A. Mellars (ed.): *The Early Postglacial Settlement of Northern Europe*. London. Duckworth, pp. 65-80.

Mellars, P.A. 1975. Fire ecology, animal populations and man: a study of some ecological relationships in prehistory. *Proceedings of the Prehistoric Society* 42, pp. 15-45.

Metcalfe, D. & K.T. Jones 1988. A reconsideration of animal body-part utility indices. *American Antiquity* 53, 3, pp. 486-504.

Mithen, S. 1987. Prehistoric Red Deer Hunting Strategies: A Cost-Risk Benefit Analysis with Reference to Upper Palaeolithic Northern Spain and Mesolithic Denmark. In P. Rowley-Conwy, M. Zvelebil & H.P. Blankholm (ed.) *Mesolithic Northwest Europe: Recent Trends*, pp. 93-108. Department of Archaeology & Prehistory, Sheffield.

Mithen, S. 1990. *Thoughtful Foragers. A Study of Prehistoric Decision Making*. CUP. Cambridge.

Moss, E.H. 1983. *The Functional Analysis of Flint Implements. Pincevent and Pont D'Ambon: Two Case Studies from the French Final Palaeolithic*. BAR International Series 177. Oxford.

Møhl, U. 1960. Sammenfatning af knoglematerialet. In K. Andersen 1960: Verup-bopladsen. En Maglemoseboplads i Åmosen. *Årbøger for Nordisk Oldkyndighed og Historie*, pp. 132-6.

Møhl, U. 1979. Faunaen omkring Flaadet-Bopladsen. En boreal bosættelse på Langeland. I J. Skaarup: *Flaadet. En Tidlig Maglemoseboplads på Langeland*. Langelands Museum. Rudkøbing.

Møhl, U. 1980. Elsdyrskeletterne fra Skottemarke og Favrbo. Skik og brug ved bore-altidens jagter. *Årbøger for Nordisk Oldkyndighed og Historie* 1978, pp. 5-32.

Mörner, N.-A. 1969. *The Late Quarternary History of the Kattegat Sea and the Swedish West Coast*. Sveriges Geologiska Undersökning, 63, 3.

Newell, R.R. 1973. The post-glacial adaptations of the indigenous population of the Northwest European Plain. In S.K. Kozlowski (ed.): *The Mesolithic in Europe*. Warsaw. Univ. of Warsaw Press, pp. 399-440.

Newell, R.R. 1984. On the mesolithic contribution to the social evolution of Western European Society. In J. Bintliff (ed.): *European Social Evolution. Archaeological Perspectives*, pp. 69-82, University of Bradford, Bradford.

Newell, R.R. 1990. Making Cultural Ecology Relevant to mesolithic Research: II. Restocking the Larder of the Later Mesolithic of Zealand, Denmark. In P.M. Vermeersch & Ph. v. Peer (eds.): *Contributions to the Mesolithic in Europe*. Studia Praehistorica Belgica 5. Leuven.

Newell, R.R., T.S. Constandse-Westermann & C. Meiklejohn 1979. The skeletal remains of mesolithic man in Western Europe: an evaluative catalogue. *Journal of Human Evolution* 8(1), pp. 1-228.

Nielsen, A.V. 1967. Landskabets tilblivelse. In *Danmarks Natur*, Bd. 1, pp. 251-344, Politikens Forlag. Copenhagen.

Nilsson, T. 1935. Die pollenanalytische Zonengliederung der spät- and postglazialen Bildungen Schonens. *Geologiska föreningen i Stockholm Förhandlingar* 57, pp. 385-562.

Nilsson, T. 1967. Pollenanalytische Datierung mesolitischer Siedlungen im Randgebiet des Ageröds Mosse im mittleren Schonen. In *Publications from the Institutes of Mineralogy, Paleontology and Quarternary Geology. University of Lund, Sweden*, 143.

Noe-Nygaard, N. 1974. Mesolithic Hunting in Denmark Illustrated by Bone Injuries Caused by Human Weapons. *Journal of Archaeological Science 1974*, 1, pp. 217-48.

Noe-Nygaard, N. 1975. Two shoulder blades with healed lesions from Star Carr. *Proceedings of the Prehistoric Society* 41, pp. 10-16.

Noe-Nygaard, N. 1977. Butchering and marrow fracturing as a taphonomic factor in archaeological deposits. *Paleobiology 1977*, 3, pp. 218-37.

Noe-Nygaard, N. 1988. Taphonomy in Archaeology with Special Emphasis on Man as a Biasing Factor. *Journal of Danish Archaeology*, 6, 1987, pp. 7-52.

O'Shea, J. 1981. Coping with scarcity: exchange and social storage. In A. Sheridan & G. Bailey (eds.): *Economic Archaeology. Towards an Integration of Ecological and Social Approaches*. BAR International Series 96, pp. 167-80.

Paludan-Müller, C. 1978. High Atlantic food gathering in northwestern Zealand, ecological conditions and spatial representation. In K. Kristiansen & C. Paludan-Müller (eds.): *New Directions in Scandinavian Archaeology*. National Museum of Denmark. Copenhagen, pp. 120-57.

Pedersen, L. 1992. Ålegård. *Skalk* 1992, 6, pp. 3-7.

Petersen, E.B. 1966. Klosterlund — Sønder Hadsund — Bøllund. Les trois Sites Principaux du Maglemosien Ancien en Jutland. Essai de Typologie et de Chronologie. *Acta Archaeologia* 37, pp. 77-185.

Petersen, E.B. 1972. A Maglemose Hut from Sværdborg Bog, Zealand, Denmark. *Acta Archaeologica*, Vol. XLII, 1971, pp. 43-77.

Petersen, E.B. 1973. A Survey of the late Palaeolithic and the Mesolithic of Denmark. In S.K. Kozlowski (ed.): *The Mesolithic in Europe*, pp. 77-127. Warsaw University Press.

Petersen, E.B. 1986. Maglemosekultur. *Arkæologiske udgravninger i Danmark 1985*, pp. 34-35. Copenhagen.

Petersen, E.B. 1989. Maglemosekultur. *Arkæologiske udgravninger i Danmark 1988*, pp. 55-7. Copenhagen.

Petersen, E.B. 1993. Maglemosekultur. *Arkæologiske udgravninger i Danmark 1992*, pp. 82-5. Copenhagen.

Petersen, E.B., C. Christensen, P.V. Petersen & K. Aaris-Sørensen 1976. Vedbækprojektet. Udgravningerne i Vedbækområdet. *Søllerødbogen*.

Petersen, E.B., J.H. Jönsson, P.V. Petersen & K. Aaris-Sørensen 1977. Vedbækprojektet. I marken og i museerne. *Søllerødbogen*.

Petersen, K.S. 1985. The Late Quarternary History of Denmark. *Journal of Danish Archaeology* 4, pp. 7-22.

Petersen, P.V. 1978. Trylleskoven. 7000 år tilbage — med S-banen. *Køge Museum 1975-77*, pp. 45-58.

Petersen, P.V. 1984. Chronological and regional variation in the late Mesolithic of Eastern Denmark. *Journal of Danish Archaeology* 3, pp. 7-18.

Petersen, P.V. & E. Brinch Petersen 1984. Prejleruptyrens skæbne — 15 små flintspidser. *Nationalmuseets Arbejdsmark*, pp. 174-9.

Plisson, H. 1982. Analyse Fonctionelle de 95 micro-grattoirs 'Tourassiens'. *Studia Prehistorica Belgica* 2, pp. 279-87.

Price, T.D. 1982. Willow tales and dog smoke. *Quarterly Review of Archaeology*, March 1982.

Price, T.D. 1981. Regional approaches to human adaptation in the mesolithic of the north European plain. In B. Gramsch (ed.): *Mesolithikum in Europa. 2. Internationales Symposium Potsdam, Bericht*. Veröffentlichungen des Museums für Ur- und Frühgeschichte, Potsdam, Vol. 14/15, pp. 217-34. Deutscher Verlag. Berlin.

Price, T.D. 1985. Affluent foragers of mesolithic southern Scandinavia. In T.D. Price & J.A. Brown (eds.): *Prehistoric Hunter-Gatherers. The Emergence of Complexity*, pp. 341-63. Academic Press. Orlando, Fl. and London.

Price, T.D. & J.A. Brown (eds.). 1985. *Prehistoric Hunter-Gatherers. The Emergence of Complexity*. Academic Press. Orlando, Fl. and London.

Renfrew, C. 1976. Megaliths, territories and populations. In S.J. de Laet (ed.): *Acculturation and Continuity in Atlantic Europe*, pp. 198-220.

Richter, J. 1982. Faunal Remains from Ulkestrup Lyng St. A Hunters Dwelling Place. In K. Andersen, S. Jørgensen & J. Richter: *Maglemose hytterne ved Ulkestrup Lyng*. Nordiske Fortidsminder, Serie B — in quarto, Bd.7. pp. 141-75.

Rosenlund, K. 1972. Zoological Material. In E. Brinch Petersen 1972: A Maglemose Hut from Sværdborg Bog, Zealand, Denmark. *Acta Archaeologica*, vol. XLII, 1971, pp. 59-62.

Rosenlund, K. 1979. Knoglematerialet fra bopladsen Lundby II. In B.B. Henriksen 1979: *Lundby-Holmen*. Nordiske Fortidsminder, Serie B — in quarto, Bd.6, pp. 128-42.

Rowley-Conwy, P. 1983. Sedentary hunters: the Ertebølle example. In G. Bailey (ed.): *Hunter-Gatherer Economy in Prehistory*, pp. 111-26. CUP. Cambridge.

Rowley-Conwy, P. 1984. The laziness of the short-distance hunter: the origins of agriculture in Western Denmark. *Journal of Anthropological Archaeology* 3(4), pp. 300-24.

Rowley-Conwy, P. 1986. Between cave painters and crop planters: aspects of the temperate European Mesolithic. In M. Zvelebil (ed.): *Hunters in Transition*, pp. 17-32. CUP. Cambridge

Rowley-Conwy, P. 1993. Season and Reason: The case for a Regional Interpretation of Mesolithic Settlement Patterns. In G.L. Peterkin, H. Bricker and P. Mellars (eds): *Hunting and Animal Exploitation in the Later Palaeolithic and Mesolithic of Eurasia*, pp. 179-88. Archaeological Papers of the American Anthropological Association no. 4.

Rowley-Conwy, P. n.d. Meat, Furs and Skins: Mesolithic Animal Bones from Ringkloster, a Seasonal Hunting Camp in Jutland.

Rowley-Conwy, P., M. Zvelebil & H.P. Blankholm 1987. Introduction. In P. Rowley-Conwy, M. Zvelebil & H.P. Blankholm (eds.): *Mesolithic Northwest Europe: Recent Trends*, pp. 1-8. Department of Archaeology & Prehistory. Sheffield.

Rowley-Conwy, P., M. Zvelebil & H.P. Blankholm (eds.): *Mesolithic Northwest Europe. Recent Trends*. Department of Archaeology & Prehistory. Sheffield.

Rust, A. 1937. *Das altsteinzeitliche Rentierjägerlager Meiendorf*. Neumünster.

Rust, A. 1943. *Die alt- und mittelsteinzeitlichen Funde von Stellmoor*. Neumünster.

Sackett, J.R. 1982 Approaches to style in lithic archaeology. *Journal of Anthropological Archaeology* 1, pp. 59-112.

Salomonsson, B. 1964. Découverte d'une Habitation du Tardiglaciaire à Segebro, Scanie, Suede. *Acta Archaeologica* 35.

Sarauw, G.F.L. 1903. En Stenalders Boplads i Maglemose ved Mullerup. *Årbøger for Nordisk Oldkyndighed og Historie*, pp. 148-314.

Schiffer, M.B. 1976. *Behavioral Archeology*. Academic Press. New York.

Schiffer, M.B. 1988. The structure of archaeological theory. *American Antiquity* 53, 4, pp. 461-85.

Schuldt, E. 1961. *Hohen Viecheln. Ein Mittelsteinzeitlicher Wohnplatz in Mecklenburg.* Deutsche Akademie der Wissenschaften zu Berlin. Schriften der Section für Vor- und Frühgeschichte 10. Berlin.

Schwabedissen, H. 1944. *Die Mittlere Steinzeit in westlichen Norddeutschland.* Wachholz. Neumünster.

Sheridan A. & G. Bailey (eds.) 1981. *Economic Archaeology. Towards an Integration of Ecological and Social Approaches.* BAR International Series 96, British Archaeological Reports, Oxford.

Simmons, I.G. 1975. The ecological setting of Mesolithic man in the Highland Zone. In J.G. Evans, S. Limbrey & H. Cleere (eds.): *The effect of man on the landscape: the Highland Zone.* Council for British Archaeology. Research Report No. 11, pp. 57-63.

Skaarup, J. 1979. *Flaadet. En tidlig maglemoseboplads på Langeland.* Langelands Museum.

Smith, A.G. 1970. The influence of Mesolithic and Neolithic man on British vegetation. In D. Walker & R.G. West (eds.): *Studies in the Vegetational History of the British Isles.* CUP, pp. 81-6.

Speth, J.D. 1983. *Bison Kills and Bone Counts.* University of Chicago Press.

Ströbel, R. 1959. Tardenoisspitze in einem Bovidenknochen von Schwenningen am Nechar. *Fundberichte aus Schwaben, Neue Folge* 15, pp. 103-6.

Sørensen, I. 1980. Datering af elsdyrknoglerne fra Skottemarke og Favrbo. *Årbøger for Nordisk Oldkyndighed og Historie* 1978, pp. 33-44.

Troels-Smith, J. 1953. Ertebøllekultur — Bondekultur. Resultater fra de sidste 10 aars undersøgelser i Aamosen. *Årbøger for Nordisk Oldkyndighed og Historie*, pp. 5-62.

Troels-Smith, J. 1957. Maglemosekulturens jægere og fiskere. *Nationalmuseets Arbejdsmark*, pp. 101-33.

Troels-Smith, J. 1960. *Ivy, Mistletoe and Elm. Climate Indicators — Fodder Plants.* Danmarks Geologiske Undersøgelse, IV, 4, 4.

Troels-Smith, J. 1963. Danmarks og den svenske vestkysts mesolitiske Stenaldersbebyggelse. *Fynd*, pp. 43-52.

Verhart, L.B.M. 1988. Mesolithic barbed points and other implements from Europoort, the Netherlands. *Oudheidkundige Mededelingen uit het Rijksmuseum van Oudheden te Leiden* 68, pp. 145-94.

Verhart, L.B.M. 1990. Stone Age Bone Points as Indicators for 'Social Territories' in the European Mesolithic. In P.M. Vermeersch & Ph. v. Peers (eds.): *Contributions to the Mesolithic in Europe*, Studia Praehistorica Belgica 5, pp. 139-52

Vita-Finzi, C. & E.S. Higgs 1970. Prehistoric Economy in the Mount Carmel Area of Palestine. Site-Catchment Analysis. *Proceedings of the Prehistoric Society* 36, pp. 1-37.

Westerby, E. 1927. *Stenalderbopladser ved Klampenborg.* Copenhagen.

White, T.E. 1952. Observations on the butchering technique of some aboriginal peoples. *American Antiquity* 17(4), pp. 337-8.

Wiessner, P. 1983. Style and social information in Kalahari San projectile points. *American Antiquity* 48, pp. 253-76.

Winge, H. 1903. Zoologiske bestemmelser i G.F.L. Sarauw: En Stenalders Boplads i Maglemose ved Mullerup. *Årbøger for Nordisk Oldkyndighed og Historie*, pp. 194-8.

Winge, H. 1919. Zoologiske bestemmelser i K. Friis-Johansen: En Boplads fra Ældste Stenalder i Sværdborg Mose. *Årbøger for Nordisk Oldkyndighed og Historie*, pp. 28-30.

Winge, H. 1924. Zoologiske bestemmelser i H.C. Broholm: Nye Fund fra den Ældste Stenalder, Holmegaard og Sværdborgfundene. *Årbøger for Nordisk Oldkyndighed og Historie*, pp. 28-30.

Winterhalder, B.P. & E.A. Smith (eds.) 1981: *Hunter-Gatherer Foraging Strategies*. University of Chicago Press. Chicago.

Wobst, H.M. 1976. Locational relationships in palaeolithic society. *Journal of Human Evolution* 5, pp. 49-58.

Woodman, P.C. 1985. *Excavations at Mount Sandel 1973-77*. Northern Ireland Archaeological Monographs: No. 2. Belfast.

Zvelebil, M. 1986. Mesolithic prelude and the neolithic revolution. In M. Zvelebil (ed.): *Hunters in Transition*, pp. 5-16. CUP. Cambridge.

Zvelebil, M. & P. Rowley-Conwy 1984. Transitions to farming in northern Europe: a hunter-gatherer perspective. *Norwegian Archaeological Review* 17, pp. 104-28.

Index of sites